Development and Structural Change in Asia-Pacific

The economic miracle in Asia-Pacific was arguably the most spectacular development experience of the twentieth century. However, in 1997–8 financial crises engulfed these 'miracle' economies, raising questions about the viability of an East Asian development model.

In this book, the authors consider how the Asia-Pacific economies have developed since the financial crises, and highlight two inter-related themes: the effects of global forces on the national Asian economies and the different development paths taken by these economies as they jointly entered this new phase.

Questions raised by the book include:

*   Is globalisation a threat to development and prosperity in Asia-Pacific, or did globalisation facilitate and accelerate the pace of industrialisation among late industrialisers in the region?
*   Is there a single Asia-Pacific development model or did the crisis show this to be false?
*   Did the financial crisis reveal structural weaknesses in an Asia-Pacific state-led model or was state leadership already in demise?

Development and Structural Change in Asia-Pacific provides a useful and relevant account of how the global economy has led to structural change within Asian economies. It will be of interest to students and researchers in Asian Studies, Economics and Development Studies.

Martin Andersson is Lecturer in Economic History and Development Economics at the School of Economics, Lund University.

Christer Gunnarsson is Professor of International Economics and Business at the School of Economics, Lund University.

RoutledgeCurzon Studies in the Growth Economies of Asia

Development and Structural Change in Asia-Pacific

Globalising miracles or end of a model?

160401

Edited by Martin Andersson and Christer Gunnarsson

RoutledgeCurzon
Taylor & Francis Group

LONDON AND NEW YORK

First published 2003
by RoutledgeCurzon
11 New Fetter Lane, London EC4P 4EE

Simultaneously published in the USA and Canada
by RoutledgeCurzon
29 West 35th Street, New York, NY 10001

RoutledgeCurzon is an imprint of the Taylor & Francis Group

Typeset in Baskerville by
HWA Text and Data Management Ltd, Tunbridge Wells
Printed and bound in Great Britain by
MPG Books Ltd, Bodmin

British Library Cataloguing in Publication Data
A catalogue record for this book is available from the British Library

Library of Congress Cataloging in Publication Data
Development and structural change in Asia-Pacific : globalising miracles or
end of a model? / edited by Martin Andersson and Christer Gunnarsson.
       p. cm.
Simultaneously published in the USA and Canada.
Includes bibliographical references and index.
   1. East Asia–Economic conditions. 2. Structural adjustment
(Economic policy)–East Asia. 3. Globalization. I. Andersson, Martin,
1969– II. Gunnarsson, Christer, 1948–
   HC460.5 .D46 2003
   338.95–dc21
                                                        2002011663

ISBN 0–415–30416–4

In Memory of Ishak Shari

Contents

Figures

Tables

Contributors

Irma Adelman is Professor Emerita at the Graduate School, University of California at Berkeley, USA.

Martin Andersson teaches economic history and development economics at the School of Economics at Lund University, Sweden.

Anne Booth is Professor of Economics at the School of Oriental and African Studies (SOAS) at London University, UK.

Chris Edwards is a Senior Fellow with the School of Development Studies at the University of East Anglia, Norwich, UK.

Christer Gunnarsson is Professor of International Economics and Business at the School of Economics at Lund University, Sweden.

Jomo K.S. is Professor of Economics at the University of Malaya, Kuala Lumpur, Malaysia.

Medhi Krongkaew is Director at the Institute of East Asian Studies, Thammasat University, Bangkok, Thailand.

The late **Ishak Shari** was Director of the Institute of Malaysian and International Studies (IKMAS), Kuala Lumpur, Malaysia, from 1997 until his death in 2001.

John Weeks is Professor at the Centre for Development Policy and Research at the School of Oriental and African Studies (SOAS) at London University, UK.

Preface

The financial crisis that hit the miracle economies of East and Southeast Asia from mid-1997 is a well-known and intensely debated phenomenon. Much has been written and debated about the causes and effects of the crisis. With regard to causes, focus has been laid upon the effects of the forces of globalisation and deregulation on the one hand, and 'moral hazards' resulting from excessive state involvement in the economic sphere, on the other. Assessments of the social consequences of the crisis have tended to focus on immediate and short-term effects such as the seemingly rapid growth of unemployment and poverty following in the footsteps of the crisis.

However, the crisis has also led to a rethinking of the so-called economic 'miracle' in the Asia-Pacific region. Once held up as a model for world development, the region's experience was later shown to the world as a deterrent. Some even took the crisis as proof that an Asian alternative to a Western development model had never existed. The countries of East and Southeast Asia were hit very differently by the crisis. Some were seriously affected, whereas others escaped rather lightly and found it easier to recover. This is a clear indication that the countries of the region never represented or followed one development model. They have, rather, been part and parcel of a regional process of industrialisation, a process in which the national economies have played very different roles depending on their individual prerequisites, levels of industrial development and social structures. Since the mid-1980s the process of industrialisation has both accelerated and become more regionally integrated as an effect of deregulation and intra-Asian globalisation. Thus, a rethinking of the crisis is also a rethinking of the Asia-Pacific model.

The idea behind this volume is to focus on international and national institutional and political factors that have shaped the different economic structures of the miracle countries and that have themselves been shaped in the very process of industrialisation and globalisation. Such structural and institutional differences came to the surface during the crisis and they are likely to have bearing on future development prospects for years to come. Thus, rethinking the Asia-Pacific economic 'miracle' in the light of the crisis means bringing in a political economy perspective as well as a broad social science perspective.

Most of the chapters contained in the present volume originate from the international conference *Social and Economic Structures and the Origins of the Asian Crisis* held at Lund University, Sweden in November 1999. This was a conference that involved not only the contributors to this volume but in addition a range of leading researchers from Asia, Europe and the United States. We wish to thank the participants for making the conference a successful and enlightening experience, and we can only regret that a number of excellent contributions could not be included in the present volume. The conference was held with financial support from the Centre for East and Southeast Asian Studies at Lund University, The Swedish Foundation for International Cooperation in Research and Higher Education, the Partnership Foundation at the Lund School of Economics and Management and the Nordic Association for Southeast Asian Studies. We gratefully acknowledge the support received.

Tragically, one of the contributors to this volume, Ishak Shari, passed away on 30 June 2001, at the age of 53. He obtained his BSc (Hons) and MSc in economics and statistics from the London School of Economics and Political Science (LSE) in 1970 and 1972. In 1985, he received his PhD in development economics from Universiti Malaya. He was Dean of the Economics Faculty at Universiti Kebang-saan Malaysia (UKM) from 1988 to 1990 and Dean of the Centre for Graduate Studies from 1994 to 1997. In 1997, he was appointed director of IKMAS, a social science research institute at UKM, a post he held until his premature death.

Ishak Shari was not only one of Southeast Asia's leading scholars on income distribution, poverty and marginalisation but also a considerate and enjoyable person. His death is a great loss. His colleagues, friends and acquaintances will remember him dearly. We dedicate this volume to Ishak's memory.

Martin Andersson and Christer Gunnarsson
Lund, Sweden
July 2002

Abbreviations

ADB	Asian Development Bank
ASEAN	Association of Southeast Asian Nations
BIS	Bank for International Settlement
BWI	Bretton Woods institution
CDRAC	Corporate Debt Restructuring Advisory Committee (Thailand)
CEPAL	Comision Economica para America Latina y el Caribe
CIS	Confederation of Independent States
EO	export-orientation
FDI	foreign direct investment(s)
FIDF	Financial Institution Development Fund (Thailand)
GATS	General Agreement on Trade in Services
GATT	General Agreement on Tariffs and Trade
GDP	gross domestic product
GFCF	gross fixed capital formation
HCI	heavy and chemical industries
HPAE	high-performing Asian economy
IO	international organisations
IMF	International Monetary Fund
IRS	Internal Revenue Service (Korea)
ISI	import-substitute industrialisation
IT	Information technology
KMT	Kuomintang
LDC	less developed country
NIC	newly industrialised countries
NIE	newly industrialised economies
NEP	New Economic Policy (Malaysia)
NGO	non-governmental organisation
NPL	non-performing loan (Thailand)
OECD	Organisation for Economic Cooperation and Development
OLS	ordinary least squares
R & D	research and development
RULC	real unit of labour cost

SEA	Southeast Asia
SME	small and medium-sized enterprises
UNCTAD	United Nations Conference on Trade and Development
UNDP	United Nations Development Programme
UNIDO	United Nations Industrial Development Organisation
VAT	value added tax
WTO	World Trade Organisation

1 Introduction

Perspectives on development in Asia-Pacific

Martin Andersson and Christer Gunnarsson

The economic miracle in Asia-Pacific was perhaps the most spectacular development experience of the entire world economy during the second half of the twentieth century. The astonishing transformation of a number of countries from agrarian and typically underdeveloped economies into industrial and modern societies has attracted enormous attention and provoked development economists and policy-makers into rethinking their theories and strategies of economic development. The growth experience of the Asia-Pacific region has rightly been held forth as a case of development worth studying and learning from. It has been the case in point for numerous empirical studies and it has generated an abundance of theorising, not least about state–market relations in economic development. The financial crisis that hit the emerging miracle economies of the region during 1997 and 1998 was therefore particularly noteworthy, not only because it challenged the notion of eternal high growth rates, but also because it raised questions about the viability of an East Asian development model.

The chapters in this volume were, in one way or another, occasioned by the financial crisis. The dramatic, and indeed unexpected, economic slowdown in the region not only made the headlines but also had a great impact in turning the course of both academic and policy debates on Asian development. The actual causes behind the crisis have been discussed in terms of either too much or too little supra-market regulation and the resulting analysis has turned out to be an outright clash between divergent explanations and policy recommendations. While some have welcomed the alleged demise of an Asian development model (Alan Greenspan, quoted in Wade 1998), others have lamented the occurrence of the crisis and blamed it on the forces of globalisation (see Wade 1998 and Singh 1999) or the interventions by the International Monetary Fund (IMF) (Sachs 1998 and Stiglitz 1997). The way the origins of the crisis are analysed has obvious implications for the debate on the prospects of development for open economies in an increasingly globalised environment. In our context, the most interesting aspect of the crisis is not what caused the financial turmoil per se, but whether any lessons can be drawn from its occurrence with regard to the mechanisms of growth and structural transformation within the Asian development 'model'. We wish to contribute to this discussion by elaborating upon the *circumstances* in which the crisis erupted, i.e. the context of both globalisation and specific historical development processes in the Asia-Pacific region.

The aim of this volume is thus to highlight two inter-related themes on the ongoing development experience in Asia-Pacific: the effect of global forces on the national Asian economies and the different development paths of these economies as they collectively entered this new phase. It is a well-established fact that up to the 1980s the economic miracle in Asia-Pacific to a large degree rested on strong government–business ties and various forms of state regulation of national markets. This is why controversies over explanations for the economic miracle have tended to be centred so much on the role in the economy played by the state. However, since the mid-1980s the pressure of globalisation has been signified by a process of integration of markets for goods and capital, fundamentally altering the scope and content of government–market relations. In the last decade and a half the tendency has been to dismantle existing national regulatory frameworks and to open up to free capital movements. In this sense the governments in Asia-Pacific have been forced to play according to the new rules of the game, rules set by international markets. This marks a great change for governments that used to be more or less in a position to set their own rules. The challenge is then how to establish a proper balance between state and market in this new global era and how to mitigate the side effects of globalisation. Future economic development in Asia-Pacific will depend immensely on the ways in which these new conditions are managed. In this sense the financial crisis does mark a watershed in the economic performance of the region. These are questions that will be discussed in part one of this volume.

In part two a related set of issues will be discussed. These deal with the tendency to over-simplify explanations for the development experiences in the region. As the processes of recovery are currently unfolding, the economies are displaying divergences regarding economic strength, political repercussions and social stability. These differences signal non-uniformity in terms of underlying structures and process-sequencing that need to be elucidated. The NICs (South Korea, Taiwan, Hong Kong and Singapore) and the ASEAN economies (in this context we refer to Malaysia, Indonesia, Philippines and Thailand) started their industrialisation processes in different periods and under different global conditions and therefore became competitive on the world markets for different reasons. To be more specific, the globalisation forces after the mid-1980s not only threatened the government–business balance in the NICs, but also provided latecomers in the region (first the ASEAN countries and thereafter China and Vietnam) with alternative development paths. This means that if there was indeed something called a development model practised by the Asian NICs in the period 1960 to 1980, it was of little relevance in the speeding up of the process of industrialisation in the ASEAN countries in the 1980s and in China in the 1990s. To acknowledge these differences should be a first step in an attempt to answer the question of what can be learned from the development experience in Asia-Pacific. However, let us first recapitulate the paradigms that have dominated the controversy about how to explain the Asian miracle and what lessons can be drawn from the debate.

The market-friendly approach

The economic miracle in East and Southeast Asia began in the 1950s and accelerated in the 1960s, but it was not until the middle of the 1970s that it attracted any greater attention outside the specialists' camps. With some noticeable exceptions (e.g. Lee 1981), the first forcible attempts to offer a grand explanation for the economic miracle were carried out by scholars affiliated with the World Bank (World Bank 1983). According to their studies, the countries in the region had followed a market-friendly strategy with limited state intervention and a high degree of openness to trade and capital movements. South Korea and Taiwan were put forward as evidence of the superiority of export-led growth vis-à-vis the model of industrialisation through import-substitution behind high tariff protection, which had been the norm in developing countries since the 1950s. With the East Asian experience as evidence, an alternative model could now be presented to Third World countries, a new way out of poverty and economic backwardness. The launching of this growth recipe was quite opportune since it was at about this time that Africa's development crisis had been set off by falling export earnings, mounting foreign debts and failed industrialisation projects. It was also the time of Latin America's debt crisis, which was to put a definite end to a model of industrialisation that had been practised with some success for several decades, but seemed to run out of steam. The East Asian example was therefore actively used as a policy device to prompt structural adjustment programmes in Africa and a reform pro-gramme in Latin America. It was also to have an immense bearing on the Indian liberalisation programme after the mid-1980s.

The export-led growth success of East Asia was not only good news for the world's poor, but also for development research. Development economics was advised to follow a completely new path after having been associated with less successful models of import-substitution and state-controlled forms of indus-trialisation, often under socialist political regimes (Little, Scitovsky and Scott 1970). Development economics, which by the early 1980s was said to be in the doldrums (Lewis 1984), could now regain strength and confidence, not least in its policy agenda. Although the structural adjustment policy was heavily attacked right from the start for being formulated as market-economic shock therapy with painful social effects, it could retain its legitimacy with the East Asian miracle as an analytical alibi and a policy promise. In a number of tone-setting academic studies (e.g. Balassa 1971, 1981, 1988, Little 1981, Riedel 1984) the East Asian success story was attributed to economic openness; in particular, to the fact that the countries of the region had successfully exploited their comparative advantages. While the NICs were not in possession of abundant natural resources of their own, they did have a comparative advantage in a hard-working, relatively well-educated, disciplined and low-paid workforce. Japan had by this time long been an established 'export-led' industrial nation, and Taiwan, South Korea, Hong Kong and Singapore appeared to be successfully following in the trail of Japan's success. This success story could be contrasted against the relative failure of a majority of developing countries where industries had been nurtured behind protectionist barriers.

4 Martin Andersson and Christer Gunnarsson

The look-east recipe for development appeared all the more relevant as other countries in the region (Malaysia, Thailand and Indonesia) also started to exhibit high growth rates during the 1980s. In common with their predecessors, they had competitive export industries and governments which, unlike other Third World governments, kept a close eye on their macroeconomic fundamentals, but did not interfere with markets or get directly involved in production. From this perspective, the role of the state was crucial for creating suitable conditions for economic growth but this role was secondary, the primary task being to maintain the working of a largely self-generating free-market dynamism. 'Getting prices right' was surely a suitable slogan for this approach.

The state-led approach

The end of the 1980s saw the emergence of an alternative type of approach, one that raised doubts about and sometimes rejected the prevailing market explanation (Johnson 1982, White 1988, Amsden 1989, Wade 1990). This approach, proffered by what was to be called the revisionist school, pointed to the fact that the state had not only been efficient in macroeconomic management but had also, and more importantly, taken the lead by adopting selective industrial policies and protectionist trade regimes. The revealed comparative advantages, therefore, had not existed initially but had largely been created by state interference in the market, an intervention sometimes referred to under the slogan 'getting prices wrong' (Amsden 1989). The state intervened in industrial policy with the objective of encouraging the export sector through tax exemptions, credits, import tariffs, and rebates on import duties on industrial intermediary goods. Initially, the export industry was concentrated on simple consumption goods, but gradually production became more sophisticated and directed towards capital goods as national capabilities were being built. New technologies were adopted with surprising ease. The East Asian state apparatus, and, above all, its bureaucracies, were considered unusually enlightened and insulated from influential interest groups. Instead, they represented a national economic interest vis-à-vis the world at large and they were in a position to 'discipline' their own capitalists. It is this argumentation that established the idea of a specific 'East Asian model' with the developmental state as a core ingredient. Developmental states were initially identified in Singapore, Taiwan and South Korea, but the concept was later to be applied in studies of the industrialising ASEAN countries as well. So, from this perspective, the East Asian model was not identical to a reliance on free market principles and Western-style institutions and forms of governance, but was rather a case of state *dirigisme*, in which some free market principles were rejected and Western institutions had been replaced.

The strife between miracle explanations

In its extreme forms this controversy reflects a fundamental conflict between, on the one hand, a sceptical attitude towards the market, with roots in the dependency paradigm, and, on the other hand, a neo-liberal market fundamentalism, which sees the state as the root of inefficiency and development failure. During the heydays of the dependency paradigm in the 1970s, underdevelopment was thought to have its origin in the prevailing capitalistic world order. The only way to pull off a process of economic development was to break away from an unfair and uneven world trade order and resort to self-reliance. The state was thereby given a completely decisive role in the building of all kinds of capacities associated with economic development, from basic needs provision to technological capabilities. The Asia-Pacific economic miracle was of course highly cumbersome for this paradigm. Reality effectively demolished all ideas of the Third World forever being doomed to underdevelopment as long as it relied on integration into the world economy. The Asia-Pacific region thus represented the antithesis of the dependency paradigm. Integration into world trade and more private initiative were better choices than protectionism and state control.

On the other hand, empirical evidence demonstrated that state intervention had been extensive and significant in the fast-growing economies of East Asia, which gradually weakened the simplistic market explanation and made its policy recommendations obsolete. So the challenge by the revisionists had to be taken seriously. In a seminal study instigated by the World Bank (World Bank 1993), the explanation proffered was that the East Asian miracle had been the result of a successful mix of market forces and state policy. Investments in human capital and infrastructure had been an important government contribution, added to which the governments had created prerequisites for the market by setting up regulatory frameworks favourable to private investments, by developing forms of co-operation between the governments and industry, and by maintaining macroeconomic stability. The role of industrial policy, accorded decisive importance for the economic miracle by the revisionist school, was thereby downplayed. A foremost conclusion was that successful state intervention could, in principle, only be observed for Japan, South Korea and Taiwan, while the state's efforts in the Southeast Asian miracle countries were regarded as being more marginal and mostly directed towards maintaining macroeconomic stability and fundamental institutions. Countries such as Malaysia, Thailand and Indonesia were said to have availed themselves less of selective measures and more of general stimulation measures, mainly with the aim of attracting foreign direct investments. In fact, it was now this 'model' and not the East Asian experience that was said to set an example for other developing countries. The reluctance to attribute a decisive, positive role to the state provoked a new wave of criticism from the revisionists, and again the argument about the fundamental role of state intervention was brought to the fore; in particular, the importance of industrial policies for building national capabilities (Fishlow *et al.* 1994). Such was the state of the debate around the mid-1990s.

The controversy takes a new turn

In 1997 the Asian financial crisis struck the world like a bolt from the blue. Decades of unbroken and even accelerating economic growth had fostered the belief that the Asian miracle was practically unlimited. Only a month or so before the crisis began, the Asian Development Bank had published a study, under the leadership of Jeffrey Sachs, extolling the virtues of the Asian growth model and expressing unbounded optimism for the future. (Asian Development Bank 1997). Similar positive assessments were made at the same time by such leading credit evaluation institutes as Standard & Poor's and Moody's. It was in this atmosphere of euphoria that the Thai government devalued the baht in response to the flight of capital and currency speculation, and in which panic suddenly spread throughout the capital and currency markets in the region. The effects, in the form of increased outflows of capital, an escalating external debt and bankruptcies, soon became evident. Investment volumes sank drastically, unemployment shot up and real incomes shrank. In some of the countries of the region the number of poor increased at record speed, with social and political unrest following soon after. The crisis was particularly hard on the urban economy, affecting, in particular, jobs in the manufacturing industries and construction sector. Prices rose dramatically, largely affecting the import-dependent urban sector, while the rural population as a rule was more lightly affected as the relative prices of agricultural products rose.

The financial crisis instantaneously gave rise to a lively debate. As with many other economic crises in history, the first reaction to the unexpected and apparently inexplicable events was one of amazement and confusion. Within the course of a few months, however, a multitude of seemingly rational and logical explanations for the crisis had come forth. It was now seen by many leading analysts as an inevitable consequence of inherent weaknesses and distortions in the Asian economies. It was even considered a natural outcome of an obsolete political–economic system. The obituaries of the Asian model became legion. Concepts such as 'crony capitalism', 'rent-seeking state', 'bad governance' and 'moral hazard' were oft-repeated expressions, and they all contributed to augmenting the picture of a model of economic development in Pacific-Asia doomed to failure (for overviews see Roubini 2002 on the Asian crisis and Wade 2002). The state was thus deemed to have been the main root of the problem. The close ties that were thought to have existed between the political apparatus and industrial and commercial circles were thought to have distorted the market allocation system. Favouritism, rather than competence, formed the basis of government intervention and, in general, transparency was virtually non-existent. Besides, firms had taken extravagant risks in the secure understanding that the government would come to their rescue. This school of thought saw the crisis as marking the end of the Asia-Pacific state-capitalistic model of development.

However, the explanation that the crisis had been an unavoidable result of distortions in the Asian model did not rest unchallenged. Some argued that the Asian model was basically sound and that the crisis was due to panic in the financial markets. The real problem was the large amounts of short-term credits in circulation. When some of the important lending institutions withdrew their loans, they started a capital flight causing the exchange rate to fall. This in turn made it rational for other lending institutions to pull out as well. Panic became a perfectly rational mode of behaviour. The efforts of the IMF, based as they were on the understanding that the crisis had been caused by distortions in the political–economic structure, which aimed at privatisation and the restriction of credits, were therefore thought to have exacerbated the crisis. According to this school of thought, inadequate government regulation and inspection of the financial system were the real causes of the crisis (e.g. Radelet and Sachs 1998). This perspective is quite compatible with a market-friendly approach to the economic miracle but a similar conclusion could also be reached on the basis of a revisionist approach. From the latter perspective it was the dismantling of the controls and regulations under the developmental state and the liberalisation and globalisation of financial markets that made economies in Asia-Pacific more vulnerable to external shocks (Wade 1998). The chapters in part one of this volume touch on these controversies. In this part the Asian economies and the crisis are analysed in the context of intensified integration and globalisation of financial markets. On this issue opinions and interpretations diverge considerably with regard to the effects of globalisation on the national economy, including the capacity of the state to carry out development programmes and policies.

One process, many models – the need for differentiated analysis

The financial crisis also disclosed the obvious but important fact that the miracle economies in Asia are not on the same developmental level. Neither have they based their economic transformation on an identical development model. This is the theme of the chapters in the second part of this volume. The fact that the economies of Asia-Pacific have been interlaced through trade, direct investments, regional co-operation and so on does not imply that their development processes from the start were identical, or even that the 'developmental state' was built on the same premises. Instead, it means that as the countries have become more regionally integrated and the preconditions for economic development have changed in fundamental ways, the demand for and scope of government policy have changed as well.

As a rule, there is an overwrought yearning to generalise and overstate the case of Asia-Pacific, either the miracle or the crisis, which leads to the impression that there is little that differentiates, for example, Taiwan from Thailand, or Thailand from Malaysia. The tendency to engage in such generalisations can, in fact, be expected to increase, especially since the crisis affected almost all the countries of the region at the same time. This would, however, be an injustice to any attempt to learn from the Asian development experience. For example, the perceived even income distribution in the region has been taken to be an outcome of an almost identical mechanism of 'shared development' at work in all countries of the region (e.g. Campos and Root 1996). This is, however, highly questionable since the industrialisation process in the region exhibits a number of individual characteristics and special features. In fact, since the 1970s poverty has declined enormously in the whole region as an effect of economic growth and structural change (Quibria 2002), but the mechanisms at work differ between periods and countries. In the early phase of industrialisation the growth process was largely linked to the transformation of the agricultural sector. The modernisation of agriculture in Japan, Taiwan and South Korea was facilitated by reforms that limited the concentration of agricultural land and encouraged the growth of a class of land-owning farmers. Private as well as public contributions in the agricultural sector increased productivity and per capita incomes to such an extent that the income gap between agriculture and industry did not grow as it usually does in developing economies (Ranis 1996). In this way the domestic market could be deepened and widened in both the production and the consumption of goods with mass-production potential, and in terms of income distribution the East Asian NICs did not exhibit a Kuznetsian inverted U-curve. The pattern in the ASEAN region appears to be more complex. When Malaysia embarked on the process of industrial-isation in the 1960s and 1970s its agricultural sector was greatly modernised, leading to productivity growth and a significant rural poverty reduction. When in the middle of the 1980s Malaysia opened up to foreign direct investments (FDI) and export-oriented manufacturing, only one-third of the labour force remained tied up in agriculture. In Indonesia and Thailand agricultural labour productivity remained much lower and by the early 1980s the agricultural sector still employed 60 per cent or more of the labour force. So when the export drive in manufacturing began in the 1980s these countries remained structurally much less developed than Malaysia, and the production of manufactured goods for international markets became an important factor at an earlier stage. This duality between a highly modern manufacturing sector and a relatively low-productive agriculture (measured in terms of the share of the labour force needed in agriculture) also found expres-sions in terms of uneven income distribution and a latent poverty problem. When the crisis struck, millions were forced into poverty in Indonesia and Thailand, which signifies that they had previously lain precariously over what constituted the poverty line.

That there are large differences between strategies and choices of development paths is an important assertion, not only for the development-theory debate, but also, above all, for what other countries can learn from the Asian miracle countries. The chapters in part two of this volume focus on the diversity of the Southeast Asian cases and on the need to rethink some of the analytical concepts that have been associated with the leading explanations for the economic miracle as well as the crisis.

Part one – global institutions and the state in Asia-Pacific

In chapter two Irma Adelman takes a broad and multidimensional approach to what we have learned about the development process, and suggests how this knowledge should be used in order to make the development process take off, in a world of radically changed global conditions. Adelman's chapter provokes interesting perspectives and questions on how to use our knowledge of past experiences as a guide to the future, both academically and in development practice.

She shows the importance of national autonomy for the creation of comparative advantages, for the ability to choose institutions and trade regimes and for using/ optimising potential resources. All lessons are permeated by the historical fact that governments matter. Of central importance in this context is the fact that the post-World War Two international system allowed latitude for this autonomy at the nation level at the same time as it promoted stability at the international level. Since the current system, according to Adelman, is flawed in these respects, she puts forward some corrective suggestions. In short, she argues for rearranging the global institutions in a development-promoting fashion (à la Bretton Woods), where stability and liquidity once again become the lodestars. Without jeopardising the virtues of recent trends toward liberalising trade and investments, enough rope must also be given to national governments so that adequate policy autonomy is secured.

In the chapter by John Weeks, attention is paid to the capricious nature of the international financial markets. In his comparison with the Latin American debt crisis of the 1980s, he examines the arguments put forward to explain the underlying causes of the Asian crisis. Basing his reasoning on a vast body of empirical material covering the main macroeconomic indicators, he tries to make sense out of the strong and impetuous reaction of the actors in the international financial markets. Weeks finds that the orthodox – wrong policy argument – does not do a good job in explaining the crisis in Asia. The 'fundamentals' did not constitute any cause for alarm, since they were positioned well inside the critical limits. The reason for the crisis is then to be sought outside the realms of rationality, since evidence suggests that the financial markets are inherently unstable. Both the Latin American and the Asian crises, Weeks claims, are signals of this kind of market failure.

Chris Edwards poses four questions and provides four answers. Could the crisis have been avoided? *Yes*. Should it have been avoided? *Yes*. Will similar financial crises occur in the future? *Yes, unless radical changes to national and international policies are adopted*. Are such changes likely to be introduced? *Probably not*. Edwards points out that the causes of the crisis and the remedies required are analysed very differently by two schools of economic thought whose ideas appeal to different fractions of capital. The views of the *neo-liberal* school are attractive to *financial* capital, while those of the *institutionalist* or *Keynesian* school are attractive to *industrial* capital. Edwards finds the analysis of the Asian crisis by the institutionalist school more convincing than that of the neo-liberals but he ends by being pessimistic as to whether the changes advocated by this group of economists are likely to be made. For the moment, the power of financial capital based in the developed countries and particularly in the USA – what Bhagwati has called the Wall Street–Treasury complex – is simply too great.

A clearly different view is delivered in Medhi Krongkaew's chapter, in which he looks at the Thai experience of intervention by the IMF. On balance, he finds more pros than cons in a general assessment of such interventions. First, Medhi suggests that it is all too simplistic to picture the IMF as the scapegoat of the Asian crisis or that its actions exaggerated the downturns as the crisis unfolded. One has to acknowledge the difficulties in dealing with such a wildfire as the Asian crisis,

Medhi argues. The counter-factual, i.e. the non-existence of the IMF, would have been much more detrimental for the region. Moreover, after establishing the importance of the IMF, we should concentrate on how to avoid, or at least how to best handle, future crises. The IMF had initially misdiagnosed the crisis by recommending a decrease instead of an increase in aggregate demand, but when the mistake was discovered it changed its plan for fiscal policy. Despite the harsh criticism from some quarters, Medhi contends that, apart from this mishap at the beginning, the IMF helped Thailand to steer out of the crisis with regard to both monetary and exchange rate policies.

Ishak Shari takes on the issue of the need, and room, for manoeuvre for the state in an era of economic globalisation. By looking at the development history of Malaysia, he discerns a case that both differs from other countries of the region and sets an example of how to reformulate the role of the developmental state. Even though data are still incomplete, available evidence shows that income distribution and other indicators of social welfare became more skewed during the crisis. But unlike, for instance, Indonesia, where matters became far worse, Malaysia maintained ethnic harmony and could keep levels of poverty from plunging into ruin. Ishak states that this was possible thanks to the extensive and deliberate efforts by the state, starting in the early 1970s, in the spheres of poverty-reduction (even if poverty was not eradicated) and income-equalising programmes in the countryside. The rapid industrialisation and expansion of education in Malaysia have also seen the rise of a middle class. When Malaysia, like many other countries in the region, started to liberalise and deregulate in the mid-1980s, she first had to take measures to rely more on the private sector in order to face the economic downturn at the time. While these efforts were quite successful, the process of liberalising and deregulating further deepened to the point where the pre-liberalisation economic arrangements were undermined. For instance, the share of portfolio investments of all inflows of capital had become increasingly dominant by the mid-1990s, and thus weakened the state's capacity to control capital flows and accumulation. This became apparent in the events of 1997–8 when the economy began to contract. However, as Ishak emphasises, the impact of the crisis seemed to be bad, but not disastrous. While the historical achievements described above give one clue as to why Malaysia had a relatively less severe crisis, another factor was her refusal to take the IMF advice of fiscal and monetary tightening. The Malaysian government went its own way instead by introducing selective capital controls and other unorthodox measures. While Ishak recognises that excessive state intervention might breed corruption, inefficiency and downright repression, an unregulated financial system might produce equally bad outcomes. The challenge is to find the balance in between, where equality, growth and stability are juxtaposed.

Part two – divergent development paths among the Asian miracles

The second part of the volume begins with the chapter by Andersson and Gunnarsson, in which some of the leading concepts to explain the economic miracle of Pacific Asia are examined and criticised. Catchy concepts such as *export-led growth*, *developmental state* and *growth with equity*, commonly found in the miracle literature, are often used in axiomatic and metaphorical ways to characterise and describe features of the miracle. Their analytical value is, however, more limited since they are used in a context of policy-choice analyses, in which the miracle is characterised and explained by the conscious choices of enlightened politicians and competent bureaucrats. Andersson and Gunnarsson argue that the concepts are given a fundamentally different meaning if used in a causal analysis of the long-term processes of economic development. Instead of assuming that outcomes are responses to policy choices in terms of trade regimes, industrial policies and distributive arrangements, we should focus on the long-term formation and demise of economic structures. From such a perspective, it is important to determine the structural characteristics of an export-led economy as well as the developmental state. Growth with equity will also have to be determined in relation to development and structural change rather than as a result of policy choices. The authors argue that export-led growth is an outcome of accelerated development and intensified international integration, and not a correct characterisation of the cause of growth. Likewise, the developmental state is a useful concept only if it is defined in terms of government control over capital accumulation, basically via controls over savings and investments. As such the concept may be useful in analyses of the economic miracle but only until the mid-1980s when the national financial systems began to crack and were overshadowed by international financial flows. The concept of growth with equity must also be determined in a structural context. One then finds that a fairly even income distribution is associated with how the initial phase of industrialisation involved a modernisation of the agricultural sector. In this respect, the path followed by Southeast Asia (with the possible exception of Malaysia) differs markedly from the East Asian experience. Due to these historically-determined differences, the countries of Asia-Pacific have responded differently to, and coped differently with, liberalisation and the movement towards higher stages of industrial development as well as the crisis that followed in their footsteps.

Anne Booth examines the educational development among the Asian high performers. She claims that the notion, commonly found in the miracle literature, of all countries having followed the path of Taiwan and South Korea, both of which educated ahead of demand, is deeply erroneous. The crisis made it clear that the actual performances in Singapore, Malaysia, Thailand and Indonesia not only differed from South Korea and Taiwan, but that they also differed among themselves. For the ex-colonies the experiences of the colonial period and the nature of the growth process naturally shaped their educational systems differently. Furthermore, even though every country has attained higher levels of human capital over the last decades, a series of shortcomings must be addressed before those countries can have a chance to reach the standards of the developed world. Booth, in this context, disputes the commonly held views of a strong relationship between growth and enrolments and that the educational systems in the countries have done a good job in reducing inequalities. By taking a closer look at the issue of education among the Southeast Asian cases, Booth aims at forming valuable lessons in order for Vietnam to cope with plausible problems that lie ahead. Vietnam, which in 1980 had a remarkably high level of enrolment rates in relation to its level of GDP, now faces problems of inequality and inefficiency not different from some of the Asian tigers. While Booth concludes that Vietnam never followed the East Asian path (nor did the other Southeast Asian economies), a closer investigation of the Southeast Asian experiences might not only dispute the conventional wisdom of a single Asian model, but also give some hints to Vietnam of what to guard against.

In a similar vein, Jomo K.S. critically examines the idea of the Asian model, as it has generally been conceived since the famous World Bank study of 1993. To understand, and extract lessons from, the dramatic changes that have occurred in East Asia during the last few decades, we need to recognise the differences between the first- and second-tier NICs. Opposed to the above-mentioned study, Jomo emphasises the inferiority of the path chosen by the latter group of countries compared to Taiwan and South Korea, by pointing to the excessive reliance on FDI and the lower technological capability in these countries. In this context, divergences with regard to the autonomy of the state to withstand pressure from *rentiers* have become particularly apparent. These countries' development after the crisis underscores this notion, as the gap left by the declining rate of FDI reveals the daunting challenge of transforming from labour-intensive to technology-intensive industrialisation. Additionally, Jomo raises concerns over the superficial analyses on the part of the international organisations (IOs) in their approach to Asian development. By acting to constrain the options for designing country-specific investment regimes, the IOs not only disregard the lessons to be learned from the East Asian success, but ultimately obstruct the possibilities for sustainable development.

In the concluding chapter Andersson and Gunnarsson relate the financial crisis to the actual development pattern in the region during the last four to five decades by placing the discourse on institutions and policy in a structural and historical perspective. Two propositions are made. First, the development experience in the region can be historically divided into two distinctly separate periods, one before the mid-1980s and one after. Second, within both periods the development patterns that have evolved vary a lot between Northeast Asia and Southeast Asia depending on the forms of substitution undertaken in the process of industrialisation. The financial crisis is interpreted as part and parcel of a long-term development process and as a consequence of events that occurred ten to fifteen years prior to its eruption. The conclusion is that the industrialisation types in the light of the structural change in the region provide relevant lessons for development, both within and beyond Asia-Pacific. It is, however, unlikely that the traditional miracle explanations will be able to contribute toward this end.

Bibliography

Amsden, A. (1989) *Asia's Next Giant: South Korea and Late Industrialization*, New York: Oxford University Press.

Asian Development Bank (1997) *Emerging Asia: Changes and Challenges*, Manila: Asian Development Bank.

Balassa, B. (1971) 'Industrial policy in Taiwan and Korea', *Weltwirtschaftliches Archiv* 106, 1: 55–77.

—— (ed.) (1981) *The Newly Industrializing Countries in The World Economy*, New York: Pergamon Press.

—— (1988) 'The lessons of East Asian development', *Economic Development and Cultural Change* 36, 3: 273–90.

Campos, J.E. and Root, H.L. (1996) *The Key to the Asian Miracle: Making Shared Growth Credible*, Washington, DC: The Brooking Institution.

Fishlow, A., Gwin, C., Haggard, S. and Rodrik, D. (eds) (1994) *Miracle or Design? Lessons from The East Asian Experience*, Washington, DC: Overseas Development Council.

Johnson, C. (1982) *MITI and the Japanese Miracle: The Growth of Industrial Policy 1925–1975*, Stanford: Stanford University Press.

Lee, E. (ed.) (1981) *Export-Led Industrialisation and Development*, Singapore: Maruzen Asia.

Lewis, W.A. (1984) 'The state of development theory', *The American Economic Review* 74, 1: 1–10.

Little, I.M.D (1981) 'The experience and causes of rapid labour-intensive development in Korea, Taiwan Province, Hong Kong, and Singapore and the possibilities of emulation', in E. Lee, (ed.) *Export-Led Industrialisation and Development*, Singapore: Maruzen Asia.

Little, I.M.D., Scitovsky, T. and Scott, M. (1970) *Industry and Trade in Some Developing Countries: A Comparative Study*, New York: Basic Books.

Quibria, M.G. (2002) 'Growth and poverty: lessons from the East Asian miracle revisited', *ADB Institute Research Paper* 33, Tokyo: ADB Institute.

Radelet, S. and Sachs, J. (1998) 'The East Asian financial crisis: diagnosis, remedies, prospects', mimeo, Harvard Institute for International Development.

Ranis, G. (1996) 'The trade–growth nexus in Taiwan's development', *Economic Growth Center Discussion Paper* No. 758, Yale University, New Haven.

Riedel, J. (1984) 'Trade as the engine of growth in developing countries revisited', *Economic Journal* 94, March: 56–73.

Roubini, N. (2002) Nouriel Roubini's homepage, http://pages.stern.nyu.edu/globalmacro.

Sachs, J. (1998) 'The IMF and the Asian flu', *The American Prospect* March–April: 17.

Singh, A. (1999) 'Asian capitalism and the financial crisis', in J. Michie and J. Grieve Smith (eds) *Global Instability: The Political Economy of World Economic Governance*, London: Routledge.

Stiglitz, J. (1997) 'How to fix the Asian economies', *New York Times* 31 October.

Wade, R. (1990) *Governing the Market: Economic Theory and the Role of Government in East Asian Industrialization*, Princeton: Princeton University Press.

—— (1998) 'The Asian debt-and-development crisis of 1997–?: Causes and consequences', *World Development* 26, 8: 1,535–53.

—— (2002) 'Gestalt shift: from "miracle" to "cronyism" in the Asian crisis', *Destin Working Paper Series* No. 02-25, London School of Economics.

White, G. (ed.) (1988) *Developmental States in East Asia*, London: Macmillan.

World Bank (1983) *World Development Report*, Washington, DC: Oxford University Press.

—— (1993) *The East Asian Miracle: Economic Growth and Public Policy*, Washington, DC: Oxford University Press.

Part I

Global institutions and the state in Asia-Pacific

2 Global institutions and economic development

What have we learned?

Irma Adelman

Introduction

Economic development, as distinct from economic growth, combines: (1) self-sustaining growth; (2) structural change in patterns of production; (3) technological upgrading; (4) social, political and institutional modernisation; and (5) *widespread* improvement in the human condition. When 'development' is used in this sense, less than half a dozen countries, mostly East Asian, have travelled the whole path from underdeveloped to developed since World War Two. Others have progressed part-way. The semi-industrial countries have achieved substantial transformations of their patterns of production, and have gone part-way in increasing the sway of markets and the democratisation of their political institutions, but have failed to share the benefits of growth widely. And some Sub-Saharan countries have attained slight growth in human capital and infrastructure but are still relying on primary production and its processing for whatever growth they experience.

The outline of the chapter is as follows: the next section summarises the main lessons about development policy relevant for globalisation, learned from the last fifty years of development. We conclude that state autonomy is critical to development. It is needed for creating comparative advantage, choosing institutions and trade regimes, and for transforming the economy and society. We further conclude that domestic governments are best situated to make the policy and institutional choices that are consistent with their own countries' current conditions and prior history. The next three sections draw the implications of these lessons for global economic institutions. We start by sketching the history and characteristics of the post-Bretton Woods global system. We then point out the severe limits that the post-Bretton Woods global system places on the economic autonomy of national states and examine the remaining broad policy options for developing-country government responses. We end the chapter with specific proposals for limited reforms in the financial architecture of global institutions, designed to allow for greater national autonomy while maintaining the benefits of international trade in goods and long-term international investment flows.[1] Our discussion of these issues is strongly influenced by East Asian experience in national development and by the Korean financial crisis of 1997–8 and its aftermath. Indeed, it is this crisis which sensitised us to the issues analysed in this chapter.

Some policy lessons from post-World War Two economic development

We concentrate primarily on the major lessons that have direct implications for the design of global institutions that are good for the national development of developing countries.[2] Since the North East Asian countries, in general, and South Korea, in particular, have incontrovertibly been the best development performers in the modern era (World Bank 1993, Stiglitz 1996) we rely heavily on their experience to illustrate the propositions in this section.

Lesson one

Perhaps the single most important lesson we have learned is that economic development of developing countries is possible.

This proposition was not obvious in the 1950s, since, prior to the end of World War Two, growth in developing countries had been purely cyclical and exogenously induced. There was little structural change in patterns of production, and even less institution-building or human-resource accumulation. Developing countries' growth was linked to the growth-cycles of metropolitan centres, and waxed and waned in response to changes in international demand for raw materials and food. The growth of overseas territories also depended heavily on the import of factors of production from industrial countries – cyclically varying inflows of investment-capital and the immigration of skilled and unskilled labour (Thomas 1946).

Lesson two

There is scope for choice in institutions, policies and in their sequencing, even at similar levels of development. The choices made, in turn, generate the initial conditions for subsequent development. This is why development policy is possible and why political and economic development are closely linked.

Institutional choices

The most important institutional choice facing developing countries concerns the pattern of government–private sector interactions. In most East Asian nations, the government has successfully played an entrepreneurial role, in much the same manner as it did in the late-comers to the industrial revolution (Amsden 1989, Stiglitz 1996 and Wade 1990). The governments of East Asian countries shaped their financial, investment, trade and commercial policies so as to promote their countries' climbing the ladder of comparative advantage. They restructured institutions to conform to their policy aims, changing old institutions or introducing new ones whenever they embarked on new policy initiatives. They exhibited high degrees of government commitment to development and enjoyed high degrees of autonomy from pressures by business or workers. At the beginning of each policy phase, their initiatives were market-incentive-distorting, though the extent of market distortions was limited by tying subsidies to firms' export performance and, once industries attained certain levels of proficiency, the government spurred competitiveness by shifting to market-conforming policies and by liberalising trade.

By contrast, Latin American governments had less autonomy, exercised less direction, and had less commitment to economic development (McGuire 1997). Their main struggle was over social reform rather than over economic development. Their governments started out as captives of landed feudal elites and the foreign interests to which they were allied (Furtado 1963), and tailored institutions, especially land tenure, to favour landed-elite interests. When urban middle-class concerns became important, they embarked on import-substitution policies, to benefit them, and stayed with these policies till the 1980s.

Policy choices

One significant type of policy choice faced by countries at similar initial levels of development is that of their accumulation strategies. Depending on their accumulation strategies during the 1950s and 1960s, developing countries subsequently achieved comparative advantage in either labour- or capital-intensive products (Balassa 1979). Their contrasting accumulation strategies resulted in divergent consequences for inequality, industrial structure, domestic price levels, international competitiveness and optimal trade policies.

Some countries, primarily in East Asia, commenced development by stressing the accumulation of human capital prior to embarking upon serious industrial-isation, with favourable effects on income distribution, growth, industrialisation and productivity. Others, especially in Africa and the Middle East, initially stressed investment in infrastructure at the expense of acquiring indigenous skills, and imported the human resources needed to initiate industrialisation. This accumu-lation strategy resulted in a narrow-based, dualistic development path: little, low-productivity, industrialisation; natural-resource-based exports; cyclically varying growth, responding to changes in world demand for raw material inputs; and shallow social change. Still other LDCs, mainly in Latin America, embarked on the accumulation of physical capital at an early stage in their development. This led to widening inequality and an insufficient domestic market for the output of manufactures. They were therefore forced into pursuing import-substitute indus-trialisation, with unfavourable consequences for total factor productivity and income inequality.

The phasing of industrialisation and trade policies diverged significantly among countries at similar levels of development. LDCs that stressed physical capital accumulation, primarily in Latin America, pushed into the second phase of import-substitution (in capital- and skill-intensive producer goods), after completing the first phase of import-substitution (in labour-intensive consumer goods) (Waterbury 2000). While they succeeded in promoting significant structural change in their economies, this was at the cost of slow growth, loss of competitiveness, and worsen-ing distributions of income (Krueger 1983). By contrast, LDCs that emphasised the early accumulation of human capital, mainly in East Asia, shifted immediately to export-led growth in labour-intensive consumer goods after a very short period of import-substitution (Adelman 1974, Kuo *et al.* 1981 and Wade 1990). These countries experienced egalitarian growth, increased competitiveness and rapid economic growth.

The histories of Sub-Saharan and intermediate-level developing countries during the last two decades offer further support for the proposition that there exist alternatives in development paths at all levels of development. Thus, while throughout the first two decades of post-World War Two development all Sub-Saharan countries pursued natural-resource intensive development strategies, during 1980–94 some Sub-Saharan countries shifted to broadly-based rural development while others continued their earlier trade-led, natural-resource-intensive, limited industrialisation patterns of narrowly-based economic growth (Adelman, 1999b). At higher levels of development, during the last two decades, some countries at an intermediate level of social development continued their previous dualistic, export-oriented, growth paths while others started concentrating on building the institutional foundations for broad-based development (Adelman 1999b).

A final indication of contrasting policy choice is offered by the varying adjustment patterns to the debt crises of the 1980s (Balassa 1989). Most developing countries in Latin America and Africa adopted restrictive import regimes, deflationary government expenditure and macroeconomic policies, restrained wages, reduced subsidies, and liberalised domestic markets. These measures were undertaken in order to cut their current account deficits, lower inflation, and increase competitiveness. But, for the countries that followed this path, this was a lost development decade, characterised by low growth and mushrooming poverty and inequality, from which they started to emerge only in the 1990s. By contrast, a few NICs, mostly in East Asia but also in Latin America (Brazil and Chile), coped with the adjustment problem by exporting their way out of the crisis. They shifted from import-substitution to export-promotion, devalued to promote expenditure-switching among imports and domestic goods, and raised interest rates to increase net capital inflows. After a short period of curtailed growth rates, these countries rebounded remarkably fast, and successfully grew their way out of the crisis.

Lesson three

Development is a path-dependent process.

Initial conditions affect subsequent development options, so that there are certain irreversibilities in the development process which create path-dependence (Chenery 1960, Chenery and Syrquin 1975, and Temple and Johnson 1998). Path-dependence implies the need to understand the country's prior history of interaction-patterns among civil society, the government, the bureaucracy and the military, how existing institutions have operated, and the legacy of prior interventions, before prescribing a blueprint for institutional change in a given country. Policy prescriptions for a particular country must be anchored in a good understanding of its particular situation at that point in time as well as how it got there, not only recently but also on a historical time scale.[3]

For example, those countries in the former Soviet Union that have only known oppressive government (such as Russia) are more likely to abuse the economic freedom granted by market institutions than countries that have known responsive democratic government before Communism, such as Czechoslovakia, or than countries whose governments have been authoritarian, but in which the government is expected to act in the social interest, such as those of East Asia.

Lesson four

Development policy consists of the creation of dynamic comparative advantage on an accelerated time scale by historical standards. A corollary of this proposition is that the development process entails continual, co-ordinated dynamic change in many aspects of the economy, society and polity: in production patterns and technology; in social, political and economic institutions; and in patterns of human development. Creative evolution, redirection and destruction constitute the essence of successful long-term development. Another corollary is that interventions may have to be multipronged: that what is good for one phase of the development process may be bad for the next phase; and that, while there are certain regularities and preferred time sequences in the process of development, universally applicable institutional and policy prescriptions are likely to be incorrect.

Economies mature through the sequential acquisition of comparative advantage (Balassa 1979) in successively more sophisticated and higher value-added branches of production. Investment patterns, human resources, institutions, culture and incentives must be continually adapted so as to foster comparative advantage in the next set of industries. As a new type of comparative advantage is realised, by mastering its technology, emphasis must be shifted to other sectors or activities.

During the past fifty years, Korea, for example, moved systematically from an agricultural economy in 1953 (when the share of agriculture in value added was 49 per cent and that of industry only 6 per cent) specialising in primary exports (85 per cent of total exports), to a manufacturing economy concentrating on the production and export of manufacturing by 1966 (14 per cent of value added and 61 per cent of exports) centring on light, labour-intensive industry (74 per cent of manufacturing), to a heavy-industry focus by 1981 (54 per cent of manufacturing and 64 per cent of exports), to a technology and knowledge-based economy.[4] It became an industrial country in 1985 (Krueger 1997). Within broad sectors, the composition of output also changed, sometimes dramatically. For example, in the 1960s, the output of the petrochemical sector consisted primarily of labour-intensive coal briquettes, produced in small shops with less than five employees; by the late 1970s, the main activities in the petrochemical sector had evolved into oil refining and agricultural and industrial chemical inputs, produced in big, capital-intensive factories, in a new urban complex of large state-owned enterprises. Similarly, in the 1980s, the primary steel firm produced mainly rolled-steel sheets, while by the early 1990s it had branched out into speciality steels.

The process leading to the acquisition of dynamic comparative advantage is complex and multifaceted. New comparative advantage is achieved through a large variety of *co-ordinated* means whose nature and magnitude change dynamically: through investment in specific factors of production (the acquisition of special skills and human capital, and the construction of plant and machinery) and in infrastructure (roads, ports, airports, electricity generation, telecommunication facilities, etc.); through the creation of an enabling policy climate which realigns incentive systems away from 'old' activities and towards 'new' ones; through the building or restructuring of institutions complementary to the 'new' sectors (financing facilities, national research institutes, trade-promotion centres, industrial processing complexes); and through technology policy. This implies that comparative advantage is man-made, not God-given.

Strategic approaches to the development of dynamic comparative advantage requires a dynamically changing, anticipatory, thrust of policy initiatives. Policy prescriptions cannot remain constant. Rather, they must change with the country's initial conditions – her resource endowments, both physical and human, her development levels, and her institutions.

The same policy prescriptions are not appropriate for all countries or even for a single country at all points of time. The main gist of development policy must change with changes in: (i) domestic conditions, including but not limited to its natural and human resources, its physical capital and its institutional infrastructure, (ii) technological and demographic trends, and (iii) national and international conditions. Policy initiatives should focus on creating the initial conditions for generating comparative advantage in the new activities one wants to promote at a given point in time while improving the productivity of existing activities one wants to retain. The created initial conditions include not only resources, both physical and human, but also the country's institutions, outlook and behaviour. In identifying which new economic activities to stress, one needs to take account of the linkages of the new activities in factor and inputs markets, their optimal scales, and the local and global initial conditions needed for them to thrive. In choosing which activities to develop one also needs to evaluate how the potential new activities might contribute to overall objectives when their direct and indirect effects and their positive and negative externalities are taken into consideration. Because of virtual markets and the globalisation of trade, local output-demand markets are becoming much less important in this decision than are local backward linkages through production.

The East Asian countries have been particularly aggressive and skilful in the acquisition of dynamic comparative advantage.[5] For example, the switch from import-substitution to outward-oriented development in both Korea and Taiwan entailed substantial devaluation (by as much as 50 per cent in Korea in 1964) and aggressive investment in new capacity and infrastructure (investment rates were raised above 20 per cent in both countries, investment in electric energy was undertaken and, in Taiwan, processing facilities for re-export were constructed). In both Korea and Taiwan, a multitude of subsidies was granted to exporters. The export incentives included: numerous quotas on imports (in Korea by commodity, in Taiwan not only by commodity but also by country of origin), automatic import licences and foreign exchange allocations for inputs used in the production of exports and their duty free entrance, access to otherwise tight credit at high nominal but subsidised real rates and, in Korea, an industry-specific wastage-allowance system that permitted the domestic sale of some portion of the raw materials imported for export purposes. In Korea, individual firms were allocated export targets and their performance relative to the target was strictly monitored by the Ministry of Commerce as well as by the President himself (Cole and Lyman 1971, Jones and Sakong 1980). If the firms exceeded their target, they were rewarded with further credit and foreign exchange allocations; if they fell short, they were admonished and, if they did not 'shape up' they were punished with sanctions ranging from turning off utilities, to IRS audits, to shutting them down by revoking their trading licences.

When, in 1973, Korea embarked on its heavy and chemical industries (HCI) drive, the government's role in promoting this reorientation from textiles and footwear towards steel, petrochemicals, shipbuilding, machinery, non-ferrous metals, and electronics became especially heavy handed. Some Koreans perceived it as a forced march, and worried about its inflationary implications, the substantial difficulties it generated for traditional exporters, and the concentration it promoted in industrial organisation in manufacturing.

The switch from the promotion of comparative advantage in the production of light, consumer goods to heavy and engineering industries entailed a second, substantial shift in policy. The special export incentives were largely withdrawn from the labour-intensive industries (indeed they became starved of credit) and shifted to capital-intensive HCIs. The HCIs received massive financial assistance: over 50 per cent of policy loans at specially subsidised rates and 47 per cent of general bank loans in manufacturing. The tax incentives for traditional exports were reduced while tax incentives for the new industries were raised, albeit tempo-rarily. Also, the HCIs benefited from a multitude of extensive industry-specific, targeted supports, granted under special laws enacted to promote each individual HCI. There was a complete shift to a classical import-substitution programme in producer-goods industries accompanied by a switch towards free trade in light consumer-goods industries.

Whether the HCI drive was desirable is debatable. On the negative side, it was certainly very expensive, it drastically increased the capital output ratio of the economy (by 50 per cent), it raised industrial concentration, it promoted industrial giantism, and it produced severe dislocations for the high-employment traditional industries. It also increased the government's role in the economy not only indirectly but also directly, since many of the HCIs were state-owned enterprises and gave a large push to the conglomerates (*chaebols*) who were 'asked' to branch out into some HCIs. It was also ill-timed, coming, as it did, just before the first oil-shock which tripled the cost of oil inputs into oil refineries and petrochemical industries. On the positive side, the economy's growth rate continued high, as did its exports, despite the world-wide recession. The potentially negative distributional effects of the reorientation towards capital-intensive growth in manufacturing were mitigated through simultaneous emphasis on labour-intensive rural economic and social development. And some of the HCIs became internationally competitive very quickly, with Korean steel displacing steel production by US Steel and Korean shipbuilding displacing Swedish shipbuilding in less than five years from their start. Other industries, especially the petrochemicals, did not become internationally competitive for ten to fifteen years. And, last but not least, by the 1980s, the HCIs had become the backbone of the economy and its predominant exports.

The consequences of failing to base policy on a dynamic approach to comparative advantage is illustrated by Latin America, where countries stuck with their focus on developing large-scale, heavy industries through ISI from the 1960s to the early 1990s. Their history indicates that countries that have used static, rather than dynamic, comparative advantage as a guide for development policy eventually stagnate.

Lesson five

The most critical factors needed to generate development are both tangible and intangible. In order of importance, they are:

Leadership commitment to economic development

This concept includes not only the willingness of the leadership to submerge personal and short-run considerations to the common long-run welfare but also the capacity of the bureaucracy and its dedication to the pursuit of common long-run goals. Adelman and Morris (1967: 241) found that, once the major economic and social obstacles to development had been overcome, inter-country differences in leadership commitment to development explained as much as 66 per cent of inter-country differences in rates of economic growth.

Similarly, in Korea, it was not until President Park, whose major commitment was to economic development, had replaced President Syngman Rhee, whose primary commitment was to achieving and maintaining political autonomy, that the economy started taking off. Prior to that Korea was considered by the US a 'basket case' and 'the hell hole of foreign assistance' (Cole and Lyman 1971). Finally, visionary leadership has been identified as a significant factor in instituting and maintaining credible commitment to institutional and policy reforms (Williamson 1994).

The level of social capital

This concept includes not only the supply of human resources but also the extent of social cohesion, and the willingness to act in the social good. 'Social capital' (Abramovitz 1986) reflects the extent of social trust, co-operative norms, and the density of inter-personal networks (Evans 1997). The critical importance of social capital for developing countries has been confirmed by Temple and Johnson (1998). Social capital generates a synergistic relation between the state and civil society

(Evans 1997) in which active states and mobilised communities enhance each others' effectiveness. The degrees of social and economic stratification, ethnic homogeneity, and religion/culture cleavages are important in determining the level of social capital in a given society and hence the society's acceptance of reform initiatives.

Kerala, however exceptional it might be in India, is a case in point. There, the interaction between state and labour in a society with high social capital generated the economic processes and political institutions for redistributive growth (Heller 1997). Similarly, Wade (1982) attributes the contrast in effectiveness of irrigation systems in Korea and Taiwan, on the one hand, and their ineffectiveness in India, on the other hand, to contrasts in their degrees of social development. Korea and Taiwan have socially cohesive citizenries while India's social structure is highly stratified. Social capital is also an important ingredient in economic reform, as social consensus for reform widens the political base for change (Williamson 1994) and thus facilitates its implementation and enhances the probabilities of reform-survival. A deeply stratified society with low levels of mutual trust is likely to fight over the distributional benefits from reform, even when the net benefits of reform are widely distributed, since different groups are unlikely to feel that commitments to sharing benefits will be honoured once reforms are implemented (Bardhan 2000).

Fortunately, however, social capital is endogenous and can be enhanced (or depleted) by the nature of interactions between the state, external agents (such as students or NGOs) and societal civic actors. To mobilise communities for the next thrust of development requires forging alliances between 'good bureaucrats', reformists within the state, the media and socially motivated groups that articulate civic aspirations and grievances, on the one hand, and civic groups, on the other.

The tangible inputs

The tangible inputs (infrastructure, physical and human capital, investment and finance), while important, tend to respond to the intangible ones. For instance, using a stochastic growth model, Uedo (2000) finds that the high investment rate in Korea between 1960 and 1980 exceeded that which would have been undertaken in response to market forces alone. The classical economists regarded investment as the critical prime mover of development. Indeed, Rostow (1960) posited that an increase in the national savings rate to above 15 per cent was a precondition for development. And the World Bank was founded to provide foreign savings when domestic savings are insufficient to finance the necessary investment push. However, the tangible inputs are the handmaidens of development, not the ultimate source of development. For example, a statistical analysis of time series for the last fifty years of development in Korea has indicated leadership commitment to development Granger-caused investment (Adelman and Song forthcoming. This is a special sense of causality. While it does not prove causality, it provides a strong presumption in its favour.). When leadership commitment to development is high, investment resources can be mobilised. But investment by itself can only contribute to economic growth, not generate development, in the sense the term is used in this chapter.

Appropriate policies

Appropriate policies, especially with respect to trade, technology, accumulation, investment and macroeconomic management, are important for both growth and development. But they must change dynamically with development and are not constant, either across different industrial sectors or across the same sector over time. They must also be co-ordinated.

Institutions and culture

Institutions and culture can either support or thwart development. Institutional modernisation, in the sense of increased emphasis on markets and trade, was stressed by the neoclassical development economists of the 1980s. Interest in the role of institutions in economic growth has been reawakened by the problems of transition in the former Soviet Union and by the Asian crisis.

The considerable quantitative importance of socio-cultural, economic and political institutions for development was first analysed by Adelman and Morris (1967) in their factor analytic studies of development in the 1960s. It was confirmed by their analyses of patterns of development during the industrial revolution (Morris and Adelman 1988).

Similarly, the World Bank (1996), in its analysis of transition processes in the former Soviet Union, attributes a large percentage of inter-country variance in economic growth rates to the degree of development of market institutions. A recent study by Aron (2000) also finds significant simple correlations between different aspects of social and political institutional modernisation and economic growth rates.

The quantitative impact of the modernisation of economic institutions on economic growth increases as countries become more developed. Adelman and Morris (1967) found that the level of development and degree of improvement in financial and tax systems accounted for 4 per cent of inter-country variance in growth rates of countries at the lowest level of socio-economic development and 50 per cent of variance in growth rates for countries at high levels of socio-economic development.

Institutional change can occur endogenously, in response to a change in transactions cost (North 1990). It can also happen in reaction to a crisis (as in India in 1991), or it can arise in answer to technological or to social change in power relations (Marx 1853). But in developing countries reforms occur mostly in response to state action, since co-ordination failures, free rider problems, risk, distributive conflicts and moral hazard impede automatic responses from the private sector through the creation or amendment of existing institutions (Lin and Nugent 1995).

The structural adjustment era of the 1980s saw substantial evolution of market institutions and liberalisation of trade in most Latin American and Asian countries; the Latin American liberalisations occurred in response to their financial crises and to pressure from international institutions urging pursuit of 'Washington Consensus' policies, and was more rapid than in East Asia. These exemplify institutional change introduced from above in response to a crisis and to external influences. A different example of institutional change is offered by Korea in the 1960s and 1970s, where each major new government policy initiative entailed creating a new institutional vehicle for its implementation. For example, the assumption of an entrepreneurial role by the state, when President Park took office, called for deep institutional reform in the bureaucracy and the strengthening of the Economic Planning Board; similarly, embarking on broad-based rural development called for the creation of a new superagency to co-ordinate and oversee the rural-animation policies of different government departments (Adelman and Song forthcoming).

Institutional and social resilience and malleability

These attributes of the society and polity are critical to successful long-run economic development because development calls for continual, non-linear dynamic change in all aspects of economy, polity and society. One therefore needs to be able to switch out of activities and institutional modes that have become unprofitable or undesirable. The need for higher adaptability has been enhanced by the intensified speed of technological change associated with globalisation (Streeten 2001).

State development initiatives are not always wise, well-timed and of appropriate scale. When mistakes are made, or when development revises the initial conditions, or when the global circumstances evolve, sufficient institutional malleability, social capital and social resilience are needed to allow what may even be a drastic about-turn. For example, the HCI drive in Korea in the late 1960s, was premature, extremely costly, and ill-timed, occurring as it did just before the formation of the oil-cartel which drastically raised the input prices for these industries. Fortunately, in 1980–1, Korea was able to abandon the subsidies to these industries and force them to become competitive. This enabled the HCI to become the backbone of the economy and to account for over 50 per cent of its exports during the mid-1980s and 1990s.

Historically, economies that cannot adapt get stuck in a particular developmental phase in which they ultimately stagnate. Most East European countries had sufficient political flexibility to enable them to introduce partial market reforms even during the Communist era; this enabled them to resume growth after a short period of adjustment to the break-up of the CIS (World Bank 1996). By contrast, during the Soviet era the Communist Party in the Soviet Union was sufficiently strong to block *all* attempts at partial market reform. Consequently, the Soviet Union started to stagnate and even decline and when it ultimately broke up, it did not have sufficient institutional development to avoid plunging into an economic tailspin.

Lesson six

The nature of trade and commercial policies is critical to development. Export-orientation promotes growth and structural change.

Trade is critical for developing countries because it is the only wild card in the deck which enables them to decouple national production from national consumption. Shortfalls in domestic production can be corrected through imports, and surpluses can be disposed of through exports. Trade is especially important for small or very low-income countries, with domestic markets that are too small to enable them to adopt an efficient production-scale. But, as we saw above, the trade incentives offered to particular industries need to be changed dynamically. Generally, infant-industry protection is required to encourage new activities, but protection must be gradually withdrawn once the infant approaches adolescence to promote efficiency. Trade policies must therefore consist of a changing mix of selective protection for some industries and free trade for others. The changing dynamic thrust of trade regimes is a direct result of developing countries' pursuit of dynamic comparative advantage. However, trade policies were never pure. In both Korea and Taiwan, the import-substitution periods emphasised exports as well as import-substitution. Conversely, selective import-substitution (e.g. in cement, fertiliser and petroleum) was also characteristic of the heyday of their export-led growth.

The evolution of trade and trade-related incentives in Korea and Taiwan illustrates this point (Scitovksy 1985). The East Asian economies pursued *four* different trade regimes. They started with import-substitution in manufactured consumer goods (1961–5 in Korea and 1952–8 in Taiwan); during this period import-substitution provided the major impetus to economic growth (in Korea, Kim and Roemer's (1979) calculations indicate that 46 per cent of growth was due to import-substitution, as compared to only 7 per cent for export-expansion). The primary focus of import-substitution policies in this phase was on labour-intensive consumer industries rather than on producer goods, though some producer-goods industries (cement, fertiliser) were also developed during this period. Economic growth and restructuring were rapid (Krueger 1997) during this first phase of import-substitution.

Next came a period of export-orientation, during which trade incentives were changed to induce the previously import-replacing consumer goods producers to reorient their sales towards exports. The stress upon export-orientation in this early phase was where the East Asian economies differed from all other developing countries, which followed up their initial import-substitution in labour-intensive consumer goods with import-substitution in capital-intensive producer goods. This difference in trade strategy is responsible for the contrast between the rapid expansion of the East Asian economies and the slow growth of the rest of the developing world.

But it would be incorrect to view this period as an 'open economy' period, since the effective exchange rate on exports was 20 per cent higher than on imports (Kim and Westphal 1977). Rather, one should view it as a *mercantilist* period (Hong 1994) of active encouragement of export-led growth in labour-intensive, consumer-goods industries, during which a multitude of price and non-price measures was used to promote exports and discourage imports.

Nevertheless, there was some trade liberalisation as well as general liberalisation of the economy during the export-led growth period. The number of items whose imports were forbidden was reduced substantially. Tariff rates were lowered. The real effective exchange rates for imports and exports, though still biased, were moved towards greater neutrality, and the incentive-bias towards imports was less than in most other developing countries or than it would become during the next trade-policy phase. Finally, the import privileges of exporters were transformed from being targeted in a discretionary manner to individual firms, to generalised, non-targeted incentives available to any exporter. Thus, the Korea–Taiwan experience suggests that a country cannot launch a successful export drive while maintaining extreme degrees of import restriction, even when international retaliatory moves are ignored.

This export-led growth period led to accelerated growth and structural change, as is typical of labour-intensive, manufacturing, export-led growth periods in most developing countries. In Korea, exports grew by a phenomenal average annual rate of 46 per cent and the average annual growth rate of real GNP rose to 9.6, almost 25 per cent higher than during the previous import-substitution period. Inequality decreased.

The third trade policy phase, the HCI phase, entailed a return to heavy-duty protectionism and intensification of government interventionism. However, despite increased emphasis on import-substitution this period was not accompanied by an abandonment of export-led growth. Rather, export growth was 'encouraged' through the imposition of firm-specific export targets rather than through exchange rate incentives. Nor did it lead to a slow-down in economic growth. In part, this was because of continued stress on exports even in the newly established HCIs, but it was also because of the increased demand for exportables due to the Vietnam War.

The average tariff rate in Korea during this phase was increased initially by 50 per cent, and then reduced gradually. The import liberalisation ratio declined from a high of 60 per cent in 1967 to 50 per cent in 1978 and there were significant increases in import restrictions on HCI-competing industries. Growth remained high but inequality rose.

The fourth and final phase in Korea's (and Taiwan's) trade policy came at the beginning of the 1980s, when most trade restrictions were dismantled and most subsidies, even to HCIs, were withdrawn. This entailed an abrupt about-face in trade policy.

The growth rate of the economy continued to be very high, especially throughout the 1980s. Growth and exports became self-propelled, rather than government-driven.

Lesson seven

The government has a central role to play in the promotion of economic development. But its functions must adapt dynamically, as development proceeds, ending up in a quasi-Smithian phase.

No area of economic development has been as contentious as the professional attitudes concerning the role of government in the economy. General professional attitudes have undergone three different phases. The first thirty years of development economics viewed government as a necessary prime mover, and reflected the view that the state represents a Platonic, social welfare-guided arbiter among conflicting interests. The state is needed to correct co-ordination failures in interdependent industrial investments and move the economy out of the low-level equilibrium trap (Leibenstein 1957).

Then, in the 1980s, came a delegitimisation of the state. It started with a recognition that, despite rapid economic growth, the government-guided development process had not delivered improvements in the living standards of the poor in Latin America, South Asia and Africa. The bias against the state was reinforced by the shift in ideology in industrial countries evident in the wholesale replacement of Democratic and Labour governments by Republican and Tory governments throughout the OECD. The Washington Consensus blamed development failures on government policies and institutions that it claimed accorded too much power to the state. State policies that distorted factor prices against wages were criticised for the failure of rapid growth and structural change to deliver commensurate increases in employment and benefits to the poor. Government focus on industry, its neglect of agriculture, and its reliance on inappropriate imported technologies that were capital-intensive and induced distortions in factor prices were held accountable. The pendulum swung against government-led development. The view of the state was amended from 'Platonic arbiter' to predatory, rent-seeking, corrupt and waste-inducing. International institutions (the World Bank and the IMF) encouraged a shift in dominant professional opinion towards a limited state, which does best for development by doing least. The universal nostrum touted as a panacea for the ills of developing countries became domestic and international institutional reform consisting of marketisation and liberalisation. GATT was established to liberalise international trade and the IMF and the United States used their influence to liberalise capital flows.

The third phase, in which we are currently, saw a partial rehabilitation of the state. This rehabilitation was due in part to a shift against socially conservative governments in OECD countries; in part to a reinterpretation of the East Asian experience (World Bank 1993); and, in part, to a general recognition of the disastrous consequences for Latin America of 'Washington Consensus' growth. There came a swing of professional opinion in favour of a more active role for the state (Stiglitz 1989, World Bank 1997).

The 'government can do no right' camp now recognises that the withdrawal of the government from the economy entails potentially damaging consequences for efforts to stimulate economic growth. It recognises that government action is critical to getting development started, that interactions between the public and the private sector are not only competitive but also complementary, and that there exists a synergy between greater governmental capacity and the development of markets. However, while now arguing for increasing the capacity of the state, the new consensus (World Bank 1997) still regards greater government capacity merely as an instrument for promoting the role of markets – reducing the distortion of market incentives, liberalising trade and promoting economic efficiency. The main role it assigns to the state is the use of its powers to generate a neoclassical world in which the private sector and market institutions predominate. Thus, the new reigning consensus continues to underplay the role of governments in stimulating dynamic comparative advantage, through mechanisms other than the liberalisation of commercial and trade policy. It also denies that the state has a legitimate interest in promoting a wider sharing of the benefits of growth and structural change, or that it can exercise its power through its regulatory and institution-creating functions.

The 'government can do no wrong' school shares with the 'government can do no right' school an enhanced recognition that too high a level of market distortions can be harmful to growth. They hold that if governments are oligarchic and personalistic, and bureaucracies corrupt, their policy interventions and the institutions they promote can harm both growth and distribution. And both see greater transparency and less discretionary interventions as preferable. Both sides further agree that, as we saw in the previous section, the government must aim at working its way out of supporting adolescent industries, so as to foster their maturing into internationally competitive activities.

If the view of development as a process of sequentially mastering comparative advantage in technologically more sophisticated industries is correct, *developmental* states must also assume an active role in industrial policy and in stimulating the acquisition of dynamic comparative advantage. Markets alone are insufficient to climb the ladder of comparative advantage, since the successful generation of new comparative advantage requires *co-ordinated and anticipatory* changes in investments, institution-creation and reform, and trade and tax-cum-subsidy policies. Only governments can correct co-ordination failures in all these manifold facets of change. In developed countries, where financial institutions and entrepreneurs are ready to undertake quite risky activities, markets alone may be adequate to the task,[6] but not in developing countries where financial institutions and entrepreneurship are inadequate and institutional change can only be promoted by government (see lesson five above).

Markets are not particularly good at predicting the future when development is non-linear. They also cannot take account of externalities, both positive and negative; to correct for this deficiency requires internalising the externalities through tax and subsidy policies, but this requires government intervention. Markets promote the efficient use of resources but only when externalities are successfully internalised and the economy is competitive. Making economies competitive, though, also requires intervention (e.g. through enforcing anti-trust legislation). Making markets work thus, in itself, requires capable, autonomous and honest governments.

The strengths of government reside in correcting co-ordination failures (Hoff and Stiglitz 2000 and Hoff forthcoming) in both investment and institution-creation, and in substituting alternatives for missing or immature institutions. Co-ordination failures in investment are due primarily to externalities and economies of scale in production; co-ordination failures in institution-building arise primarily from collective action difficulties (free rider problems, distributional conflicts, and the fact that losses are almost always immediate while gains are usually delayed). Collective action problems are usually more severe in developing countries that are plagued by lack of social capital, ethnic, religious and regional disparities, high levels of economic and political inequality, and major resources devoted to rent-seeking.

Since the strengths of markets and governments are largely complementary, a dynamically evolving mix of the two is needed. The relative roles of the governments and markets should unfold with development, not only overall but also in particular sectors. Initially, the state must take a more active role in the economy; once the growth habit becomes entrenched in a sector or in the economy as a whole, markets should assume ascendancy.

During the first forty post-World War Two years, the East Asian states relied most on government for their economic development, as did the successfully industrialising follower-countries during the industrial revolution (Morris and Adelman 1988). They all employed three major types of instruments: market and non-market incentives; discretionary and non-discretionary bureaucratic interventions; and moral persuasion. Korea's economic growth was not a case of simply 'getting prices right' (Amsden 1989). In addition to price policy, Korea's government made use of a multitude of market and non-market, discretionary and non-discretionary, incentives to achieve both general and specific industrial-policy goals. Neither was it a case of 'getting prices wrong'. Rather, Korea's economic development consisted of a creative dynamic mix of prices that were almost right with subsidies, targets, directives, regulations and controls that provided just the right blend of carrots and sticks. The mix among instrument-types varied over time and by sector, but even now Korea's institutions do not fit the purely neoclassical, laissez-faire, mould.[7]

The importance of government for long-run development has several corollaries. The first corollary is that a government with substantial autonomy, capacity and credibility is required for successful long-term economic development. A certain degree of independence from pressures emanating from entrenched economic elites is necessary to implement the switches among policy regimes (e.g. from import-substitution to export-led economic growth) or to engineer the fundamental changes in economic institutions required for the pursuit of dynamic comparative advantage. Such policy-regime switches inflict inescapable injuries upon some entrenched economic interests, such as entrepreneurs and workers in the protected import-substitute enterprises, while only *promising potential benefits* to other groups, such as the would-be exporters and their workers, and that only after painful restructuring to become export-competitive. Popular support for major policy-regime switches is therefore unlikely, especially over a time-frame long enough for the new policy regime to become effective. Repeated abortive trade-liberalisation efforts in Latin America and recent elections of Communist leaders in some reforming Central European countries underscore this point.

The second corollary is that of the nature of the state and its relation to civil society matter. This statist-capitalism approach will not have much of a chance of success if the domestic political/bureaucratic actors are not capable, honest and committed to modernisation. It must pursue increases in the welfare of all its citizens by representing national rather than particularistic, elitist, ethnic or religious special-group interests. A strong state that adopts self-serving, divisive, or simply misconceived economic policies and/or institutions can generate economic disasters. The last twenty-five years of indifferent, poorly distributed economic growth in most African nations, in a large number of Latin American countries and in the non-defence sectors of the former Soviet Union underscore this point. A non-activist government would have been preferable to a strong, captive government promoting bad policies.

However, these are not the only alternatives. The economic histories of Japan, the four little tigers, the seven flying geese, and post-1980 China suggest rather strongly that the combination of a developmental state with good economic policy is unbeatable. Their experience underscores that a technocratically-influenced developmental state, that is relatively autonomous from special interests, with an economically-literate meritocratic bureaucracy, is key to long-run success in broad-based economic development.

Corrupt, rent-seeking, venal states can be transformed into developmental states. This can be done from above, by leaders committed to development, as in Korea and Taiwan. When the Kuomintang was expelled from the Chinese mainland, it realised that this was in great part due to its corruption, rampant inflation, and maldistribution of benefits from growth. It therefore set out to create a develop- mental state when it assumed power on Taiwan through measures such as redistributive land reform and the imposition of severe penalties for corruption on civil servants and the military. Similarly, when President Park assumed power in Korea, he quickly transformed the corrupt, self-serving bureaucracy he had inherited into a meritocratic one by a combination of firing and jailing corrupt bureau-chiefs and enterprise owners and retraining the rest. Alternatively, states that are self-serving can be induced to become more developmental by exposing them to external pressures through international aid conditionality based on human rights and distributional provisions, and through the activities of NGOs (Streeten 2001). They can also be subject to pressures by civil society from below. But this is a risky course, for the pressures for reform of the state may escalate into humanly very costly civil wars. Or they may end by the mere replacement of authoritarian, particularistic governments responding to one set of special interests with authori- tarian, particularistic governments responding to the interests of another group, ethnicity, or religious or secular ideology.

The third (and final) corollary stemming from the critical and dynamically changing role governments must play in the economic development of their countries is that they must have sufficient autonomy not only from domestic political constraints but also from international constraints on their economic actions. This proposition is sufficiently important to warrant stating it as a separate lesson of post-World War Two economic development for globalisation.

Lesson eight

The prospects for economic development are intimately linked not only to the countries' own institutions but also to the global economic and political institutional conditions.

What is needed is a global environment that affords sufficient autonomy to developmentally-oriented national states.[8] Economic development became feasible only after World War Two, when developing countries acquired an unprecedented degree of autonomy in managing their economic destinies thanks to political independence, a benign global system, subsidised capital and technical assistance from developed countries, and rapid global economic growth. Thus five countries that were developing in the 1950s (Israel, Japan, Korea, Singapore, and Taiwan) became developed by the 1990s and about twenty, mostly Latin American, countries in which manufacturing played only a minor role at the end of World War Two became semi-industrial by the 1980s. By contrast, since the Bretton Woods global system crumbled there has been little progress in development, if any. Indeed, the 1980s were known as the lost development decade.

The emergence of the current global economic system and its characteristics

After the end of World War Two, the global economic system was redesigned so as to offer scope for increased economic interdependence while allowing national governments to pursue their own welfare and development goals. The architect of the post-war global system, Lord Keynes, knew well that the pursuit of national full employment required a global system that would permit governments to embrace anti-cyclical domestic policies; set wage policies and undertake anti-poverty measures that would be consistent with the particular government's social goals; and choose how fast it wanted to increase its rate of economic growth. He also knew that these pursuits required global economic stability and would be facilitated by enlarging the scope of world trade. The system he designed, known as the Bretton Woods system, was one of fixed, but adjustable, exchange rates with a lender of last resort and an international arbiter of when national exchange rates were systematically under- or over-valued (the IMF). The Bretton Woods system stressed trade liberalisation but explicitly encouraged barriers to international short- and long-term capital flows. National governments thus acquired autonomy in setting the macroeconomic framework for their growth. They could choose the particular combinations of exchange rates, fiscal and trade deficits, domestic unemployment, inflation, interest rates, and wage and welfare policies that suited their special social traditions and current economic goals. They could also choose their trade and commercial policies.

Between 1947 and 1973 (and for the first time in history), the global system extended the necessary degree of economic autonomy not only to developed countries but also to the newly decolonised under-developed nations. For them, the system offered even greater autonomy than it did for industrialised nations by designing national and international institutions to augment their meagre supplies of saving and foreign exchange earnings through multilateral and bilateral aid and by exempting them, for a time, from free-trade requirements. The result was a Golden Era of economic development. It combined full-employment growth in developed countries with the development of LDCs, consisting of a combination of economic growth and structural change, in the politically, socially and economically more advanced developing countries. The result was the emergence of about twenty semi-industrial countries, poised for entry into the club of industrialised nations.

This permissive, benign global economic system broke down abruptly in 1973, with the first oil crisis. The seeds for its breakdown had been laid earlier. Towards the end of the 1960s, the liquidity needs of the world trading system could no longer be satisfied by the US dollar-based Bretton Woods system. The supply of the international reserve currency (the US dollar) became inadequate for the growing needs of international commerce. Also, there had been a slowdown in the growth of productivity in industrial nations; national wage settlements had started to exceed the growth of productivity; inflationary pressures were mounting; and a bunch of price shocks, in oil and grain prices, were imposed exogenously. The Bretton Woods system broke down and was replaced by a flexible exchange rate system with progressively more open capital markets and commodity trade, in which governments lost their economic autonomy.

Macroeconomic policies now had to become co-ordinated. For developed countries the co-ordination is accomplished through international negotiations among them. At the regular, periodic consultations among the G7 industrial nations, agreement is reached on the general thrust of national macroeconomic policies. They decide in a concerted fashion whether to stress macroeconomic stability (fight inflation and achieve balance of payments equilibrium), or pursue full employment and growth. Nations that try to do it alone are severely disciplined by the world's financial markets. As to developing countries, under the new global system, those with relatively open capital markets or those requiring economic assistance from international agencies have to passively accept globally-established interest and exchange rates. This means that they cannot devalue strategically, in either nominal terms or through changes in domestic inflation, to encourage exports; and they cannot unbalance their government budgets or loosen monetary policy beyond modest degrees to subsidise or finance domestic investment. Otherwise they will experience large, disequilibrating short-term capital outflows or inflows, which can quickly turn into devastating financial and banking crises, and greatly amplify cyclical swings in their real economies. The 1980s in Latin America, and the late 1990s in East Asia and Russia, dramatically demonstrate the validity of this proposition.

Since 1980, three-quarters of the IMF's member countries, developed and developing alike, have been hit by financial crises. Indeed, of the over seventy financial crises that have occurred lately, fully one-third were in developed countries. Why are financial crises so frequent now while absent before 1973? Largely because in 1973, when the supply of US dollars became woefully inadequate for world trade, the global financial system was changed drastically. Flexible exchange rates replaced fixed ones and, under US and IMF pressure, open capital markets are increasingly replacing closed short-term capital markets and regulated foreign investment flows. These changes have provided the conditions enabling financial crises to take place by robbing countries of their economic autonomy.

The proximate triggers for these financial crises have been massive capital outflows, which the architecture of the global financial markets enables, if not stimulates. Unfortunately, the architecture of these markets is faulty. As pointed out by Tobin (1974), international markets for foreign exchange are too smooth, permitting the transfer of vast sums to be carried out instantaneously; they are much too large, enabling immense amounts of cash to be brought to bear on any currency at any moment in time; and they also have an inherent tendency to overshoot, generating waves of overly optimistic risk-assessments, leading to over-lending, followed by overly pessimistic risk-assessments, leading not only to the cessation of new loans but also to huge withdrawals of foreign currency. They are thus pro-cyclical in nature, amplifying both domestic and international recessions and prosperity. Controlling short-term capital movements would short-circuit the start of the process (Adelman and Yeldan 2000). Without them, neither a currency appreciation due solely to foreign capital inflows, nor a currency depreciation due to capital flight, could get started.

The magnitude of the potential problems generated by short-term international financial flows becomes obvious when one realises that according to the Bank for International Settlement's figures, during 1993–5, *daily* foreign exchange trans-actions averaged 1.3 trillions. By 1997, the daily volume of foreign exchange transactions had increased to 1.5 trillion. The daily volume of foreign exchange transactions is six times the value of *annual* private long-term foreign investment. Moreover, 40 per cent of international foreign exchange transactions are reversed within two days (and 80 per cent within seven days) and are thus clearly speculative in nature. The volume of speculative foreign exchange transactions in 1997 was 600 billion per day! No country, however large and however developed (transparent and accountable) its domestic financial institutions, is immune from currency attacks. The enormous swings in gross capital flows that ensue constitute the essence of financial crises. In turn, these crises lead to banking failures, instability in asset prices, deep depressions, and rapid increases in poverty. The induced volatility of exchange rates is also an impediment to other kinds of globalisation: it discourages foreign trade in goods and services as well as private direct investment.

In the post-Bretton Woods global payments regime, governments of both developed and developing countries are precluded from pursuing independent economic policies. They cannot set an exchange rate which does not equilibrate the country's current account balance (i.e. is out of alignment with its international competitiveness and economic reputation), or an interest rate which is out of alignment with world market interest rates adjusted for a country-risk premium. With respect to interest rates, if, as happened in Korea during the 1990s, the domestic interest rate is set significantly above the world market in order to mobilise more domestic savings, redirect them into the banking system, and fight inflation, then the result is a build-up of foreign private indebtedness. If, as happened in Japan and more recently in Canada, the domestic interest rate is set substantially below the world market, the result is an outflow of domestic savings in the form of portfolio investment in foreign bonds and securities and of real investment abroad; the consequence is lower domestic economic growth. Likewise, globalisation of short-term capital markets in a fluctuating exchange rate regime is also incompatible with an independent exchange rate policy, especially one that attempts to peg the exchange rate. Attempts to maintain an over-valued currency (as in Mexico and Turkey in the early 1990s and Korea in the late 1990s) require using foreign exchange reserves to sell foreign currency to prevent a devaluation; eventually, the supply of foreign exchange reserves will be exhausted and the currency will devalue anyway, frequently much below its equilibrium rate. Attempts to maintain an under-valued currency (as in Japan in the 1990s) will, in the absence of restrictions on currency outflows, cause an outflow of domestic currency with adverse effects on domestic investment and domestic growth. Thus financial globalisation imposes severe fundamental constraints on the policy levers which governments can exercise in their management of the domestic economy, thereby creating a crisis of the state.

The current limits upon government economic policy

The present financial architecture of the global economy threatens the capacity of national governments to perform their functions. It penalises not only domestic institutional inadequacies and policy mistakes but also the self-defeating efforts of governments to pursue policies of economic independence in macroeconomic management and social policy. It also introduces an unacceptable degree of economic instability into the global economy (for more extensive discussion of this topic see the special issue of *World Development* 2000 devoted to this problem, see also Streeten 2001).

Limits upon developing-country government actions to promote dynamic comparative advantage

Development policy is constrained not only by financial liberalisation but also by the globalisation of trade in commodities and services. Membership in WTO and adherence to GATT rules, which the more developed developing countries are pressured to obey, loses developing countries most of their instruments of commercial trade policy. They cannot use tariffs and quotas, or sector-specific subsidies, to promote climbing the ladder of comparative advantage. They cannot increase the effective exchange rate for exports through the subsidised allocation of scarce resources, such as credit or foreign exchange or tax and tariff rebates for exporters. The effective exchange rate for exports and imports must be the same and must be uniform across sectors. Thus WTO members lose most market, non-discretionary instruments. GATT members also lose most major non-market, industry-specific, non-discretionary measures. They cannot grant exporters virtual monopoly in the domestic market; if exported goods sell domestically at above export price, they are deemed to engage in dumping on the world market. They also cannot impose export targets on firms for the same reason. Thus the combination of GATT with the liberalisation of capital markets constrains developing countries from using most market-oriented instruments for economic development. Neoclassical development economists would argue that these constraints on LDCs' commercial and trade policies are all to the good. But this view is contradicted by the lessons of development experience articulated in the previous section. It is also subject to analytical errors (Stretton 2000 and Stiglitz 2000).

True, even under WTO, countries wishing to climb the ladder of comparative advantage can still use less polite (and less efficient and more error-prone?) non-market, discretionary pressures on entrepreneurs to push them to invest in some particular types of factories. They can also continue to carry out direct government investment in specific public enterprises and/or court certain types of foreign investments. And they can also continue to generate externalities by investing in public education, research and infrastructure and by creating export-facilitating institutions. But the ability of developing countries to induce structural change in patterns of production and generate movement to higher-productivity activities and sectors, a major element of economic development, is nevertheless severely curtailed.

Limits on government macroeconomic policies

With regulated foreign capital inflows typical of the Bretton Woods period, countries could choose two out of three of the following instruments: the exchange rate regime (managed float or flexible) and, with a managed float, the exchange rate level; the interest rate level (above or below world market); or the rate of inflation. They could not choose all three because, as evident from the discussion below, the three instruments are interconnected. By contrast, with the unrestricted foreign capital inflows typical of the post-Bretton Woods era, countries lose control over all three of these instruments. Governments become unable to employ their traditional macroeconomic policy instruments (interest rates, government expenditures, and exchange rates) unilaterally. For, if they do, this will generate a financial crisis. The financial crises induced by attempts to engage in autonomous macroeconomic policy are endogenous, with the prosperity phase causing the conditions leading to the massive economic decline of the crisis phase.

For example, raising interest rates above world-market levels triggers a large foreign capital inflow, setting the stage for a subsequent financial crisis. The inflow induces an exchange rate appreciation; this leads to a loss of international competitiveness, decline in demand for domestic manufacturing and increase in demand for imports; this raises the trade deficit and reduces the current account surplus (phase one of the process). As this process continues the current account surplus is transformed into a current account deficit, which mounts persistently. Eventually, both domestic capitalists and foreign speculators lose confidence in the currency. They rapidly withdraw massive amounts of liquid capital from the domestic economy, leading to a massive flight from domestic currency (phase two of the process) and the crisis starts. The exchange rate tumbles. The burden of foreign debt service, denominated in foreign currency, escalates. There is a scramble for liquidity and foreign exchange to service the debt and asset values tumble, as real estate prices and stock markets crash. Eventually, the corporate sector becomes illiquid and possibly even insolvent. Banks are also hit by the increase in value of their foreign debt, and by the decline in quality and prices of their assets. A banking crisis arises. A deep depression develops. Conversely, fixing interest rates below world markets triggers a large foreign capital outflow, setting in motion the start of a financial crisis and initiating the second phase of the previous process. Thus governments lose autonomy over domestic interest rate levels unless they are willing to court a financial crisis, which would destroy their previous developmental and macroeconomic gains.

Similarly, under a managed-float exchange rate regime, setting exchange rates above equilibrium levels leads to a current account deficit, as exports lose competitiveness and imports become more attractive. This raises the trade deficit and reduces the current account surplus, positioning the economy in phase one of the process described in the previous paragraph. An early devaluation, returning the exchange rate to equilibrium levels, could short-circuit the process by restoring export competitiveness and raising the price of imports. But it is risky, because exchange rate markets might take the devaluation as a signal of economic weakness. This could precipitate capital flight and start the financial crisis. By contrast, fixing exchange rates below equilibrium leads to fear of domestic inflation and stimulates capital flight and investment abroad, producing the financial crisis and initiating the process of severe and prolonged depression in phase two of the process described in the previous paragraph.

Thus governments cannot set their exchange rate levels either, without triggering a financial crisis and severe depression, even under a managed float. Of course, with flexible exchange rates, countries give up the exchange rate as an instrument up front and must accept whatever exchange rate the global system generates. In addition, flexible exchange rates may also amplify the effects of short-term international capital flows: by stimulating speculation on foreign exchange, markets have become excessively large, excessively liquid, excessively volatile, imperfectly informed, and subject to herd psychology.

Finally, running a budget deficit, to stimulate growth, combat recession or provide social programmes more generous than the international average, causes capital flight. Domestic actors fear inflation and international actors fear a devaluation, and the economy is positioned in phase two of the process described earlier.

The loss of economic autonomy resulting from unregulated short-term capital flows afflicts both developed and developing nations, but has more severe consequences for developing ones. Developed countries are walking an economic tightrope in which they cannot afford to have a unilateral recession, for fear of capital flight which would start the process of phase two, but have lost the ability to use counter-cyclical policy except with multilateral agreement for the same reason. And developing countries with open and unregulated capital markets are extremely constrained in the extent to which their governments can stimulate further development. All countries, developed and developing alike, are left with economic responsibilities but without instruments they can control. It is therefore hardly surprising that, periodically, governments ignore the global constraints on their economic freedoms and trigger a financial crisis and real depression. The global financial system therefore urgently requires reform.

What are the policy options open to developing countries?

So what are developing-country governments to do in the post-Bretton Woods era? Fundamentally, governments have four types of choices.

One, they can relinquish their economic autonomy and renounce their responsibilities for macroeconomic management, economic development and social policy. But this is hardly an appealing, or indeed a responsible, choice. For, as we saw in the section describing the lessons of development, to enable governments to play their developmental roles successfully, they must have sufficient economic and political autonomy to shift among policy regimes as the requirements of economic development change and as shifts in domestic and international conditions take place.

Two, developmentally-oriented governments can limit themselves to the instruments they retain. In particular, having lost control over more neutral indirect means of promoting structural change, they can rely increasingly on direct, targeted and untargeted, mostly non-market mechanisms for achieving economic development. More specifically, they can use disguised subsidies to industry, through education, infrastructure investment, cheap food, and low-wage, anti-union policies (but some of these actions have unequalising effects on the distribution of income). They can use targeted subsidies in the form of tax rebates and/or monopoly privileges to specific industries, regions and firms (but here they may invite retaliation from OECD countries, under WTO rules). They can create generalised externalities in the form of investment in education, skill-import enticements, state-supported research, and tax holidays to promote local and foreign direct investment. They can build the physical and legal infrastructure for processing zones and industrial parks. The least developed among developing countries that still retain the capacity to impose infant-industry protection under WTO can use selective tariffs to promote climbing the ladder of comparative advantage. Finally, as was done in Korea, Meiji Japan, and Communist China, they can create national commitment to development, through the educational system and by using the media and national campaigns to motivate workers, entrepreneurs, bureaucrats and households to exert themselves and work hard, and to save and invest in the interest of the modernisation of their countries. Of course, the national commitment route presupposes a culture that is amenable to this, leadership commitment to development and a distribution of assets, and access to accumulation opportunities that are relatively egalitarian.

Nevertheless, the pace of modernisation that developing countries will be able to achieve through the concerted (and co-ordinated) use of this battery of direct instruments will be much slower than it was during the Bretton Woods era. They will be constrained by a relatively restrictive monetary and fiscal regime and by fear of international retaliation. And development will most likely be more costly, as some of the targeted efforts may be economically inappropriate, premature, ill-timed or of the wrong scale. This method of development will also require state institutions for co-ordinating industrial policies, not unlike the development agencies of the 1960s and 1970s. It also assumes world-wide economic growth, so that world demand for imports from developing countries is expanding.

It is ironic that this 'do what you can' approach, which is the most statist and interventionist, is stimulated by too liberal an international milieu imposed on economies that are not ready for endogenous growth and endogenous structural change institutionally, socially or politically.

Third, developing countries can work to convince the international community that the current global financial system requires reform. Their efforts along these lines can be augmented by lobbying by developmentally-oriented national and international aid establishments of OECD countries. It can further be aided by a more realistic evaluation of the benefit–cost ratios of financial liberalisation by development economists and Keynesian macroeconomists, as provided by Streeten (2001), Stretton (2000), Stiglitz (2000), Davidson (2000) and Tobin (1974 and 2000). International aid establishments of OECD countries can further this drive by adding their voices to those of developing-country advocates of impediments to, and the re-regulation of, global short-term capital markets.

Since both developed and developing countries suffer from crises and loss of economic autonomy, there is common ground for agreement among them that the reform of short-term international financial markets to reduce their volatility and restrict the volume of largely speculative short-term foreign exchange trans-actions is desirable. Iconoclastic as it may sound to neoclassical economists enamoured by efficient-market theories of capital markets, some mix of regulation, disincentives, or other impediments to short-term capital mobility is required to generate global institutions that are robust, less volatile, allow more scope for national macroeconomic and social policies, and are more friendly to economic growth and economic development. There are scattered, very recent, signs that a few prominent thinkers, of both socialist and conservative persuasion, in developed countries are coming to realise the need to curb short-term capital flows. In a recent editorial in the *Financial Times*, Felix Rohatyn (2001) has argued for an international conference, including both developing and developed countries, to redefine the roles of international institutions. Jospin, past President of the European Union, has urged the adoption of a Tobin tax (reported in *Economist* 2001). And, in his assessment of globalisation, Kissinger (2001) has stated that the volume and pace of capital flows are making the effective management of the global economy increasingly difficult.

Note that the imposition of constraints on short-term capital movements does not require international agreement. It merely requires reducing the inordinate pressures emanating from the United States, the IMF and the OECD to liberalise trade in financial services and free short-term capital flows. The threat of retaliation against countries imposing barriers to the financial liberalisation of short-term capital markets must be lifted, and that requires at least tacit international co-operation.

Fourth, developing countries could unilaterally de-link from international capital markets to preserve their economic independence and stability. They could, like Malaysia and Russia, eliminate convertibility of their currencies on capital accounts entirely. Alternatively, *à la* India and China, they could delay convertibility of their capital accounts until their economic and financial systems are sufficiently mature. Eichengreen (2000) argues for this phased approach to financial liberalisation. Or, like Chile, they could, unilaterally, introduce differential taxes and higher reserve requirements on short-term capital inflows and foreign deposits, and impose controls on foreign borrowing. Tobin (2000) and Stiglitz (2000) favour this approach. These measures would make it more expensive to engage in short-term foreign borrowing and exchange rate speculation, and thereby provide a greater degree of state independence. But unilateral de-linking may also invite retaliation in the form of trade sanctions and may reduce long-term foreign investment, since the investment climate in countries imposing these measures may be regarded as unfriendly to foreign investment.

None of these classes of approaches are mutually exclusive. To my mind, the third, financial-system-reform approach, would be the most desirable. But it would also take longest to implement. Meanwhile, developing countries that want to develop will have to muddle through using a mix of approaches two and four. But unless they stay within internationally acceptable monetary and fiscal constraints, or unless they adopt both measures two and four simultaneously, they will continue to suffer from periodic financial crises with devastating real consequences to the economy, to the people, and to the state.

Recommendations for reform

My personal list of advisable reforms is motivated by a desire to restore global conditions analogous to the Bretton Woods system, while maintaining some of the virtues of the liberalised trading and investment climate introduced by more recent globalisation. The Bretton Woods system supported the Golden Age of development for developing countries and unprecedentedly high, stable growth for developed ones. It would therefore seem desirable to approximate it as closely as possible.

The international financial system must have three basic properties: liquidity (it is the violation of this property which led to the downfall of the Bretton Woods system); stability (it is the violation of this property which is bringing down the economies of one country after another, with depressing frequency and devastating consequences); and it must provide for some policy autonomy (it is the failure of the present system to provide for monetary and fiscal autonomy which, when governments try, unsuccessfully, to use macroeconomic instruments, is plunging one country after another into financial followed by real crises).

The package of actions required to improve the faulty current architecture of the global financial system, presented below, is purposely kept minimal and modest for two reasons. First, the political forces making for liberalisation of commodity and service markets (other than financial services) are strong, despite popular protests against it. Second, a complete restructuring seems to be very difficult to engineer; agreement on it will be hard to reach and time consuming. I therefore favour measures that can be taken mostly unilaterally or by concerted agreement among only a small number of countries. The package I recommend consists of:

One, to provide for greater policy autonomy and stability, the US and IMF must stop pressuring countries against regulating or taxing portfolio investment, foreign borrowing, and transfers of liquid balances into or out of foreign exchange. This set of measures falls far short of capital market de-linking. It merely spreads out in time and makes less profitable international short-term capital movements, thereby lengthening the maturity structure of national foreign debt. Several market-oriented developing countries are already, in effect, taxing or regulating short-term capital flows. Of course, this set of measures will not by itself suffice to eliminate foreign-instigated financial crises. Only complete de-linking could do that.

Note that I do not argue for a completely closed capital market, both because long-term capital flows (i.e. direct foreign investment) are, on the whole, generally beneficial to developing countries and, to maintain them, the financial system must allow for the repatriation of profits. In essence, I am arguing for a return to the Bretton Woods world of constraints on short-term capital flows, including portfolio investment, combined with relatively free international trade.

Two, to mitigate the severity and frequency of financial cycles when conditions are ripe, the international community must require greater financial transparency of financial institutions. In OECD countries, in addition to currently provided information, developed-country banks should be required to disclose lending to hedge funds and foreign loans and, in LDCs, banks must be required to provide more accurate and timely reporting of foreign-exchange-denominated obligations, foreign exchange positions and foreign borrowing, and improve bank governance.

Greater financial transparency can bring about corrective actions sooner, but it is also a two-edged sword. On the one hand, greater transparency may reduce the temptation to pursue greater profits through riskier portfolios. This, in turn, may reduce the magnitude of adjustments needed to restore financial soundness and reduce the amplitudes of crises. On the other hand, by providing financial markets with greater amounts of common information, greater transparency is likely to contribute to herd psychology, by generating one-sided expectations. These increase the amplitude of foreign exchange flows and exchange-rate and asset-price fluctuations. It is hard to say, a priori, which of these two effects will predominate in practice. This may well vary on a case by case basis. But even if the net effect of greater transparency is always to reduce the amplitude of crises, it too cannot, by itself, eliminate internationally-triggered financial crises entirely. Only complete de-linking is likely to achieve this end.

Three, for international currency stability, the US, the EU and Japan should pre-commit to stable (though not necessarily fixed) euro–dollar and yen–dollar exchange rates – the currencies of the three largest trading blocks. This is necessary to provide a stable anchor not only for these currencies but also for the domestic currencies of other countries. Once the credibility of the euro becomes established, some countries will opt to peg their currencies to the euro, others to the yen, others to the dollar, and still others to a trade-weighted basket of these currencies. A trilateral pre-commitment to stable euro–dollar and yen–dollar exchange rates can be credible, since the US has an infinite supply of dollars while the European Monetary Union and Japan have infinite supplies of euro and yen respectively. They can use their currencies to stabilise the exchange rate, if they are willing to accept the impacts of their stabilisation efforts on their domestic currencies and price levels. (Observe that a unilateral commitment to a stable exchange rate is not enough because the US does not have an infinite supply of euro or yen and vice versa; nor can a sterilised commitment be effective.)

Four, since even if all these proposals are implemented, financial crises will nevertheless develop, there should be some contingency planning for handling incipient crises so as to make them less devastating once they start. At the national level, the contingency plans may include standby borrowing arrangements and the maintenance of larger foreign currency reserves. At the international level, one must create a new institution, analogous to a World Central Bank, such as an expanded Bank for International Settlements or a revamped and re-capitalised IMF, with capacity to provide quick liquidity to several countries undergoing crises simultaneously. This requires the commitment of reserve funds by the major OECD countries or, as Davidson (2000) suggests, a clearing-union arrangement.

None of the recommended measures, taken singly, will suffice to avoid international financial crises entirely. Only complete de-linking of national financial markets can succeed in doing that. Even the combination of all four classes of measures will not eliminate financial crises resulting from abrupt changes in foreign capital inflows, or contagion, or world-market conditions: the combination of these measures will merely reduce the frequency and amplitude of financial crises. After all, one cannot regulate against economic stupidity, leading to misguided policies; one cannot avoid domestic real fluctuations or international trade cycles entirely; even with regulation, malfeasance due to the combination of greed with corruption, can only be punished *ex post facto*; and accidents, due to geographic proximity, due to similarity to other crisis-hit countries, or triggered by exogenous events which give rise to a domestic recession or increase a country's risk-premium, cannot be avoided. At best, all one can hope to achieve by reform is less numerous and less devastating financial cycles. But this is a goal well worth striving for.

Notes

1   A broader, multidimensional appraisal of the benefits and costs of globalisation is to be found in Streeten (2001). Streeten also offers institutional remedies other than increasing state autonomy (international cooperation, transnational NGOs) and new supranational institutions for reducing some of the costs of globalisation.

2   For a more comprehensive review of development lessons see Adelman (2001), in French.

3   David Landes (1998) makes a convincing case that the current travails of transition to a market economy in Russia have their roots in the social structure prevailing in Russia under the tsars, in which the division of society into oppressed serfs, on the one hand, and profligate and incompetent noblemen, on the other, imprinted cultural

attitudes which are inimical to interactions between labour, management and government based on honesty, public spiritedness and hard work.

4 The numbers in this paragraph are computed from Bank of Korea Statistical Yearbooks, various years.

5 The information on Korea and Taiwan in this and subsequent sections is based on Adelman and Song (forthcoming) and Adelman (1999a).

6 The creation of CNN by Ted Turner is a case in point. But he almost went bankrupt while waiting for needed complementary investments to materialise.

7 It is indicative that several current economic Ministers and government advisers to President Kim Dae Jung on financial crisis management and institutional restructuring are graduates of the Economic Planning Board that directed the private sector during the heyday of industrial policy.

8 Paul Streeten (2001), however, is dubious about increasing the power of national states, since he views them as promoting civil wars through their internally divisive, unequalising national policies. Instead he argues for international cooperation and specialised supranational institutions to promote equalising growth and development.

Bibliography

Abramovitz, M. (1986) 'Catching up, forging ahead, and falling behind', *Journal of Economic History* 46, 2: 385–406.

Adelman, I. (1974) 'Korea', in H. Chenery, M. Ahluwalia, C. Bell, J. Duloy and R. Jolly (eds) *Redistribution with Growth*, Oxford: Oxford Press.

—— (1999a) 'State and market in the economic development of Korea and Taiwan', in E. Thorbecke and H. Wan (eds) *Taiwan's Development Experience: Lessons on Roles of State and Market*, Norwell: Kluwer Academic.

—— (1999b) 'Society, politics and economic development, thirty years after', in J. Adams and F. Pigliaru (eds) *Economic Growth and Change*, Chelthenham: Edward Elgar.

—— (2001) 'Cinquante ans du développement économique' (in French), *Revue d'Economie du Développement* 1,2: 65–114.

Adelman, I. and Morris, C.T. (1967) *Society Politics and Economic Development: A Quantitative Approach*, Baltimore: Johns Hopkins University Press.

Adelman, I. and Song, B.N. (forthcoming) *Korea: The Visible and Invisible Hand*, Singapore: Scientific Press.

Adelman, I. and Yeldan, E. (2000) 'The minimal conditions for a financial crisis: a multi-regional intertemporal CGE model of the Asian crisis', *World Development* 28: 1,087–110.

Amsden, A. H. (1989) *Asia's Next Giant*, New York: Oxford University Press.

Aron, J. (2000) 'Growth and institutions: a review of the evidence', *World Bank Research Observer* 15,1: 99–136.

Balassa, B. (1979) 'A stages approach to comparative advantage', in I. Adelman (ed.) *Proceedings of the Fifth World Congress of the International Economic Association*, London: Macmillan.

—— (1989) 'Exports, policy choices and economic growth in developing countries after the 1973 oil shock', reprinted in B. Balassa (ed.) *Comparative Advantage, Trade Policy and Economic Development*, London: Harvester Wheatsheaf.

Bardhan, P. (2000) 'Distributive conflicts, collective action and institutional economics' in G.M. Meier and J.E. Stiglitz (eds) *Frontiers of Development Economics*, Oxford: Oxford University Press.

Chenery, H. (1960) 'Patterns of industrial growth', *American Economic Review* 50: 524–54.

Chenery, H. and Syrquin, M. (1975) *Patterns of Development 1950–1970*, London: Oxford University Press.

Cole, D.C. and Lyman, P.N. (1971) *Korean Development: The Interplay of Politics and Economics*, Cambridge, MA: Harvard Press.

Davidson, P. (2000) 'Is a plumber or a financial architect needed to end global international liquidity problems?', *World Development* 28: 1,117–32.

Economist, The (2001) (4 September).

Eichengreen, B. (2000) 'Taming capital flows', *World Development* 28: 1,105–32.

Evans, P. (ed.) (1997) *State Society Synergy: Government and Social Capital*, Berkeley: University of California Press.

Furtado, C. (1963) *The Economic Growth of Brazil*, Berkeley: University of California Press.

Heller, P. (1997) 'Social capital as a product of class mobilization and state intervention: industrial workers in Kerala India', in P. Evans (ed.) *State Society Synergy: Government and Social Capital*, Berkeley: University of California Press.

Hoff, K. (forthcoming) 'Beyond Rosenstein-Rodan: the modern theory of under-development traps', *World Bank Economic Review*.

Hoff, K. and Stiglitz, J.E. (2000) 'Modern economic theory and development', in G.M. Meier and J.E. Stiglitz (eds) *Frontiers of Development Economics*, Oxford: Oxford University Press.

Hong, W. (1994) *Trade and Growth: A Korean Perspective*, Seoul: Kudara International.

Jones, L.P. and Sakong, I. (1980) *Government, Business and Entrepreneurship in Economic Development*, Cambridge, MA: Harvard Press.

Kim, K.S. and Roemer, M. (1979) *Growth and Structural Transformation*, Cambridge, MA: Harvard Press.

Kim, K.S. and Westphal, L. (1977) 'Industrial policy and development in Korea', *World Bank Staff Working Paper* 263.

Kissinger, H. (2001) *Does America Need a Foreign Policy? Towards a Diplomacy for the 21st Century*, New York: Simon and Schuster.

Krueger, A.O. (1983) *Trade and Employment in Developing Countries: Synthesis and Conclusions*, Chicago: University of Chicago Press.

—— (1997) 'Korean industry and trade over fifty years', in D.S. Cha, K.S. Kim and D.H. Perkins (eds) *The Korean Economy 1945–1995*, Seoul: Korea Development Institute.

Kuo, S., Ranis, G. and Fei, J.H. (1981) *The Taiwan Success Story*, Boulder: Westview Press.

Landes, D.S. (1998) *The Wealth and Poverty of Nations*, New York: W.W. Norton.

Leibenstein, H. (1957) *Economic Backwardness and Economic Growth*, New York: Wiley.

Lin, J.Y. and Nugent, J. (1995) 'Institutions and economic development', in J. Berman and T.N. Srinivasan (eds) *Handbook of Economic Development*, Amsterdam: Elsevier.

Marx, K. (1853) *Capital*, Reprinted in 1906, Chicago: Kerr and Co.

McGuire, J.W. (1997) *Rethinking Development in East Asia and Latin America*, Los Angeles: Pacific Council on International Policy.

Morris, C.T. and Adelman, I. (1988) *Comparative Patterns of Economic Development: 1850–1914*, Baltimore: Johns Hopkins University Press.

North, D.C. (1990) *Institutions, Institutional Change and Economic Performance*, New York: Cambridge University Press.

Rohatyn, F. (2001) 'Editorial', *Financial Times* 20 August.

Rostow, W.W. (1960) *The Stages of Economic Growth: A Non-Communist Manifesto*, Cambridge: Cambridge University Press.

Scitovsky, T. (1985) 'Economic development in Taiwan and South Korea 1965–1981', *Food Research Institute Studies* 19,3.

Stiglitz, J.E. (1989) 'The economic role of the state', in A. Hertye (ed.) *The Economic Role of the State*, London: Basil Blackwell.

—— (1996) 'Some lessons of the East Asian miracle', *World Bank Research Observer* 11: 151–77.

—— (2000) 'Capital market liberalization, economic growth and instability', *World Development* 28: 1,075–86.

Streeten, P.P. (2001) *Globalization – Threat or Opportunity?* Herndon: Copenhagen Business School Press.

Stretton, H. (2000) 'Neoclassical imagination and financial anarchy', *World Development* 28: 1,061–73.

Temple J. and Johnson, P. (1998) 'Social capability and economic development', *Quarterly Journal of Economics* 113: 965–90.

Thomas, B. (1946) *Migration and Economic Growth*, 2nd edn, Cambridge: Cambridge University Press.

Tobin, J. (1974) *The New Economics one decade Older*, Princeton: Princeton University Press.

—— (2000) 'Financial globalization', *World Development* 28: 1,101–116.

Uedo, A. (2000) 'A growth model of "miracle" in Korea', *Journal of Policy Modeling* 22, 1: 43–60.

Wade, R.E. (1982) *Irrigation and Agricultural Politics in South Korea*, Boulder: Westview Press.

—— (1990) *Governing the Market: Economic Theory and the Role of Government in the Industrialization of East Asia*, Princeton: Princeton University Press.

Waterbury, J. (2000) 'The long gestation period and brief triumph of import-substituting industrialization', *World Development* 27, 2: 323–42.

Williamson, J. (1994) *The Political Economy of Policy Reform*, Washington, DC: Institute of International Economics.

World Bank (1993) *The East Asian Miracle*, New York: Oxford University Press.

—— (1996) *World Development Report: From Plan to Market*, New York: Oxford University Press.

—— (1997) *World Development Report 1997: The State in a Changing World*, New York: Oxford University Press.

—— (1999/2000) *Entering the 21st Century*, Washington, DC: World Bank.

3 A tale of two crises

Latin America in the 1980s and the 'HPAEs' in the 1990s

John Weeks

Introduction

This chapter reviews the Latin American growth disaster of the 1980s and considers its implications for the causes of the Asian financial crisis. The impressive growth performances of a small group of Asian countries made those countries an ideological battlefield (Wade 1996). For those of a neoclassical persuasion, it became important to demonstrate that the so-called miracles achieved their miracles by following orthodox policy dogma, especially 'sound macro fundamentals'. It was equally important to the heterodox school to claim the 'miracles' as their own. When 'show case' countries transubstantiated into 'basket cases' (see Pincus and Ramli 1998), each school sought an explanation consistent with its particular political economy.

It would be an analytical step forward if one did not find commentators taking predictable positions on the Asian crisis. With few exceptions, those who saw the miracles as paragons of orthodox virtue explain the crisis by an alleged failure to maintain this orthodoxy previously ascribed to them (Corsetti, Pesenti and Roubini 1998). Those of a 'structuralist' persuasion single out the deregulation of capital markets as their perpetrator of preference (Kregel 1998 and Palma 1998). That writers take predictable positions does not make their analysis wrong, but shifts of position take on particular credibility. For example, given his previous work on stabilisation and structural adjustment in Latin America, Poland, and Russia, one would not have expected Sachs to view the Asian crisis from a notably heterodox point of view (for example, Radelet and Sachs 1998).

This chapter does not champion a cause of the Asian crisis. It considers a narrower, empirical issue: can one credibly argue that the failure to follow orthodox macro fundamentals explains the Asian debacle? The answer reached is 'no'. If this is not unexpected, given the author's arguments elsewhere (Weeks 1999), it is potentially productive for the pursuit of causality, which requires some common ground between the two political economies. It may be that the fundamental cause of the crisis was internal, e.g. the putative 'cronyism'; or external, e.g. an inherent instability of international financial markets. Internal or external, the crisis was not a result of bad behaviour on the 'fundamentals'.

In pursuit of the role of 'sound macro fundamentals' in crises, we first review the relative growth records of two groups of countries, eighteen in Latin America and four so-called high-performing Asian economies (HPAEs). The orthodoxy attributes the difference in performance between the Latin American countries and the HPAEs to basic differences in policy-orientation: it holds that the HPAEs pursued sound macro policies, while Latin American governments persisted with 'closed economy', import-substitution regimes characterised by heavy state intervention.[1] This interpretation has been the source of considerable mischief in policy-advice from international organisations. If the Latin American governments failed on the macro basics, while the HPAE governments excelled prior to some crisis period, then it provides a superficial explanation for the Latin American crisis and, by implication, for the later Asian crisis. The Latin American crisis would be explained by unwise policy choices over several decades, and the Asian crisis by deterioration in what had previously been sound policy fundamentals. Errant behaviour by the HPAEs would need to be established empirically but, prior to this, it must be established that the differences between the two groups of countries, before the Asian crisis, can be explained by policy differences.

Inspection of the statistics yields somewhat unexpected conclusions. Some of the oft-quoted 'stylised facts' prove invalid: on average, fiscal deficits were not higher in the Latin American countries, and nor did government expenditure take a significantly larger share of national income. The empirical evidence leads to an inspection of the relative burden of external debt for the two regions. To pursue this point further, the results of a previous modelling exercise are summarised, which support the view that debt service was central to the explanation of Latin America's performance.[2] At that point, the chapter turns to a discussion of the Asian crisis.

A comparison of the evidence

Growth and exports

The conventional wisdom on the relative performance of Latin American countries and HPAEs is that the latter achieved an outstanding growth record compared to the former on the basis of an 'orthodox' policy framework (World Bank 1993: 2, 5). To sustain or reject this hypothesis, we employ the straightforward statistical technique of the difference-of-means test. The two relevant groups are the eighteen Iberian-American countries (excluding only Cuba) and the four crisis-struck HPAEs: Indonesia, Korea, Malaysia and Thailand.[3]

Table 3.1 presents the statistics for the rate of growth of gross national product, measured in constant US dollars of 1987. Over the thirty-five years, the mean for all Latin American countries was 3.4 percentage points below the mean for all HPAEs, both for GDP and per capita GDP.[4] While it is incontestable that the HPAEs grew faster, it is also the case that the difference in growth rates is not statistically significant at the standard 10 per cent level of probability, except for 1980–4. The measurement of the statistically significant difference in means indicates the periods during which the two groups of countries can be treated analytically as behavioural groups. This is clear, for example, for 1970–4 compared to 1980–4. Of the twenty-two countries during 1970–4, the three with the highest growth rates were in Latin America: Brazil, the Dominican Republic, and Ecuador,

Table 3.1 Growth of real GDP for Latin American and four HPAEs, 1960–94 (constant $US)

Means and standard deviations	1960–4	1965–9	1970–4	1975–9	1980–4	1985–9	1990–4
Latin America							
Mean	5.2	4.9	5.3	4.1	–0.3	2.3	3.8
Std dev	2.0	1.6	3.4	3.0	2.8	3.1	2.3
HPAEs							
Mean	5.5	7.5	8.0	7.9	6.3	7.3	8.3
Std dev	2.2	2.2	0.6	0.8	0.6	2.3	1.1
Differences in means, significance:	nsgn	nsgn	nsgn	nsgn	**0.05**	nsgn	nsgn

Source: Weeks (2000).

Note:
For this and subsequent tables, Latin America includes all Spanish-speaking countries but Cuba, plus Brazil. The HPAEs are Indonesia, Republic of Korea, Malaysia, Taiwan, and Thailand.

leaving Korea to take fourth place. Assume that in this period, the twenty-two had been pooled, and two randomly-selected groups of four and eighteen countries created. The probability is overwhelming that the average growth rates of the two groups would have been virtually the same as for the groups selected on the basis of geography. On the other hand, during 1980–4, the probability is that such a random selection of groups would have produced averages significantly different from the averages based upon geographic location. While the mean growth rates of the HPAEs were above the mean of the Latin American countries, the dispersion of individual countries around their respective means suggests that before the 1980s *the two sets of countries could have been drawn from the same population* (the null hypothesis); selection on the basis of geography does not correspond to selection based upon performance.

The non-significance of differences in growth rates results from the uneven performance of the Latin American countries. In some time periods, some Latin American countries had strong growth performances, but no country had a strong performance across most or all periods. In each period there were Latin American 'high performers', but the high performer in one period not infrequently suffered low growth during another period.[5]

Central to the conventional wisdom story of the Asian growth miracle is the claim that the HPAEs exhibited extraordinarily high rates of growth of exports, and that it was this 'outward orientation' that in part explains the high GDP growth rates. Table 3.2 demonstrates this point, with an important caveat: *for none of the periods is the difference in means in export growth between Latin America and the HPAEs statistically significant.* This does not contradict the claim that exports grew faster for the HPAEs. Rather, it indicates the great variation across Latin American countries, and over time for particular countries. In some Latin American countries exports performed well in some periods, while in others the performance was poor.[6] The same point applies to 'openness', measured by the share of exports in GDP (Table 3.3).[7] On average, the HPAEs had higher export–GDP ratios, *after the 1960s*, but for no time period does the t-statistic approach the required level for statistical significance. Inspection of country data shows that as late as 1970–4 three of the four HPAEs (Indonesia, Korea, and Thailand) had export shares below the *average* for Latin America. In the 1990s Indonesia's percentage was below that of seven Latin American countries. This does not deny the greater export-orientation of the HPAEs, but suggests that judgements about relative 'openness', in the quantitative sense, need to be related to structural characteristics such as size of economies and composition of GDP.[8]

Along with the emphasis on the greater outward orientation of the HPAEs has gone an equally strong supposition that rates of investment were extremely high in those countries. The World Bank (1993) cited high rates of fixed capital investment as a 'major engine' of miraculous growth (see also Kuznets 1988).[9] One finds that during the 1960s, when the HPAEs began their rapid growth, the investment rates for the two regions were virtually the same on average, with the Latin American mean slightly *higher* for both halves of the decade (Table 3.4).[10] In the 1970s, the HPAE mean was above the Latin American, but non-significant. During the debt crisis the situation changed: the difference in means increases in significance, falling below the 10 per cent probability for 1980–4 and 1990–4. On average for the fifteen years 1980–94, the investment rate in the HPAEs was considerably higher than for the Latin American countries, 9 to 13 percentage points, compared to 2 to 3 for the 1970s. Thus it appears that one cannot explain the higher *long-term* growth of the HPAE countries by *long-term* differences in investment rates (i.e. they were substantially higher for less than half the thirty-five year time period). If one had inspected the statistics of the two groups in 1980, the observer would not have been struck by differences in investment rates.

Higher investment rates have been attributed to higher *savings* rates, with the implication that the latter facilitated the former in the HPAEs and, further, that Latin America's debt crisis in part reflected countries 'living beyond their means' in terms of domestic resources. This conclusion derives from a macro framework in which saving is treated in a full-employment, general equilibrium context. If one adopts a quantity-constrained framework, then the level and rate of savings in national income are the *ex post facto* consequence of the rate of autonomous expenditure, of which investment is usually the major component. Several authors have argued that in the HPAEs the high savings rates reflected retained earnings by corporations (Singh 1996), derivative from accumulation, and were not its cause.[11] The disagreement over causes may be academic, because the evidence shows that savings rates in the HPAEs were not significantly above those in Latin America until the debt crisis (Table 3.5). As for investment rates, the share of savings in GDP was higher for the Latin American group during the 1960s, and only slightly lower for the 1970s.

Table 3.2 Growth of the volume of exports, Latin America and four HPAEs, 1960–94 (constant $US)

Means and standard deviations	1960–4	1965–9	1970–4	1975–9	1980–4	1985–9	1990–4
Latin America							
Mean	4.7	5.6	5.9	6.5	0.4	4.2	6.3
Std dev	5.4	3.8	7.0	5.4	6.7	4.7	2.8
HPAEs							
Mean	8.4	13.1	13.2	11.2	6.7	9.0	10.7
Std dev	8.1	12.3	6.4	5.2	5.8	2.0	2.5
Difference in means, significance	nsgn	nsgn	nsgn	nsgn	nsgn	nsgn	nsgn

Source: Weeks (2000).

Table 3.3 Exports as a percentage of GDP for Latin America and four HPAEs, 1960–94 (constant $US)

Means and standard deviations	1960–4	1965–9	1970–4	1975–9	1980–4	1985–9	1990–4
Latin America							
Mean	17.7	18.3	19.6	22.1	20.3	22.2	22.6
Std dev	7.9	8.6	8.4	9.0	8.1	7.9	9.0
HPAEs							
Mean	19.1	19.7	24.7	31.1	34.8	38.1	43.6
Std dev	17.6	14.6	9.5	12.9	14.2	16.9	22.3
Difference in means, significance	nsgn	nsgn	nsgn	nsgn	nsgn	nsgn	nsgn

Source: Weeks (2000).

Macro policy indicators

The review of growth, export, investment and savings performance between the two groups of countries showed that while the indicators were stronger for the HPAEs, there was substantial variation within groups. It does not appear that these indicators can account for Latin America suffering a crisis in the 1980s, while the HPAEs did not. This raises the question: does the evidence support the conclusion that the HPAEs pursued 'fundamentally sound macroeconomic policies' to an extent that Latin American did not?[12] Comparable data on policy variables exist for fiscal deficits, a key measure of 'sound' macroeconomic policy. In the orthodox view, slippage on the deficit results in inflation and the crowding out of private investment.

Table 3.4 Gross domestic investment as a percentage of GDP for Latin America and four HPAEs, 1960–94 (current prices)

Means and standard deviations	1960–4	1965–9	1970–4	1975–9	1980–4	1985–9	1990–4
Latin America							
Mean	18.2	19.0	21.4	23.7	20.4	18.8	19.9
Std dev	6.3	4.6	4.5	5.1	4.3	4.8	4.2
HPAEs							
Mean	15.8	18.8	23.7	26.8	29.9	28.6	35.9
Std dev	3.9	6.8	2.9	2.7	3.4	4.2	5.8
Difference in means, significance	nsgn	nsgn	nsgn	nsgn	0.10	nsgn	**0.10**

Source: Weeks (2000).

Table 3.5 Saving as a percentage of GDP for Latin America and four HPAEs, 1960–94 (current prices)

Means and standard deviations	1960–4	1965–9	1970–4	1975–9	1980–4	1985–9	1990–4
Latin America							
Mean	17.1	18.1	19.4	22.5	19.7	18.5	17.0
Std dev	8.7	8.9	8.9	7.5	6.6	7.0	7.7
HPAEs							
Mean	14.1	17.1	21.7	27.3	27.7	26.2	31.7
Std dev	9.9	10.1	6.2	4.1	4.0	4.1	2.3
Difference in means, significance	nsgn	nsgn	nsgn	nsgn	nsgn	**0.10**	**0.05**

Source: Weeks (2000).

The evidence indicates that fiscal deficits in Latin America were not significantly different from those in the HPAEs; indeed, hardly different at all until the second half of the 1980s.[13] This is shown for the overall fiscal deficit, in Table 3.6, which covers both the current and capital account (including the domestic currency equivalent of foreign debt service). There are no comparable data for the 1960s. The results for the 1970s show that Latin American fiscal deficits were slightly *lower* than for the HPAEs: when the HPAEs began their rapid growth (see Table 3.1), they ran, on average, slightly *higher* deficits than the Latin American countries. If small deficits gain good marks for fiscal management,[14] then the Latin American governments were on average better students of orthodox macroeconomics than the governments of the HPAEs in the 1970s, and not much worse in the early 1980s. The Latin American fiscal deficits in the 1970s would not appear to be harbingers of the hyper-inflation suffered by several countries in the 1980s. The evidence on deficits implies that it is necessary to reconsider the argument that high inflation in Latin America resulted from the excesses of 'populist' macro-economics. During some years some Latin American governments ran large fiscal deficits; most did not.[15] The Latin American deficits exceeded those in the HPAEs by the greatest amount during the last two periods; that is, during and after Washington Consensus adjustment policies.

As a further indication of sound macro policy in the HPAEs, it has been suggested that the size of the state in GDP has been notably small compared to other developing regions (Kuznets 1988). A smaller state, some argue, stimulates a more vigorous private sector by reducing 'crowding out' and fostering private incentives via lower tax levels.[16] Whatever the merit of such arguments, state expenditure as a percentage of GDP was virtually the same in both regions (Table 3.7, where the variation within regions is so great as to reduce the t-statistics to near zero). The perception that the Latin American region was characterised by large state sectors derives from a small number of countries, none of which maintained large ratios of public expenditure to GDP throughout the twenty-five years.[17] While there is a correlation between the size of the public sector and the accumulation of external debt, it is quite low, suggesting that other factors dominate.[18]

Inspection by country reveals that the share of total government expenditure in GDP was astoundingly low for many of the Latin American countries. While none of the HPAEs had shares less than 15 per cent of GDP for all five time periods, there were three such countries in Latin America (Colombia, Guatemala and Paraguay). Further, government expenditure accounted for more than 30 per cent of GDP in Malaysia during the last three time periods, and only two Latin American countries averaged over 30 per cent in as many as two time periods.[19]

These statistics on deficits and government expenditure do not necessarily invalidate the conventional wisdom about the HPAEs having relatively small states. They indicate that conclusions cannot be drawn on the basis of simple calculations. Research has shown that both state expenditure and revenue are correlated with structural characteristics of countries, such as the importance of mineral production in the economy. Just as any conclusion about relative degree of openness should be based on adjustment for size of country (the most obvious influence), so should conclusions about the relative size of the state be derived from an analytical framework.

The final macro indicator we consider is the real exchange rate. We follow the common practice of treating it as an index with no presumption as to its equilibrium value,[20] so it does not lend itself to the analysis of Tables 3.1–3.7. The question is, to what extent was the crisis of the 1980s exacerbated by over-valued exchange rates? Appreciating exchange rates do not in and of themselves establish that the exchange rate contributed to the crisis. But the absence of appreciating rules this out. There are eighteen countries to consider, and exchange rate movements during

Table 3.6 Overall fiscal deficit as a percentage of GDP for Latin America and the HPAEs, 1972–94 (current prices)

Means and standard deviations	*1970–4*	*1975–9*	*1980–4*	*1985–9*	*1990–4*
Latin America					
Mean	−2.6	−2.6	−5.1	−4.4	−1.5
Std dev	2.70	2.47	4.25	5.12	2.58
HPAEs					
Mean	−3.1	−3.5	−4.7	−2.0	0.9
Std dev	2.4	1.9	4.2	1.6	1.1
Difference in means, significance	nsgn	nsgn	nsgn	nsgn	nsgn

Source: Weeks (2000).

Table 3.7 Total government expenditure as a percentage of GDP for Latin America and four HPAEs, 1972–94 (current prices)

Means and standard deviations	*1972–4*	*1975–9*	*1980–4*	*1985–9*	*1990–4*
Latin America					
Mean	15.6	17.4	21.7	21.2	19.0
Std dev	5.0	5.5	9.2	9.4	7.6
HPAEs					
Mean	14.3	16.9	22.6	22.0	21.6
Std dev	5.0	5.4	8.6	7.3	9.2
Difference in means, significance	nsgn	nsgn	nsgn	nsgn	nsgn

Source: Weeks (2000).

1960–80 were quite diverse. To make the issue manageable, we focus on the five major countries, Argentina, Brazil, Chile, Mexico, and Venezuela (see Figure 3.1). There was some appreciation of the Mexican peso in the 1970s, but considerably less than one might have expected given that the country was a petroleum exporter.[21] The other petroleum producer, Venezuela, did experience a substantial appreciation in the 1970s. Though counterproductive in the long run, this appreciation can hardly be assigned to policy failure, given movements in the price of petroleum. This leaves the three non-petroleum-exporters as candidates for a crisis-enhancing mismanagement of exchange rates. Chile can be excluded, for its exchange rate depreciated sharply during 1974–5, then remained well below its 1973 level to the end of the decade. In this case, it was exchange rate mismanagement *during* the

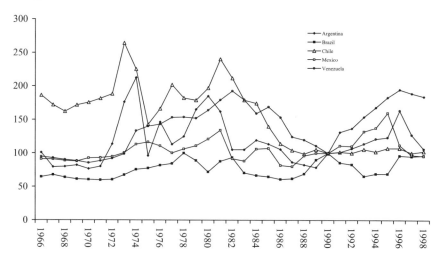

Figure 3.1 Latin America, major countries: real exchange rate for exports, 1966–98 (1990 = 100, a rise shows an appreciation)

crisis that made matters worse (that is, in the early 1980s). Argentina and Brazil did have appreciating exchange rates in the 1970s, without the push of petroleum prices. However, we shall see below that during the 1970s two HPAEs experienced even greater exchange rate appreciations (Indonesia and Malaysia), and they did not suffer an economic collapse in the 1980s. Prior exchange rate over-valuation may account for part of the Latin American crisis of the 1980s, but a regional generalisation is not possible.

Debt service between groups

The foregoing supports an obvious point: there was a debt crisis in Latin America and not for the HPAEs because the debt service of the former countries was so much larger than of the latter; this is rendered non-trivial by the discovery that basic macro indicators provide little guide to the cause of the difference. We now consider how much larger the Latin American debt service was.

Table 3.8 provides the statistics on debt service as proportion of export earnings. Even without disaggregation, the differences between the two regions are substantial, averaging 11 percentage points cross all five periods. A clear pattern presents itself, with the difference in debt service high and rising during 1970–84, then sharply narrowing in the second half of the 1980s, with the latter a harbinger of a crisis to come for the HPAEs. The sharp reduction in the difference between the two groups was the result of both increased debt service for the HPAEs (especially Indonesia),[22] and a decline for the Latin American countries, in part due to debt rescheduling. The group average for Latin America conceals great variations. Analytically we can divide the eighteen countries into three sub-groups: those whose ratio of debt service to GDP averaged over 30 per cent across the five periods ('highly indebted', seven countries); those whose average lay between 20 and 30 per cent ('moderately indebted', six); and those whose average was below 20 per cent ('lowly indebted', five).[23] The first group accounted for 75 per cent of the Latin American population in the mid-1990s, and the second group for 18 per cent. Thus the vast majority of Latin Americans lived in highly-indebted countries.

For the high debt countries, debt service as a proportion of export earnings was significantly higher (10 per cent probability or lower) than for the HPAE countries during three time periods, 1975–9, 1980–4, and 1990–4, and quite close to the 10 per cent probability during 1970–4.[24] Somewhat surprisingly, the highly-indebted Latin American countries had a *relatively* greater debt burden compared to the HPAEs in the 1970s than the 1980s. Indeed, in the second half of the 1980s, the difference in debt burdens between the Latin American highly-indebted countries and the HPAE was less than in the first or second half of the 1970s.

To estimate the quantitative impact of debt service on Latin America's growth, an expanded Harrod–Domar model was formulated, with a partial adjustment to equilibrium mechanism. Given the four arguments of debt service, gross domestic investment, foreign investment, and export growth, the model shows that debt service accounts for 20 per cent of the difference between HPAE and Latin American growth rates, 1970–94, and is the largest single factor.[25] When secondary effects of the debt service burden are included, manifested primarily in demand compression, the total debt effect accounted for 40 per cent of the difference in growth rates between the two regions. This modelling indicates that the Latin American 'debt crisis' was exactly that. It was a depression brought on by excessive debt burdens (see Weeks 1989), and exacerbated by what De Pinies called 'over-adjustment' (De Pinies 1989). Demand-depressing monetary and fiscal policies reduced imports in order to generate trade surpluses, following the Washington Consensus. Figure 3.2 emphasises this point, presenting the annual average growth rate across eighteen countries, the three-year moving average of that growth rate, and (in the negative quadrant) the number of countries with negative growth rates. From 1961 through 1980, the average growth rate varied in a narrow range, between 4.5 and 6 per cent, with no more than three countries with negative rates in any year. During 1991–8, the performance was significantly less robust,[26] but the number of countries with negative growth was never more than four (in 1998). Indeed, were these two periods joined in an interrupted chain, they would appear to be part of a relatively stable growth process, perhaps leaving one to wonder why the radical reforms of the 1980s were required. The years 1981–90 were disastrously different: in 1982 thirteen countries suffered negative growth, twelve did in 1983, and five did in three of the next seven years.

Thus in the 1980s the Latin American countries suffered more than a growth interruption; the decade was a debt disaster. Debt, not policy mismanagement, caused the Latin American crisis. On this issue, we agree with Palma, that the Latin American debt crisis resulted from 'over-lending and over-borrowing [that] are basically endogenous market failures of over-liquid and under-regulated financial markets' (Palma 1998: 789). We now turn to the Asian crisis, to investigate whether it can credibly be attributed to macro policy errors.

Table 3.8 Foreign debt service as percentage of exports for Latin America and four HPAEs, 1970–94 (current prices)

Means and standard deviations	1970–4	1975–9	1980–4	1985–9	1990–4
Latin America					
Mean	22.5	27.9	36.7	32.0	28.5
Std dev	13.33	17.15	15.36	13.38	13.79
LA, high debt					
Mean	34.8	45.5	51.3	41.8	31.5
Std dev	12.86	11.2	10.59	12.55	7.35
LA, moderate debt					
Mean	17.1	20.0	34.1	28.0	33.9 (26.3)
Std dev	6.35	9.55	6.18	12.85	19.25 (5.55)
LA, low debt					
Mean	11.9	12.7	19.4	22.8	17.9
Std dev	2.87	4.71	5.52	4.47	7.98
HPAEs					
Mean	12.4	14.2	18.6	28.5	17.3
Std dev	5.58	3.87	5.89	7.51	12.17
Differences in means: LA – HPAEs					
significance	nsgn	nsgn	nsgn	nsgn	nsgn
LA HD – HPAEs					
significance	nsgn	**0.05**	**0.05**	nsgn	**0.10**
LA MD – HPAEs					
significance	nsgn	nsgn	**0.10**	nsgn	nsgn
LA LD – HPAEs					
significance	nsgn	nsgn	nsgn	nsgn	nsgn

Source: Weeks (2000).

Notes:
The Latin American countries are divided on the basis of their average ratio of debt service to exports across all periods. High debt (HD): greater than 30 per cent; Argentina, Bolivia, Brazil, Chile, Mexico, Peru, and Uruguay (7); Moderate debt (MD): between 20 and 30 per cent; Colombia, Costa Rica, Ecuador, Nicaragua, Panama, and Venezuela (6); and Low debt (LD): less than 20 per cent; Dominican Republic, El Salvador, Guatemala, Honduras, and Paraguay (5).

The Asian crisis considered

Growth performance

Unlike the Latin American crisis, the Asian growth collapse was unexpected, virtually up to the moment of its onslaught.[27] This in itself casts doubt upon the macro fundamentals hypothesis: if the world's most sophisticated risk assessors signalled no cause for worry, why would one expect their private sector subscribers to do so? It might be argued that while the famous rating agencies pursued a

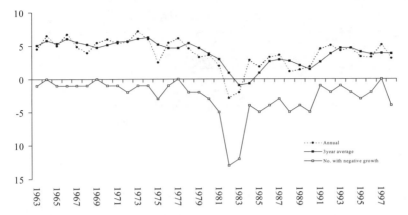

Figure 3.2 Latin America: growth rates and number of countries with negative growth, 1963–98

Pollyanna-like delusion, negative signals from the four miracles were reaching international corporations. These accumulated doubts intensified, until there came a collapse of confidence. This interpretation has an unsettling hint of perfect hindsight and, if valid, implies that there were clear indications of approaching instability. The empirical evidence for this argument is considered below.

Table 3.9, part A, shows the growth rates of the four countries by five-year periods. Indonesia, the country whose GDP decreased most in 1998, grew faster in the 1990s than in the 1980s. In two of the four countries growth rates were higher in the first half of the 1990s, and for a third, Korea, the rate was the same as during the second half of the 1980s. Figure 3.3 shows that for only one, Thailand, might a pessimistic observer have concluded that the growth miracle was coming to an end. Even for Thailand, 1994–5 brought a recovery to near double-digit growth rates. Indeed, to the extent that one might have divined a fall in growth rates for the countries in the 1990s, a rational observer might well have interpreted this a cyclical phenomenon, or an adjustment to a more realistic and sustainable long-term rate. Figure 3.4 averages the growth rates across the four countries, and applies a three-year moving mean. The average performance during 1990–6, 'smoothed out' for external shocks, fits well into a longer-term cyclical pattern. However, a rational observer would have asked whether the growth could be sustained, and would have looked to relevant indicators to answer this question.

Basic macro indicators and policy outcomes

Since the orthodox macro fundamentals hypothesis assumes that agents are rational, it would be fair to assume that the rational agent would have had some model of growth determination. A rational agent would not be panicked by a negative signal from one, or even several indicators, but would weigh such information in a system-atic manner. A reasonable approximation of such a model would include the rate of investment, export performance, and debt service. Should any of these manifest

Table 3.9 Macro indicators for four 'miracles', by time period

A. GDP growth

Period	Indonesia	Korea	Malaysia	Thailand	Average
1960–64	2.3	6.1	6.7	7.0	5.5
1965–69	4.9	10.0	6.4	8.5	7.5
1970–74	8.2	8.4	8.2	7.1	8.0
1975–79	7.4	9.0	7.2	8.0	7.9
1980–84	6.7	6.3	6.9	5.6	6.3
1985–89	6.0	9.5	4.7	9.0	7.3
1990–94	8.0	7.6	8.7	9.0	8.3
1995–98	1.9	3.8	4.5	0.9	2.8
Average:	5.9	7.7	6.7	7.0	**6.8**
(thru 1996)	*6.4*	*8.2*	*7.1*	*7.7*	*7.0*

B. Investment/GDP

Period	Indonesia	Korea	Malaysia	Thailand	Average
1960–64	10.5	14.7	19.8	18.4	15.8
1965–69	9.2	23.3	19.5	23.3	18.8
1970–74	19.3	25.8	24.9	25.0	23.7
1975–79	24.0	30.5	26.1	26.6	26.8
1980–84	26.2	29.7	34.8	29.0	29.9
1985–89	27.5	30.6	26.3	29.9	28.6
1990–94	29.5	36.7	36.5	40.9	35.9
1995–98	27.0	32.8	38.6	35.9	33.6
	21.8	28.2	28.3	28.7	**26.7**

C. Exports/GDP

Period	Indonesia	Korea	Malaysia	Thailand	Average
1960–64	11.2	5.3	44.1	15.9	19.1
1965–69	9.8	11.3	41.0	16.7	19.7
1970–74	19.4	21.3	40.3	17.9	24.7
1975–79	25.4	29.6	49.3	20.2	31.1
1980–84	28.3	35.1	53.2	22.6	34.8
1985–89	23.5	36.6	63.2	29.1	38.1
1990–94	26.9	29.2	81.5	36.7	43.6
1995–98	33.5	37.2	98.6	47.1	54.1
	22.2	25.9	58.2	25.5	**33.0**

D. Debt service/Exports

Period	Indonesia	Korea	Malaysia	Thailand	Average
1960–64	na	na	na	na	na
1965–69	na	na	na	na	na
1970–74	14.5	17.4	4.5	13.3	12.4
1975–79	18.2	12.5	8.9	16.6	14.2
1980–84	16.9	21.7	10.2	21.9	18.6
1985–89	36.4	22.9	22.6	24.1	28.5
1990–94	32.9	8.6	9.3	14.0	17.3
1995 98	28.7	8.2	7.7	11.2	14.0
	29.7	15.2	11.6	17.6	**17.7** \Contd

Table 3.9 continued

E. Fiscal deficit/GDP

Period	Indonesia	Korea	Malaysia	Thailand	Average
1960–64	na	na	na	na	na
1965–69	na	na	na	na	na
1970–74	−2.1	−1.5	−6.7	−2.1	−3.1
1975–79	−3.0	−1.6	−6.2	−3.3	−3.5
1980–84	−1.4	−2.2	−10.6	−4.4	−4.7
1985–89	−2.0	0.2	−4.5	−1.6	−2.0
1990–94	0.4	−0.4	0.4	3.2	0.9
1995–98	−0.1	−1.4	1.3	0.6	0.1
	−1.4	−1.1	−4.4	−1.3	**−2.0**

F. Trade balance/GDP

Period	Indonesia	Korea	Malaysia	Thailand	Average
1960–64	1.3	−9.7	4.7	−1.5	−1.3
1965–69	−4.4	−10.4	4.7	−2.2	−3.1
1970–74	2.1	−7.7	2.0	−2.4	−1.5
1975–79	4.6	−4.2	6.5	−4.7	0.5
1980–84	5.2	−3.1	−3.2	−5.1	−1.6
1985–89	2.4	5.1	8.4	−0.8	3.8
1990–94	2.8	−0.9	−0.4	−5.2	−0.9
1995–98	−0.7	−1.9	−0.5	−3.8	−1.7
Average:	1.8	−4.2	2.9	−3.2	**−0.7**

G. External current account balance

Period	Indonesia	Korea	Malaysia	Thailand	Average
1980–84	−3.9	−3.3	−9.9	−5.6	−5.7
1985–89	−2.5	4.3	2.4	−2.0	0.5
1990–94	−2.2	−1.1	−5.1	−6.5	−3.7
1995–97	−2.9	−2.8	−6.4	−6.0	−4.5
Average:	−2.8	−0.4	−4.3	−4.9	**−3.1**

H. Real exchange rate producer prices

Period	Indonesia	Korea	Malaysia	Thailand	Average
1970–74	164	95	114	106	120
1975–79	189	103	120	100	128
1980–84	150	92	133	98	118
1985–89	100	90	124	95	102
1990–94	104	99	97	104	101
1995–96	116	101	97	113	107

Source: World Bank (1999).

an unhealthy movement, the rational agent might then look to other indicators: the fiscal deficit, inflation, the external balance, and the real exchange rate. Thus we ask the question: in early 1997, with the information from 1996, would a rational agent have had cause for concern?

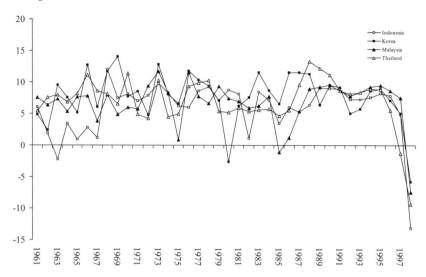

Figure 3.3 Growth rates of four 'miracles', 1961–98

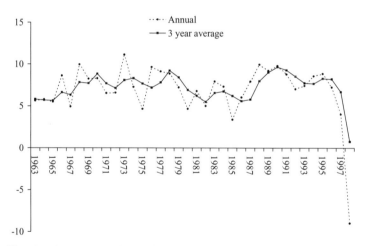

Figure 3.4 Average growth rate for four 'miracles', 1961–98

The agent would have discovered that, during 1995 and 1996, the rate of investment was higher in three of the four countries than in the immediately previous
years (Korea being the exception). For every country there was a statistically
significant, long-term upward trend. It would have been a pessimist, indeed, who
would have foreseen an imminent fall in investment in any of the countries.

Some have identified the fiscal deficit, the external account, and the real
exchange rate as signalling macro instability in the miracle countries just prior to
the crisis. In order to consider the rational response to these, it must be noted that
they are not policy variables as such, but policy outcomes. Governments have
influence over these outcomes indirectly. As a result, the movement in the indicators

can reflect random shocks as well as purposeful policy. A rational agent would seek to discriminate between policy and shocks, in order to avoid over-reacting.

The typical approach to assessing the macro signals from the miracle countries has been to undertake a review, indicator by indicator, and pass judgement as to whether the movement in the indicator in question should be interpreted as a harbinger of the subsequent crisis, i.e. whether a rational agent would have viewed them with alarm. This is a fundamentally subjective approach, mere story-telling with an implicit political economy bias. As a result, different judgements can be reached on the same statistics, influenced by the assessor's ideological predilections. Further, if one believes firmly that macro instability reflects the mistakes of governments, there is a tendency to apply criteria that will generate this conclusion in each specific case. Such political economy assessments are informative, but lack the methodology to discriminate between competing explanations.

A theoretically rigorous approach would be to analyse indicators within a formal model, such that the model itself would generate the assessment rather than the subjectivity of the observer. However, in practice formal models are derivative from the author's political economy perspective, particularly with regard to closure conditions. Perhaps the closest one can come to objectivity is to explicitly state assumptions and pursue these logically. For the analysis we employ the following assumptions, that rational agents:

1   viewed the policy indicators for the four miracles as 'sound' during the five-year period 1990–4;
2   sought to discriminate between movements of indicators due to policy measures and movements due to random shocks;
3   made their judgements on the eve of 1997 by comparing the indicators during 1995–6 to 1990–4; and
4   employed the judgement criterion that a 1995–6 value less than one standard deviation from the 1990–4 average was 'stochastic', and a variation in excess of one standard deviation (in the 'dangerous' direction) suggested an 'unsound' policy framework.

Other reasonable and theoretically credible assumptions could be made. For example, it may be that the agents whose actions precipitated the financial crisis operated on a much shorter time-horizon, and we should be specifying the rules in terms of quarters not years. It may be that one standard deviation is too great (or too small) as a yardstick for discriminating between policy and shocks. However, the approach has the advantage of generating objective judgements, and alternative criteria could be provided within this approach. Tables 3.9E–3.9H show the basic statistics, and Table 3.10 provides the results of the method of assessment. First, for the fiscal deficit (see also Figure 3.6), in both 1995 and 1996 each country had a deficit to GDP ratio well within one standard deviation of the mean value for 1990–4. If an agent had asked the question 'Given the values of the fiscal deficit for 1995 and 1996, what is the probability that 1995–9 will not be significantly different?', the answer would have been '60 to 80 per cent'.

Assessment of the trade balance as a percentage of GDP would have been mixed (see Figure 3.7). For two of the countries, Malaysia and Thailand, the deficit was well within one standard deviation of the relevant average, but it was outside this range into the 'danger' zone for Indonesia and Korea. However, if the agent had made his or her assessment on the basis of the current account deficit, only Korea would have given cause of anxiety (see Figure 3.8). With regard to debt service, all four countries were well within the postulated stochastic region in 1995 and 1996 (Figure 3.9).

After the four countries began their economic free-fall, some quite definitive judgements were made alleging over-valuation of exchange rates in the four countries as either the proximate or fundamental cause of the crisis (Figure 3.10). It would appear that these judgements rest more on predilection than fact, for it is difficult to assess this indicator by strictly quantitative criteria. As the annex to this chapter shows, different measures of the real exchange rate show different movements. For example, if one used the index preferred by Corsetti, Pesenti and Roubini (1998), there would have been no cause for concern in any of the four countries. With Radelet and Sachs' measure, Indonesia and Malaysia would have been outside the stochastic zone, but not Korea and Thailand. With the index preferred here, based on manufacturing purchasing power parity, only Indonesia appears to have a non-stochastic over-valuation.

Since rational agents would have been interested in indicators of competitiveness, and each of the countries was an exporter of manufactures, the final indicator we consider is real unit labour cost. A rational agent could have obtained an estimate of this by going to the relevant UNIDO manufacturing database and calculating average wages and constant price productivity, then adjusting with the nominal exchange rate. The relevant calculation would be:

$[\text{RULC(Exch adj)}]_{it} = [W_{it}/L_{it}][L_{it}/VA_{it}]E_{it}$
Where $[W_{it}/L_{it}]$ = total wages divided by total employment,
$[L_{it}/VA_{it}]$ = employment per unit of output,
E_{it} = nominal exchange rate, and i is country and t is year.

The result of the calculation is shown in Figure 3.11, for the countries with data. Inspection of the time series in the chart would show, as expected, a strong negative correlation between real unit labour costs and exports for two of the countries, and a weak negative correlation for the third.[28] If one treated these correlations as credible, Figure 3.11 would give no cause for concern. For Korea and Malaysia, real unit labour costs for 1995–6 were well below the average for 1990–4 (Korea), or virtually the same (Malaysia). The rational agent would have found no data for 1996 for Indonesia. If he or she had taken 1995 as the relevant indicator, there would have been no cause for worry, for this value was 3 per cent below the 1990–4 average. As for the other indicators, the available information on real labour costs would have not sent out a danger signal to a rational agent.

To carry our analysis to an overall assessment, subjectivity enters, because we have specified no weights to the elements in Table 3.10. Perhaps, at a minimum,

Table 3.10 provides quantitative judgements that can be generally accepted; namely, that it was *highly unlikely* at the end of 1996 that macro indicators from Malaysia would have provoked serious concern by rational agents, *unlikely* for Korea and Thailand, but not absurd; and *somewhat likely* for Indonesia.

Summing up

Any rational agent observing relevant macro indicators of the major Latin American countries at the end of 1981 would have immediately and unambiguously concluded that an extremely costly financial and economic adjustment was in the offing. While the Mexican government's famous announcement in autumn 1982

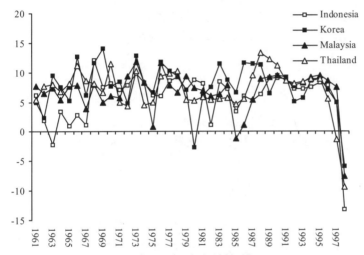

Figure 3.5 Inflation rates in four 'miracles', 1969–98

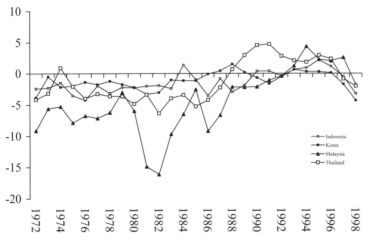

Figure 3.6 Fiscal deficits as a percentage of GDP for four 'miracles', 1972–98

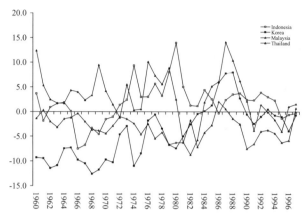

Figure 3.7 The trade balance in GDP for four 'miracles', 1960–97

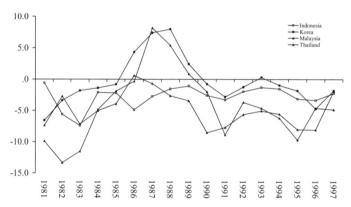

Figure 3.8 Current external account balance in GDP for four 'miracles', 1981–97

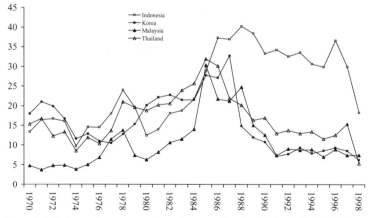

Figure 3.9 Debt service as a portion of exports for four 'miracles', 1970–97

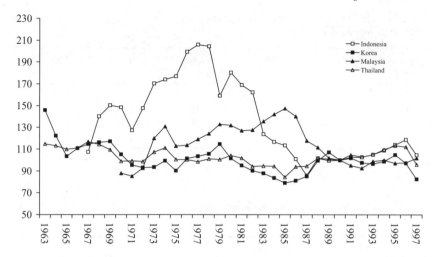

Figure 3.10 Real (PPP) exchange rates for four 'miracles', 1963–97 (1990 = 100, a rise shows an appreciation)

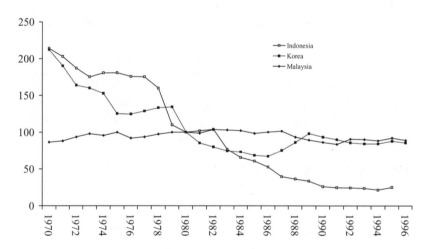

Figure 3.11 Exchange rate adjusted real unit labour costs in manufacturing, three 'miracles', 1970–96 (natural logs, 1980 = 100)

Table 3.10 Evaluation of policy outcomes for four 'miracles': was 1995–6 within one standard deviation of average for 1990–4?

Country	Fiscal deficit	Trade balance	Current account	Debt service	Exchange rate
Indonesia	yes	no	yes	yes	no*
Korea	yes	no	no	yes	yes
Malaysia	yes	yes	yes	yes	yes
Thailand	yes	yes	yes	yes	no*

Note:
*At least one index shows no significant appreciation. See text for discussion.

Table 3.11 A likely assessment of signals from macro indicators at the beginning of 1997, for four 'miracles'

Is it likely that a problem would have been perceived?					
Indicator	Indonesia	Korea	Malaysia	Thailand	Comment
GDP growth	no	no	no	perhaps	
Inv/GDP	no	perhaps	no	no	
Exports/GDP	perhaps	no	no	no	Export share was rising for three of four
Debt/GDP	perhaps	no	no	no	Indonesia's debt service ratio was high, but well below the 1980s
Inflation	perhaps	no	no	no	Rate in each country below what research suggests would be detrimental
Fiscal Deficit/GDP	no	no	no	no	During 1992–4 all four had surpluses
Trade balance/GDP	no	yes	no	no	Deficit lower in 1996 than 1995, except Korea
Current account/ GDP	no	no	no	perhaps	Thailand had persistent deficits, 1995–6 same as 1990–1
Exchange rate	perhaps	no	no	perhaps	Depends on the index chosen
Manufacturing competitiveness (Exch rate adj RULC)	no	no	no	no data	No notable change in mid–1990s
Summary	Most likely	Unlikely	Least likely	Unlikely	

came as a shock, it was not a surprise. Similarly, just over ten years later, the extraordinary current account deficits run by Mexico should have signalled to any rational observer that a currency collapse was highly probable.

In contrast, an extremely high degree of pessimism and Cassandra-esque foresight would have been required to prompt serious anxiety about the state of the four miracles at the end of 1996. If private agents read policy mismanagement into the macro indicators from these four countries at the end of 1996, the probability of any country consistently sending positive signals to 'financial markets' lies somewhere between slim and none. Stochastic variation alone would undo the best efforts of policy-makers if 'markets' demand such a narrow range of outcomes.

As noted at the beginning of this chapter, a review of opinions on the Asian financial crisis reveals a polarisation, between explanations that attribute the crisis to policy mismanagement (the orthodoxy), and explanations that attribute it to the inherent instability of international financial markets (the heterodoxy). The statistics presented in this chapter indicate that the dichotomy is false. If, as argued here, in 1997 'financial markets' were alarmed, then driven to panic, by variations in policy indicators that were within the range stochastic fluctuations, then the 'policy mismanagement' argument collapses. Governments can hardly be blamed if financial markets expect them to maintain indicators within ranges that are too small for the inherent effectiveness of the policy instruments available to those governments. In other words, if the so-called investors expect a performance that the science and practice of economic policy cannot reasonably deliver, those markets are, by definition, unstable.

Annex on exchange rates

This annex demonstrates that judgements about whether exchange rates in the four miracles were over-valued at the end of 1996 depends on what index one uses. For all four countries the following three indices are presented:

1   the producer price parity index, compiled by the author, which is the nominal exchange rate multiplied by the domestic price index for manufacturing, and divided by the US producer price index (PrdPrI);
2   the index used by Radelet and Sachs (1998), which is the nominal exchange rate weighted by trade, multiplied by the domestic consumer price index, divided by a 'foreign' wholesale price index (Sachs); and
3   the index used by Corsetti, Pesenti and Roubini (1998), which is cited as being from J.P. Morgan (CP&R).

For Thailand, the real effective exchange rate from the *World Development Indicators 1999* is also included. Inspection of Figures 3.A1–3.A4 show considerable variation in the measured degree of appreciation during 1990–6. For each country there is a measure, and not always the same one, which indicates a quite small appreciation.

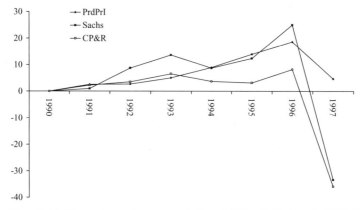

Figure 3.A1 Alternative exchange rate indices (1990 = 0): Indonesia 1990–7

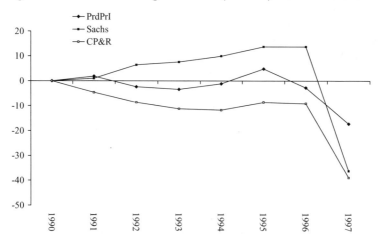

Figure 3.A2 Alternative exchange rate indices (1990 = 0): Korea 1990–7

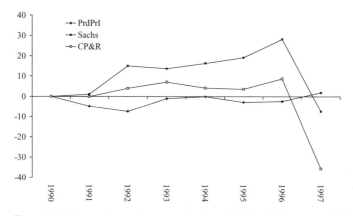

Figure 3.A3 Alternative exchange rate indices (1990 = 0): Malaysia 1990–7

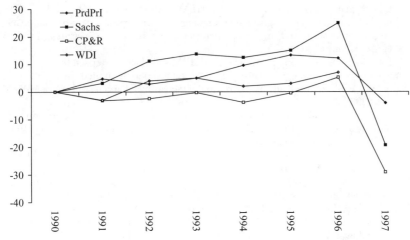

Figure 3.A4 Alternative exchange rate indices (1990 = 0): Thailand 1990–7

Notes

1   Bulmer-Thomas argues that it is an exaggeration to characteriste the region by this term (Bulmer-Thomas 1992).
2   For a sympathetic presentation of the Washington Consensus (albeit by another name), see Rodrik (1996).
3   The application of the difference in means test is justified in some detail in Weeks (2000). The data sources are given in that paper. The most important is the World Bank's *World Development Indicators 1999* (CD-ROM). In that paper the two groups are the same as here, with the exception that Taiwan is included in the Asia set for most tables.
4   For GDP itself, the average for the thirty-five years was 7.1 for the HPAEs and 3.6 for Latin America. Per capita GDP growth was 5.1 per cent per annum compared to 1.6.
5   During most of the 1970s Chile's growth rate was quite low, and it was low in the early 1980s. Subsequently it enjoyed growth rates comparable to the 'miracles'.
6   As with national income, export growth was uneven in Latin America, across countries, and over time for specific countries. Non-oil-exporting countries with export growth in excess of 10 per cent per year were: Brazil and Costa Rica during 1970–4; Argentina, Chile, and Uruguay during 1975–9; Brazil and the Dominican Republic during 1980–4; Colombia and Paraguay during 1985–9; and Bolivia, Chile, Costa Rica, the Dominican Republic, and Nicaragua during 1990–4.
7   The stress given to 'openness' derives from the view that 'open economies do grow faster' (Dollar 1992). Pritchett (1996) demonstrated that the various measures of openness used in empirical work are not correlated with each other. For another critique of the usual measures, see Subasat (1999).
8   The conclusion that the HPAEs were more open might be strengthened by such an analysis, since several of the Latin American countries are quite small and, for several, minerals dominated exports. Both of these tend to inflate the export–GDP ratio.
9   All writers do not stress high investment rates. See, for example, Kagami (1995) and Institute of Developing Economies (1990), where it is noted that Latin American and East Asian rates of capital accumulation were quite similar.
10   The surprisingly low average for the HPAEs during 1960–4 is partly the result of the low investment rate in Indonesia during the last years of the Sukarno government.
11   Palma argues that higher saving rates in the HPAEs than in Latin America can largely be explained by state policies to coerce a lower consumption level and foster corporate

retained earnings. He concludes that the HPAE performance is explained by 'forced household savings, massive government savings as in Singapore, credit restrictions on luxury consumption and mortgage operations, or attractive long-term returns on savings' (Palma 1996: 44).

12   'More that most developing countries, the HPAEs were characterised by responsible macroeconomic management. In particular, they generally limited fiscal deficits to levels that could be prudently financed without increasing inflationary pressures' (World Bank 1993: 12).

13   This casts doubt upon the concept of 'macroeconomic populism' in Latin America, especially as set out by Dornbusch and Edwards (1991). Kaufman and Stallings (1991) also view the concept sceptically.

14   Which, evidently, they do in the judgement of the World Bank. See the 'Fiscal Policy Stance Index' in World Bank 1994: 48.

15   In a 1998 speech, Stiglitz repeated the standard view of Latin American deficits: 'Budget deficits were very high – *many* were in the range of 5 to 10 per cent of GDP [in the early 1980s]' (Stiglitz 1998: 2, emphasis added). Across the eighteen countries and five time periods (ninety observations) there were sixteen cases in which deficits averaged over 5 per cent of GDP, six during 1980–4 and five during 1985–9. Only five countries averaged over 5 per cent in more than one time period, two of which were major countries (Mexico and Brazil, the others being Honduras, Nicaragua, and Panama). The HPAE group had a persistent offender, Malaysia, with deficits in excess of 5 per cent during 1970–84. During the 1980–4 period, only two Latin American countries had deficits greater than Malaysia's (Nicaragua and Bolivia).

16   This is suggested in some World Bank reports (1993 and 1994), but one finds a more nuanced approach in World Bank (1997).

17   Due to petroleum revenues, Venezuela had a large state sector for the entire thirty-five years.

18   A simple OLS regression of public expenditure as a portion of GDP and debt service as a portion of exports, across the eighteen countries and over the five time periods, yields an elasticity of 0.4, a correlation coefficient of 0.07, and the regression coefficient is significant at 0.05 probability.

19   The ratio was over 30 per cent for Brazil during 1985–9 and 1990–4, Nicaragua during 1980–4 and 1985–9, and Chile 1980–4, and for no others during any of the periods.

20   In the absence of explicit modelling, the base year for an exchange rate has no normative implications, and movements from that base year, whether up or down, cannot be judged as movements toward or away from the optimum exchange rate. For example, an appreciating exchange rate implies unsound policy if and only if it is a movement away from, not towards, the equilibrium level.

21   The exchange rate index for 1974–80 was 5 per cent higher than for 1965–73, according to the CEPAL 'real effective exchange rate for exports'.

22   According to World Bank figures, Indonesia's debt service as a portion of export earnings was: 1975–9, 19 per cent; 1980–4, 17 per cent; and 1985–9, 36 per cent. For Korea, Malaysia, and Thailand, debt service rose sharply in the 1980s, but briefly, with rapid export growth and rescheduling reducing the percentages to 10 to 15 per cent in the early 1990s. Taiwan had a net positive external capital account.

23   In the first group, only for five observations out of thirty-five was debt service less than 30 per cent of exports. Two of these were during 1970–4, before the major debt accumulations (Bolivia and Chile), and two during 1990–4, after the debt reduction measures of the late 1980s (Brazil and Chile). The fifth, for Peru during 1985–9, reflected the Garcia government's policy of limiting debt service payments. For the 'moderate' group, the debt service ratio was *more* than 30 per cent in eleven time periods, five of which were during the debt crisis period of 1980–4. For the 'low' group, the ratio was over 30 per cent in only one time period (Honduras, 1990–4),

and above 20 per cent in only eight. Honduras is a marginal case with an average for the five periods just over 20 per cent.

24 Only one country among the HPAEs had debt service over 30 per cent of export earnings, Indonesia during 1985–9 and 1990–4, which is not unrelated to the country's financial crisis during 1997–8. Even with Indonesia, the HPAE group is in the 'low debt' category in all time periods except 1985–9.

25 The model was estimated for five-year periods, with some variables lagged. See Weeks (2000).

26 A trend analysis with a shift term for 1991–8 shows a negative and significant coefficient of 1.2 percentage points.

27 Radelet and Sachs point out that the Asian collapse was not anticipated by financial markets:

> The credit rating agencies…provide an on-going assessment of credit risk in the emerging markets. If the markets expected a financial crisis…the ratings of bonds

Table 3.12 Exports and real labour costs

Country	Elasticity, exports and RULC	Significance of T-statistic	R^2 and DF
Indonesia	−0.15	0.00	0.87 24
Korea	−0.51	0.00	0.90 32
Malaysia	−1.04	0.08	0.12 25

> should have fallen in the run-up to the crisis. Instead…we find that the rating agencies did not signal increased risk until after the onset of the crisis itself.
>
> Radelet and Sachs 1998: 18–19

28 The relevant statistics for the simple regressions are given in the table below. The dependent variable is the natural logarithm of level of exports measured in constant US dollars of 1995 (from *World Development Indicators 1999*). The independent variable is exchange rate adjusted real unit labour costs, as defined in the text (UNIDO 1998).

Bibliography

Bulmer-Thomas, V. (1992) *Life After Debt? The New Economic Trajectory in Latin America*, London: Institute of Latin American Studies.

Corsetti, G., Pesenti, P. and Roubini, N. (1998) *What Caused the Asian Currency and Financial Crisis?* New York: NBER WP.

De Pinies, J. (1989) 'Debt sustainability and overadjustment', *World Development* 17, 1: 29–43.

Dollar, D. (1992) 'Outward-oriented developing economies really do grow more rapidly: evidence from 95 LDCs, 1976–85', *Economic Development and Cultural Change* 40, 3: 523–44.

Dornbusch, R. and Edwards, S. (1991) 'The macroeconomics of populism', in R. Dornbusch and S. Edwards (eds) *The Macroeconomics of Populism in Latin America*, Chicago: University of Chicago Press.

Institute of Developing Economies (1990) 'IDE Paper: prospects and tasks for the Pacific Basin economy', in Fukuchi, Takao and M. Kagami (eds), *Perspectives on the Pacific Basin Economy: a comparison of Asia and Latin America*, Tokyo: Institute of Developing Economies.

Kagami, M. (1995) *The Voice of East Asia: Development Implications for Latin America*, Tokyo: Institute of Developing Economies.

Kaufman, R.R. and Stallings, B. (1991) 'The political economy of Latin American populism', in R. Dornbusch and S. Edwards (eds) *The Macroeconomics of Populism in Latin America*, Chicago: University of Chicago Press.

Kregel, J.A. (1998) 'Derivatives and global capital flows: applications to Asia', *Cambridge Journal of Economics* 22, 6: 677–92.

Kuznets, P.W. (1988) 'An East Asian model of economic development: Japan, Taiwan, and South Korea', *Economic Development and Cultural Change* 36, 3: 11–43.

Palma, G. (1996) 'Whatever happened to Latin America's savings? Comparing Latin American and East Asian savings performances', project on *East Asian Development: Lessons for a New Global Environment*, Geneva: United Nations Conference on Trade and Development.

—— (1998) 'Three and a half cycles of "mania, panic and [asymmetric] crash": East Asia and Latin America compared', *Cambridge Journal of Economics* 22, 6: 789–808.

Pincus, J. and Ramli, R. (1998) 'Indonesia: from showcase to basket case', *Cambridge Journal of Economics* 22, 6: 723–34.

Pritchett, L. (1996) 'Measuring outward orientation in LDCs: can it be done?', *Journal of Development* 49, 2: 307–35.

Radelet, S. and Sachs, J. (1998) *The Onset of the East Asian Financial Crisis*, Harvard: NBER WP 6680.

Rodrik, D. (1996) 'Understanding economic policy reform', *Journal of Economic Literature* XXXIV (March): 9–41.

Singh, A. (1996) 'Savings, investment and the corporation in the East Asian miracle', project on *East Asian Development: Lessons for a New Global Environment*, Geneva: United Nations Conference on Trade and Development.

Stiglitz, J. (1998) 'More instruments and broader goals: moving toward the post-Washington Consensus', *The 1998 WIDER Annual Lecture*, Helsinki: WIDER.

Subasat, T. (1999) 'Export-led Development: A Theoretical and Empirical Investigation', London: School of Oriental and African Studies PhD Dissertation in Economics.

UNIDO (1998) *Industrial Statistics* (Three 3.5 inch disks).

Wade, R. (1996) 'Japan, the World Bank, and the art of paradigm maintenance: The East Asian Miracle in political perspective', *New Left Review* 217 (May/June): 3–36.

Weeks, J. (1989) 'Losers pay reparations: how the third world lost the lending war', in J. Weeks (ed.) *Debt Disaster?*, New York: New York University Press.

—— (1999) 'Stuck in low gear? South African macro policy, 1996–1998', *Cambridge Journal of Economics* 23, 6: 795–811.

—— (2000) 'Latin America and the "High Performing Asian Economies": growth and debt', *Journal of International Development* 12, 5: 625–54.

World Bank (1993) *The East Asian Miracle: Economic Growth and Public Policy*, Oxford: Oxford University Press.

—— (1994) *Adjustment in Africa: Reforms, Results, and the Road Ahead*, Oxford: Oxford University Press.

—— (1997) *World Development Report 1997*, Oxford: Oxford University Press.

—— (1999) *World Development Indicators* (CD-ROM), Washington: World Bank.

4   Neo-liberalism on the defensive but not defeated?

A comparative review of the Asian crisis and lessons for the future

Chris Edwards

The crisis in East Asia – an introduction

Table 4.1 shows both the miracle of East and Southeast Asia and the extent of the crisis in 1998.[1] In 1998 the average fall in GDP for the four worst-affected countries (Indonesia, South Korea, Malaysia and Thailand) was 9 per cent. In terms of a deviation from the average for 1985–96, the loss averaged 17 per cent, equivalent, for these four countries, to more than 140 billion US dollars. In 1998, the population of these four countries was about 330 million so that the average per capita loss was over $400. This would be bad enough if the burden of the crisis fell equally. But the poor were hit disproportionately. Thus in September 1998, Stiglitz, the Chief Economist of the World Bank until late 1999, argued that: 'prior to the crisis there were 30 million people living on less than $1 a day in Indonesia, Malaysia, the Philippines, and Thailand. By 2000 that number could easily double to 60 million' (Stiglitz 1998c).

This chapter asks four questions.

The first two are 'Could the crisis have been avoided?' and 'Should it have been?' The answer to both of these questions is 'yes'. First, there are policies which could have prevented the crisis being so sharp (see section 'The IMF made it worse' below). Second, and more importantly, there are policies which could and should have been in force to prevent the crisis occurring (see section 'The East Asian crisis in a broader context – the necessity for change' below).

The third question is 'Will similar financial crises occur?' The answer is 'yes' (see section 'The crisis in East Asia in a broader context – a crisis of world capitalism?' below), unless certain radical changes to international and/or national policies are adopted.

Finally the fourth question is 'Are such changes likely to be introduced?' The answer is 'probably not', since there are still powerful, neo-liberal forces aligned against such radical changes (see section 'The prospects for radical change' below).

Since the onset of the crisis in mid-1997 there have been a large number of papers written which attempt to explain the crisis and set out policy prescriptions to deal with the problems.

In this chapter I look at the diverse ways in which the crisis has been analysed. I argue that the analyses and their prescriptions can be equated with schools of economic thought which themselves represent certain interest groups or social classes. The beginning of the chapter is structured around these schools of thought. I start with neo-liberalism.

Neo-liberalism on the defensive

What is 'neo-liberalism' (or 'neo-classicism')?

The main ideas of this school of thought can be briefly summarised as follows. The adherents are in favour of:

- Free markets, both nationally and internationally;
- Stable price levels (that is, low rates of inflation) because the movements of relative prices are delicate and will otherwise be drowned out by the 'noise' of general rises in prices;
- A stable demand for money because inflation is thought to be caused by an excess supply of money. The link here is the argument that the demand for money is stable so that an excess supply of money will be reflected in either domestic inflation and/or a balance of payments deficit;
- High real interest rates to avoid 'financial repression', a situation in which it is claimed savings are discouraged and investment quality is affected by rationing of funds.

The views of this school of thought are particularly attractive to, and propagated by, financial capital, the form of capital which is most mobile and footloose. In general this is the fraction of capital best served by high real interest rates and financial liberalisation.

The high point of neo-liberalism in the post-war period was in the early 1980s. This was the period when it was said that Brazil only developed at night because that was when the government was sleeping. It was when UNCTAD was being mocked as standing for 'Under No Circumstances Take A Decision'. It was from the 1980s that a 'Washington Consensus' became dominant, with programmes of stabilisation (action on the demand side, associated with the IMF) being co-ordinated with programmes of structural adjustment (withdrawal of the state on the supply side associated with the World Bank). In general, the policy conditionality associated with these programmes was neo-liberal and after the debt crisis of the early 1980s these programmes became more widespread.

The view of neo-liberalism on growth and development was that neo-liberal policies generated the fastest growth. The high point of this view was given by the World Bank's 1983 *World Development Report*. But then, through the rest of the 1980s and into the 1990s, this view was forced on to the defensive as study after study (the major ones in the English language were those of Amsden 1989, Wade 1990 and White 1988) argued that the neo-liberal version of events was wrong.

After an altercation between the World Bank and the Japanese government, the *East Asian Miracle* study was carried out by the World Bank (see World Bank 1993). We were left with two neo-liberal versions. One, the dominant World Bank view, was that directed credit and industrial policy played their parts in the miracle but could not be replicated elsewhere. The second was that the miracle took place in spite of these internal structural deficiencies, implying that without the intervention, growth would have been even faster. But even the less extreme World Bank view was attacked sharply by a large number of economists (see Fishlow *et al.* 1994, Rodrik 1995 and *World Development* 1994).

With the East Asian crisis, the neo-liberals counter-attacked by arguing that internal structural deficiencies were largely to blame for the crisis. As Corsetti *et al.* 1998a (p.1) put it: 'the ... view – advanced in this paper – [is that] the crisis reflected structural and policy distortions in the countries of the region. Fundamental imbalances triggered the currency and financial crisis in 1997'.

Thus the neo-liberal view was that the crisis was a solvency, not merely a liquidity, problem. In spite of these arguments, neo-liberalism came under attack not only for its analysis of the crisis but also for its policy recommendations. The IMF in particular went on the defensive. I look at the conflicts around IMF policies in section 'The IMF made it worse' below. There were signs that the Washington Consensus was under strain, as institutionalist views rose to prominence. It is time to look at these.

The rise of institutionalists' views

The neo-liberal views and the policies of the IMF view have been heavily criticised by writers within what broadly may be called the school of institutional or Keynesian economics.

The main ideas of this school of thought are as follows:

- Markets need institutional regulation since they adjust at different speeds;
- Markets also need institutional modification since many markets have inherent imperfections which demand particular attention. Most obviously, financial markets suffer from information asymmetries and the associated agency conflicts and moral hazard (see Gibson and Tsakalotos 1994, Stiglitz and Weiss 1981, and Stiglitz 1994);
- The cost of inflation is overstated by the neo-liberal school. It is argued that only high inflation (above 40 per cent per annum) is costly, that inflation does not in general have a tendency to accelerate, and that even when it does accelerate, it is not difficult to control (see Stiglitz 1998a). The institutionalists argue that neo-liberals understate the importance of growth, employment and income distribution. Furthermore they argue that there is a policy asymmetry, it being much easier through monetary and fiscal policy to engineer a contraction in GDP than an increase (see Stiglitz 1998c);
- Interest rates are the outcome of the demand and supply for money; that is, the *form* in which savings are held (see Keynes 1976, chapter 16). Real interest rates should be kept low and stable so as to encourage investment. Thus the focus of attention is on investment and the conditions that generate it. Savings are a function of income which itself is generated by income-generating

expenditures such as investment and consumption (personal, government and foreign);

- The emphasis is more on competitive rather than comparative advantage. Since competitive advantages can be created, there is a case for trade being managed in association with industrial policy;
- Because of the interdependence of regional and national economies, there is a strong argument for the co-ordinated regulation and management of the world economy.

The views of this school of thought are particularly attractive to, and propagated by, *industrial capital*, capital which is (at least relative to that of financial capital) fixed. For Keynes the industrialist tends to be squeezed between the demands of employees and the vagaries of the financial market. Stability of prices, of exchange rates, of interest rates – these are the necessary (but not sufficient) conditions for a growing economy favoured by this fraction of capital.

The institutionalist views have become more dominant in the 1990s as the neo-liberal dominance has weakened. There were attacks on both stabilisation and structural adjustment programmes in the 1980s (see Killick 1984, Mosley *et al.* 1995) and the Washington Consensus began to weaken in the 1990s.

The view of the institutionalists on development has been that backward economies need institutional support to grow. From the views of Gerschenkron in the 1950s and 1960s (Gerschenkron 1962) through to the detailed studies on the East Asian economies in the 1980s and the 1990s, the emphasis has been on the role of the state in promoting investment in import-substituting industries as a launching pad for export growth. However, many writers have emphasised that although there were some common factors in the East Asian growth story (such as the role of Japan as the leader of the 'flying geese'), there were also varying characteristics between countries within the region. Thus Perkins has emphasised that at least three groups of countries could and should be distinguished in East Asia. These are first Japan, Korea and Taiwan, second the natural-resource rich countries of Indonesia, Malaysia and Thailand and third Hong Kong and Singapore (Perkins in *World Development* 1994). In addition, some economists have taken great care to emphasise the importance of the initial conditions. Thus Rodrik (1995) has stressed the importance of the emphasis on primary education and the relatively equal income distribution in Taiwan and South Korea effected through land reform. Many others have stressed the geo-political conditions – not just Japan as the 'leading goose' but also the massive aid from the USA and the war in Vietnam as a stimulus, especially to Korea (see Bagchi 1987).

Thus in the institutionalists' view, the role of the state has been crucial in directing credit, in promoting investment accumulation (Akyuz and Gore 1996), in building up exports from an import-substituting base (especially in Korea and Taiwan), in assisting the assimilation of technology (Nelson and Pack 1999) and in developing human resources. The institutionalists recognise the considerable, historically-specific differences between East Asia and other parts of the less developed world but, as Stein argues:

the central lesson of … Asia's industrialization … is that there is no alternative to the state. International agencies need to move away from the policy lending based on flawed economic theories toward financing the public goods and state capacities which are prerequisites for private initiatives in industry.

Stein 1995: 21

When we come to look at the East Asian crisis, there are a large number of papers written from what may broadly be called an institutionalist perspective. The next section looks at the different threads within the institutionalist cloth.

Financial liberalisation and the East Asian crisis – institutionalist perspectives

A number of papers have argued that the crisis was not due, in general, to macroeconomic mismanagement (see Brownbridge and Kirkpatrick 1999, Furman and Stiglitz 1998, and Radelet and Sachs 1998). All four worst-affected countries had strong economic growth and the IMF would have approved of their low rates of inflation and fiscal surpluses, or at least only small budget deficits, in the run-up to the crisis. Thus between 1990 and 1997 all four had average inflation rates of below 10 per cent and over the same period three of the four governments ran fiscal surpluses. It is worth noting that China, the country in East Asia with the highest rate of inflation over this period, has not suffered from the crisis, at least in terms of GDP growth.

Thus the general institutionalist argument is that the main problem did not lie in structural weaknesses. As Singh (1998) has pointed out, it is ironic that the very features of the Asian model which were identified previously as the basis for its economic success – strong government and competent bureaucracy equipped with the right policies – began to be seen as the root cause of the crisis. So in the institutionalist view, the cause of the crisis was not in general due to macroeconomic mismanagement nor to crony capitalism, but to capital liberalisation.

Thus in the run-up to the crisis, as a result of capital liberalisation, the East Asian countries experienced strong inflows of foreign, mostly short-term, capital attracted by high interest rates (especially compared to Japan) which led to rapid increases in the external indebtedness of the domestic corporate and financial sectors. An investment boom led to strong growth in domestic absorption, while export growth began to slow, partly as a result of the slow-down in the Japanese economy and partly due to the maintenance or even appreciation of real exchange rate indices. In 1995 and 1996, the real exchange rate indices were maintained in spite of large deficits on the current account of the balance of payments. In 1996 these deficits (as a percentage of GDP) were 3 per cent in Indonesia, 5 per cent in Korea, 5 per cent in Malaysia and 8 per cent in Thailand.

The current account deficits were covered by massive capital inflows. An indication of the inflows is given by Radelet and Sachs, who point out that for these four countries, plus the Philippines, private net inflows soared, rising from $US41 billion in 1994 to $US93 billion in 1996. In 1997 this was reversed and there was a net *outflow* of US$12 billion. They point out that this swing of US$105 billion was equivalent to about 11 per cent of the pre-crisis GDP of these five countries (Radelet and Sachs 1998: 2).

The institutional economists tend to argue that it was this massive inflow which propped up the real exchange rates. By contrast, the neo-liberals tend to argue the reverse. Thus according to Corsetti *et al.* (1998a: 21): 'the decision to maintain a stable currency led to large capital inflows attracted by favourable interest rate differentials and expectations of low exchange rate risk'.

Thus the neo-liberals emphasise the misplaced decision of these countries to keep their currencies pegged to the dollar. When the dollar appreciated against the yen, by more than 20 per cent through 1996 and 1997, these currencies also appreciated against the yen.

The institutionalists argue that the crisis was not caused (in general) by public sector deficits and/or public sector debts but by the external liberalisation of the financial sector. Chang, Palma and Whittaker (1998: 649) argue that the crisis resulted generally from under-regulated and over-liquid international financial markets, and Brownbridge and Kirkpatrick (1999: 254) point out that: 'Although financial liberalisation had begun in the 1980s in a number of Asian countries, its pace accelerated in the 1990s'.

It was in the context of financial liberalisation that the vast capital inflows took place. These inflows were particularly threatening since a major proportion of them were short term. As a result, by 1996, the short-term external debt of three (Indonesia, Korea and Thailand) of the four worst-affected countries were all equal to or greater than their foreign reserves.

It needs to be emphasised that this financial liberalisation was combined with other factors to bring about the crisis. It is beyond the scope of this chapter to look at each of the four worst-affected countries in great detail, but the following paragraphs highlight some of the major points.

Indonesia was the most seriously-affected country in the East Asian crisis. The proportion of the population below the poverty line rose to 40 per cent and fifteen million workers were estimated to have lost their jobs (Pincus and Ramli 1998). They argue that:

> Although triggered by external factors, the roots of the economic collapse can be traced to a series of policy errors and to the nature of economic policy-making under Suharto ... including the attempt of a weak, 'patrimonial' Indonesian state to carry out a wide-ranging programme of financial liberalisation. The reforms failed to dismantle the patron–client system and increased the risks of financial collapse.
>
> Pincus and Ramli 1998: 723

They argue that, far from dismantling the patronage networks that tied capitalists to the regime, liberalisation expanded the range of opportunities available to these groups to profit from their political connections.

Liberalisation was also important in Korea. Chang, Park and Yoo (1998) argue that it was the dismantling of the traditional mechanisms of industrial policy and financial regulation, rather than the perpetuation of the traditional regime, that generated the crisis. From the early 1990s, the Korean government started significantly relaxing its control over the financial sector and, under the Kim Young Sam government, which came to power in 1993, the liberalisation process was greatly accelerated, partly because of pressure from the USA (see Chang, Park and Yoo 1998) and in the context of Korea's push for OECD membership (Wade and Veneroso 1998). Chang, Park and Yoo reject the argument put forward by Krugman (1998) that moral hazard was a particular problem for Korea because of the implicit guarantee of bail-out provided by the government. They point out that in the past two decades there had been numerous instances of *chaebols* failing and no instance of a bail-out. Chang, Park and Yoo also cast doubt on the argument of Baily and Zitzewitz (1998) that the cause of the crisis was structural because bad investment decisions had led to profitability in Korea being at a very low level by the mid-1990s. Chang, Park and Yoo point out that Korea's corporate profitability before interest payments was not low by international standards. The same point is made by Bosworth (1998a) in commenting on Baily and Zitzewitz's paper. However, the high debt ratios of the corporations which had served the country well until the crisis (see Wade and Veneroso 1998) made it vulnerable to the external exposure encouraged by the financial liberalisation. Chang, Park and Yoo (1998: 744) argue that: 'had it not been for the ill-designed financial liberalisation policy and the demise of industrial policy that led to over-investment, high corporate debt in Korea would not have produced a crisis'.

In an article on the crisis in Malaysia, Jomo (1998: 718) argues that: 'The Malaysian currency and financial crises since mid-1997 can be traced to financial liberalisation and its consequent undermining of national monetary and financial governance'. On the same page, he adds that: 'Government efforts to "bail out" politically influential business interests ... to protect and advance such interests – usually at the expense of the public ... – have exacerbated the crisis in Malaysia'.

In the case of Thailand, Brownbridge and Kirkpatrick (1999) downplay the significance of moral hazard, pointing out that Thailand had experienced a wave of failure of finance companies in the mid-1980s with twenty-five being closed, and their depositors having to bear 50 per cent of the losses. They emphasise that in the late 1980s and early 1990s, the Thai government abolished interest-rate ceilings, relaxed foreign exchange controls, granted offshore banking licences, eased the rules governing some financial institutions, and expanded the scope of permissible capital market activities. Thus foreign currency exposures were crucial in the crisis with 17 per cent of domestic credit comprising loans which had been funded by foreign currency borrowing by banks operating on the Bangkok International Banking Facility. As a result, by 1996 the foreign currency liabilities of Thai banks and finance companies were 775 per cent of their foreign currency assets (ibid. 250).

It is clear from this brief review of the four worst-affected countries that in the views of institutional economists, the financial distress in the East Asian crisis countries was triggered by financial liberalisation. Those countries that were moving more slowly to open their financial markets had far fewer problems; thus Taiwan had no capital convertibility and no crisis (see Bosworth 1998b in reply to Radelet and Sachs 1998: 82). The crisis in the four worst-affected countries was caused by financial liberalisation, combined with excessive lending to high-risk sectors such as real estate and the share market in Indonesia, Malaysia and Thailand and to highly geared conglomerates (*chaebols*) in Korea, insider lending (especially in Indonesia), and over-exposure to short-term foreign currency risks. The general view of the institutionalists is that the crisis was a liquidity, not a solvency, crisis which was made worse by the IMF's 'rescue' policies.

The IMF made it worse – the institutional economists argue

There have been sharp criticisms of the policies adopted by the IMF in reaction to the crisis. Radelet and Sachs (1998) argue that:

- The IMF imposed the wrong conditionality in respect of financial markets. In 1998, the IMF itself had recognised that the authorities were mindful of the risk that bank closures could induce a run on other healthy institutions, and yet, according to Radelet and Sachs, this is exactly what happened. They argue that, across the region, even relatively strong banks came under intense pressure as foreign creditors refused to roll over loans and depositors fled to state- and foreign-owned banks.
- The IMF failed to achieve confidence and exchange rate stability in East Asia because of its approach to fiscal and monetary policy. The IMF put great emphasis on the need for strong fiscal contraction in order to ensure a fiscal surplus in 1998, even though the crisis countries were already hit hard by the contractionary withdrawal of foreign credits. Thailand was asked to move from a deficit of 1.6 per cent of GDP in 1996–7 to a surplus of 1 per cent in 1997–8; Indonesia was required to contract fiscally by 1 per cent in 1997–8 and by 2 per cent in 1998–9; and Korea was asked to make a fiscal contraction of 1.5 per cent of GDP in 1998–9. Radelet and Sachs argue that there is no evidence that the currency markets reacted at all favourably to the fiscal targets.
- The IMF programmes failed because the loan packages provided only a weak shadow of lender-of-last-resort facility. The loans were too little and too late. In commenting on Radelet and Sachs, Bosworth points out that there was a sharp difference between the international response to the Mexican crisis of 1994–5 and the response to the East Asian crisis. Mexico was provided with $US52 billion in loans with only limited conditions. It drew US$32 billion of those funds within a few weeks, and by the middle of the year had started repaying the US and Canada. By contrast, the funds offered to the Asian countries were highly conditional and the amounts actually made available were far less than the US$100 billion prominently reported in the press. According to Bosworth, the IMF used the crisis to force the East Asian countries

to adopt its own agenda for financial market and other reforms (Bosworth 1998b: 83, see also Feldstein 1998).

- The IMF programmes failed partly because they did not insist on restructuring the debt. In other words the IMF put too little pressure on the creditors to roll over their loans. As a result, Radelet and Sachs claim, even after the IMF loans, the banking sector remained illiquid and heavily under-capitalised in each of the crisis countries.

- The IMF's programmes did not inspire confidence, partly because of secrecy and partly because of reputation. The initial loan programmes were not released to the public and this secrecy, combined with the reputation of the IMF for contractionary policies, were unlikely to inspire confidence. Radelet and Sachs (p.61) argue that the arrival of the IMF 'gives all the confidence of an ambulance arriving at one's door'.

In response to criticisms from Feldstein, Fischer (the First Deputy Managing Director of the IMF) defends the IMF's programmes, arguing that structural conditionality was imposed because structural problems were at the heart of the economic crises in Indonesia, Korea and Thailand. Fischer argues that the macroeconomic parts of these programmes consisted of tight money to restore confidence in the currency and a modest firming up of fiscal policy to offset in part the massive costs of financial restructuring (see Fischer 1998). He also claims that:

> After these initial (fiscal) adjustments, if the economic situation in a country weakens more than expected, as it has in these three Asian countries, the IMF has generally agreed to let the deficit widen and the stimulus of increased social spending and deficit expenditure to take place.
>
> Fischer 1998: 105

Fischer argues that creditors did take much of the adjustment strain, bearing considerable losses in the stock markets. He admits, however, that:

> Some short-term creditors, notably those involved in the interbank market, were protected for a while because the IMF sought to avert a formal debt moratorium for fear it would lead to a rapid withdrawal of funds from other countries.
>
> Fischer 1998: 106

By contrast, the institutionalists argue that the IMF's policies were wrong. As Stiglitz puts it: 'There is a growing consensus ... that the actual crisis-response measures exacerbated the downturn' (Stiglitz 1999: 3). Stiglitz argues that the policies were not only beggar-thy-neighbour. This would be bad enough. But they were also beggar-thyself. And he implies that the IMF's neo-liberal policies beggar belief since they were intellectually incoherent. Stiglitz considers and rejects the argument for deflation to prevent competitive, contagious devaluations, claiming that:

'Competitive devaluations, offset by successive cuts in interest rates, would serve as a mechanism for restoring the strength of the world economy' (ibid. 15). He accuses the neo-classicists of intellectual inconsistency because, while they recognise that foreign exchange markets tend to over- and under-shoot and are subject to market failure, they fail to recognise market failure in other markets.

If this is the case, Stiglitz asks, why were the policies advocated? He concludes that the real concern behind the neo-classical policies was the threat the crisis posed to lenders, arguing that a large devaluation may make it impossible for a country to repay foreign-denominated debt. He claims that even though the rescue package failed to achieve the objective of preventing a debt moratorium, in the short run, the gains to Western capital markets were clear, and the decision to liberalise was consistent with those interests being more effectively addressed than broader global interests.

I come back in the last two sections to how broader global interests can be addressed, but before that, I look briefly at the East Asian crisis in the broader context.

The crisis in East Asia in a broader context – a crisis of world capitalism?

Brownbridge and Kirkpatrick (1999) have argued that a common characteristic of banking crises in developing countries is poor supervision and regulation. They argue that Hong Kong and Singapore escaped the crisis because of the stronger prudential systems that were enforced. The affected East Asian countries suffered not so much from weak systems but rather from non-compliance.

There is some truth in this, but a quite different view of the East Asian crisis is to see it in the context of liberalisation and business cycles, in which case one is left with less optimism about the prospects for economic stability. Radelet and Sachs have argued that this was a crisis of world capitalism rather than a crisis 'only' of East Asian capitalism

The further one moves to the left of the institutionalists the stronger this view is held. The argument is that the rising profitability in the boom phase of the cycle encourages the expansion of trade credit. If profitability tails off at the height of the boom, trade credit is replaced by bank credit. The increased demand for bank credit will tend to raise interest rates and, as interest rates rise to meet falling net profitability, a crisis ensues. Rising costs of credit and worsening prospects of profitability force bankruptcy among capitalists who have taken too much speculative risk. In this situation, the stock market is likely to collapse as it did in East Asia in 1997.

The most vivid expression of the crisis is the flight by capitalists towards money. As Marx graphically expressed it: 'On the eve of the crisis, the bourgeois, with the self-sufficiency that springs from intoxicating prosperity, declares money to be a vain imagination. But now [in a crisis] the cry is everywhere; money alone is a commodity' (Marx 1970: 138).

Marx also stated that: 'The sudden transformation of the credit system into a monetary system adds theoretical dismay to the actually existing panic' (Marx 1977: 146).

In the crisis, there is a credit crunch and with the credit crunch even many of the previously profitable go under. Crisis represents short and sharp turmoil but in the ensuing recession, competition is frequently exacerbated and the falling prices are likely to depress the rate of profit (see Fine *et al.* 1999). The significance of the institutional structure of the financial system – whether it is an Anglo-Saxon stock-market-based system or whether it is a German–Japanese bank-based system – to the accumulation cycle is crucial here, as has long been recognised (see Cable 1985, Levine 1997, Mayer 1988 and Stiglitz 1994).

This cyclical analysis of crisis is rooted in the conflict between the financial and industrial fractions of capital. Two major changes in the global economy have sharpened this conflict:

- The first, which dates from the 1970s, is the financial liberalisation that has taken place in both the developed and developing countries. Financial liberalisation started in the early 1970s in both the USA and the UK with the relaxation of quantitative controls (see Fine *et al.* 1999), but financial liberalisation also occurred in Japan and in many developing countries through the 1970s and 1980s (see Lapavitsas 1997). Interest rate controls were abolished widely, the process being legitimised by the McKinnon–Shaw literature on financial repression (see Fine *et al.* 1999).
- The second change that has taken place since the late 1970s is the application of information technology (IT) which has been much faster in the financial than in the industrial sector. Thus while the efficiency of the financial sector has increased dramatically, IT has had much less impact in the industrial sector. However, large corporations have increasingly moved in to the financial sector, often establishing their own financial departments even though most of their funds for investment have come from retained funds (see Corbett and Jenkinson 1997). Thus the remarkable growth of the financial system during the 1980s and 1990s has not come from an increase in lending to industry but instead has been associated with trading in foreign currencies, stock market securities and real estate. One crude indicator of this is the rising ratio of the dealings on the foreign exchange markets to the value of world trade (see Table 4.2). The increasing speed and volatility of financial markets is a major aspect of globalisation in the late twentieth century (see UNDP 1999).

This liberalisation in international finance, in relative autonomy from industrial accumulation, regularly creates bubbles of partly fictitious prosperity. When these burst, the entire economy is thrown into turmoil. It might be argued that the East Asian crisis passed reasonably quickly (see Table 4.1), that none of these changes is needed and that nothing needs to be done. However, nothing could be further from the truth. The East Asian crisis is unlikely to be the last.

The world economy is in a fragile state. There is considerable imbalance with (in 2001) the US running a huge deficit on the current account of its balance of payments (more than 4 per cent of GDP), the UK economy running a substantial deficit (1.5 per cent of GDP), Euroland in balance and Japan running a surplus (just under 2 per cent of GDP). The US deficit (which has been above 1 per cent of GDP in every year between 1992 and 2001) continues to be financed by capital inflows which have contributed to the seemingly inexorable rise in the stock market. But the US stock market has not been the only one to have shown a sharp increase between 1995 and 1999. The stock markets in France, Germany and the UK also rose sharply over the same period, while the stock market index in Japan has grown slowly (see Table 4.3). But here I focus on the US stock market since the collapse of that market would be the most serious.

Is such a collapse likely after 2001? The answer to this is 'probably'. At the very least, a major correction is likely. Even in late September 2001, after the Standard & Poor 500 index had fallen following the attack on the World Trade Centre in New York, the price–earnings ratio was 32, which was almost double the average of 16.7 of the 1954 to 1994 period (IMF 2000: 83).

The effect of a major fall in the US stock market is difficult to estimate precisely but the recessionary effect on personal expenditure of a cut in asset values is likely to be considerable. A large fall in the US stock market is likely to have serious repercussions on the US economy since something like 28 per cent of US household wealth is held in the form of equities (compared to 20 per cent in the UK and only about 6 per cent in Germany and Japan).

Thus the world economy is in a fragile state. In particular, there are serious implications for national economies which stem from the present, largely privatised and deregulated, financial system. Alongside the privatised international financial system, there is considerable pressure on developed, and particularly on developing, countries to maintain open financial systems and to maintain low rates of inflation and high real interest rates.

The East Asian crisis in a broader context – the necessity for change

It is clear to a large number of institutional economists that changes are needed at both the international and national levels. At the international level, the financial system has swung well away from the original conception of Keynes, Hansen, White and others. Among their proposals for the Bretton Woods institutions (BWIs) were a World Central Bank which would impose a tax on surplus countries and provide unconditional liquidity to deficit countries to maintain full employment. The BWIs have evolved very differently, as discussed by Singer (1995), and there is now a need for changes in the international financial architecture. Four major changes are required, as follows:

- More liquidity must be provided for a lender of last resort. The IMF cannot provide such a role effectively because of its lack of resources. In September 1998, it was warning that any large-scale request for assistance from Brazil could leave it with insufficient resources to deal with the world's other financial flashpoints (*The Guardian*, 17 September 1998). Not only are more resources needed for a lender of last resort but also loans should be made for balance of payments support, with no other conditionality (see Feldstein 1998: 20). If the IMF is to continue to impose conditions they should swing away to safety nets and income distribution and to more (not less) inflationary policies. As Stiglitz has pointed out: 'it is harder to pull an economy out of recession, than to push it into one' (1999: 27).

- There needs to be a greater emphasis on surplus countries to adjust.
- There needs to be more emphasis on creditors adjusting and not just on borrowers, since every reckless borrower implies a reckless lender. Radelet and Sachs (1998) argue that international workout arrangements could be modelled on the Chapter 11 process in the USA so that when a sovereign borrower faces imminent default, a standstill on debt servicing would be triggered (and be officially approved by the IMF's Executive Board).
- A spanner needs to be thrown into the cogs of international finance. As Davidson, the neo-Keynesian economist, has put it: 'In the real world, efficient markets are not liquid and liquid markets are not efficient' (quoted in the *The Guardian*, 27 September 1998). At the international level, there is a need for a Tobin tax on foreign exchange transactions (see UNDP 1994).[2] The idea of a tax on 'speculative activity' is not new. Keynes in his *General Theory* claimed that the relative absence of speculation on the London Stock Exchange as compared with that in New York owed something to the heavy transfer tax in the UK. In the absence of controls at the international level, there needs to be a recognition that controls on short-term capital inflows and outflows are desirable at the national level. As argued in section 'Financial liberalisation and the East Asian crisis' above, the critical variable in explaining the incidence and the spread of the East Asian crisis was open, short-term capital accounts. There is little evidence that full capital-account liberalisation brings benefits in terms of contributions to investment or growth that outweigh the risks (Rodrik 1998 and Stiglitz 1999). Yet, in spite of the strong arguments against full-scale capital liberalisation, the IMF has continued to push for them both before and after the crisis (Radelet and Sachs 1998, Wade and Veneroso 1998).[3] A common objection to exchange controls is that they are unlikely to be watertight, but Corsetti *et al.* (1998b) admit that Chile's capital controls do appear to have affected the composition of loans in favour of long-term loans and foreign investment and as Stiglitz has pointed out: 'It is better to have a leaky umbrella on a rainy day than no umbrella at all' (Stiglitz 1998b).

Without these changes and especially the controls on financial capital, there is likely to be crisis after crisis where the burden of adjustment will fall on the poorest, especially if beggar-thyself policies are followed. In such crises, the pressure grows for beggar-thy-neighbour protectionist policies (such as the tariffs on steel imports into the USA proposed in 2002) which the World Trade Organisation (WTO) will find difficult, if not impossible, to forestall.

The prospects for radical change

The East Asian crisis was not the first crisis. It will not be the last.

There is a Chinese saying which is 'May you live in interesting times', but the characters for these are somewhat similar to those for 'May you burn in hell' (Thurow 1996: 232). The state of the economies of East and Southeast Asia in 1997 may be said to have been both interesting and hellish. The same can be said of the world economy.

Unfortunately, it is easier to state the changes that are needed to prevent further crises than to see them emerging. On the political front, wage labour and the peasantry have little muscle whether in individual states or in the world. The best hope for change is for the adoption of proposals which will manage capitalism on behalf of long-run industrial interests. But even here there are few grounds for optimism.

It is not just the liberalisation of capital markets which is favoured by powerful financial interests. Alongside this campaign, the same interests have supported the WTO's efforts to liberalise financial services and the OECD/WTO attempts to push ahead with a Multilateral Agreement on Investment. As Wade and Veneroso argue, such measures will preclude many of the policies of the developmental state (see Wade and Veneroso 1998). Bhagwati (1998) has argued that the case for capital liberalisation has been heavily backed by what he calls the Wall Street–Treasury complex (see Bhagwati 1998).

It is evident that the neo-liberals have lost many of, if not all, the intellectual battles. But they have not yet lost the war. Ideologically, they are on the defensive but, regrettably, they are far from defeated.

Table 4.1 The rise and fall of GDP in East Asia (percentage per annum)

	1960–85	1985–96	1997	1998	1999
The four worst-affected countries					
Indonesia	3.7	6.8	4.7	−13.6	0.8
Korea	5.9	8.6	5.5	−5.8	10.9
Malaysia	4.0	7.8	7.8	−7.5	5.8
Thailand	3.8	9.0	−0.4	−10.2	3.3
Others					
China (mainland)	9.9[a]	9.9	8.8	7.8	7.2
China (Hong Kong)	6.1	6.3	5.3	−5.1	3.0
Philippines	3.7[b]	3.7	9.7	−0.4	3.4
Singapore	6.0	8.4	7.6	0.3	6.9
Taiwan	6.4	6.5	6.8	4.7	5.3

Sources: Corsetti *et al.* 1998(a), table 4; IMF *International Financial Statistics;* World Bank 1983, p. 53

Notes:
a 1978–85;
b 1968–85.

Table 4.2 World exports and world forex dealings

(*$USbn*)	*1985*	*1989*	*1992*	*1995*	*1997*
Total world exports	1,849	2,966	3,723	5,014	5,546
Daily world exports	7	12	15	20	22
Daily forex dealings	250	500	800	1300	1500
Ratio of forex to world trade	**34**	**42**	**54**	**65**	**68**

Sources:
Total world exports from IMF 1996 and IMF 1998
Daily world exports are total world exports for the year divided by 250 days
Forex (foreign exchange) dealings – Krugman and Obstfeld 1997, p. 337

Table 4.3 Share price indices – 1984–99 (1985 = 100)

Year	*Germany*	*France*	*USA*	*Japan*	*UK*
1984	73	78	86	82	81
1985	100	100	100	100	100
1986	141	166	127	133	124
1987	123	181	154	196	164
1988	104	156	139	214	147
1989	133	221	167	258	177
1990	156	224	169	218	173
1991	141	209	191	185	190
1992	138	217	211	137	199
1993	147	241	231	153	228
1994	168	255	235	160	245
1995	164	222	270	139	255
1996	187	253	331	160	289
1997	264	329	447	147	358
1998	357	441	517	123	429
Average % pa increase					
1984–98	12.0	13.2	13.7	3.0	12.6
1995–8	29.7	25.6	24.3	−3.8	18.9

Sources:
for 1984–7, *Eurostatistics*, 11/12, 1988, p. 94
for 1987–90, *Eurostatistics*, 12, 1991, p. 93
for 1990–3, *Eurostatistics*, 11, 1994, p. 117
for 1993–6, *Eurostatistics*, 8/9, 1997, p. 156
for 1997 and 1998, *Eurostatistics*, 8/9, 1999, p. 157

Notes

1   The countries listed in Table 4.1 are in East and Southeast Asia but in this chapter, I refer to these countries collectively as East Asia.
2   Davidson argues that quantitative regulations on capital movements would be more effective than a Tobin-style tax (*The Guardian*, 14 September 1998).
3   In September 1998, Camdessus (the then Managing Director of the IMF) was reported to have expressed concern about the exchange controls imposed in Malaysia in the wake of the crisis and to have stated that state controls were no substitute for sound economic policy (*New York Herald Tribune*, 24 September 1998). However, it is worth noting that Michael Mussa, Director of the IMF's Research Department, stated in 1998: 'No country, no matter how soundly managed its economic policies, no matter how solid its banking system, can maintain an open attitude toward international capital flows in the face of that type of system disturbance' (quoted in Brownbridge and Kirkpatrick 1999: 243).

Bibliography

Akyuz, Y. and Gore, C. (1996) 'The investment-profits nexus in East Asian industrialisation', *World Development* 24,3: 461–70.
Amsden, A. (1989) *Asia's Next Giant; South Korea and Late Industrialisation*, New York: Oxford University Press.
Bagchi, A. (1987) 'Industrialization', in J. Eatwell *et al.* (eds) (1989) *The New Palgrave; A Dictionary of Economic Development*, London: Macmillan.
Baily, M.N. and Zitzewitz, E. (1998) 'Extending the East Asian miracle: microeconomic evidence from Korea', *Brookings Papers on Economic Activity*.
Bhagwati, J. (1998) 'The capital myth', *Foreign Affairs* (May–June): 7–12.
Bosworth, B.P. (1998a) 'Comments' on Baily and Zitzewitz (1998), *Brookings Papers on Economic Activity*: 309–12.
—— (1998b) 'Comments' on Radelet and Sachs (1998), *Brookings Papers on Economic Activity*: 80–4.
Brownbridge, M. and Kirkpatrick, C. (1999) 'Financial sector regulation: the lessons of the Asian crisis', *Development Policy Review*: 243–66.
Cable, V. (1985) 'Capital market information and industrial performance: the role of West German banks', *Economic Journal* 95 (March): 118–32.
Chang, H.J., Palma, G. and Whittaker, D.H. (1998) 'The Asian crisis: introduction', *Cambridge Journal of Economics* 22: 649–52.
Chang, H.J., Park, H.J. and Yoo, C.G. (1998) 'Interpreting the Korean crisis; financial liberalisation, industrial policy and corporate governance', *Cambridge Journal of Economics* 22: 735–46.
Corbett, J. and Jenkinson, T. (1997) 'How is investment financed? A study of Germany, Japan, the UK and the US', *The Manchester School Supplement* LXV: 69–93.
Corsetti, G., Pesenti, P. and Roubini, N. (1998a) *What Caused the Asian Currency and Financial Crisis? Part I: A Macroeconomic Overview*, (September) Cambridge, MA: NBER.
—— (1998b) *What Caused the Asian Currency and Financial Crisis? Part II: The Policy Debate*, (September) Cambridge, MA: NBER.
Eurostatistics (1988, 1991, 1994, 1997, 1999).
Feldstein, M. (1998) 'Refocusing the IMF', *Foreign Affairs* (March/April): 20–33.
Fine, B., Lapavitsas, C. and Milonakis, D. (1999) 'Addressing the world economy; two steps back', *Capital and Class* (Spring): 47–90.
Fischer, S. (1998) 'In defense of the IMF', *Foreign Affairs* (July/August): 103–6.

Fishlow, A. *et al.* (1994) *Miracle or Design?: Lessons from the East Asian Experience*, Washington, DC: Overseas Development Council.

Furman, J. and Stiglitz, J. (1998) 'Economic crises: evidence and insights from East Asia', *Brookings Papers on Economic Activity*: 1–135.

Gerschenkron, A. (1962) *Economic Backwardness in Historical Perspective*, Cambridge, MA: Harvard University Press.

Gibson, H. and Tsakalotos, E. (1994) 'The scope and limits of financial liberalisation in developing countries: a critical survey', *The Journal of Development Studies* 30, 3: 578–628.

Guardian, The (1998) 14, 17, 27 September.

IMF (1996) *International Financial Statistics*, Washington, DC: IMF.

—— (1998) *International Financial Statistics*, Washington, DC: IMF.

—— (2000) *World Economic Outlook* (May), Washington, DC: IMF.

Jomo K.S. (1998) 'Malaysian debacle; whose fault?', *Cambridge Journal of Economics* 22: 707–22.

Keynes, J.M. (1976) *The General Theory of Employment, Interest and Money*, London: Macmillan.

Killick, T. (ed.) (1984) *The Quest for Economic Stabilisation; the IMF and the Third World*, London: ODI and Gower.

Krugman, P. (1998) 'What happened to Asia?', mimeo, Dept of Economics, MIT.

Krugman, P. and Obstfeld, M. (1997) *International Economics*, New York: Harper Collins.

Lapavitsas, C. (1997) 'Transition and crisis in the Japanese financial system: an analytical overview', *Capital and Class* 62: 21–47.

Levine, R. (1997) 'Financial development and economic growth', *Journal of Economic Literature*: 688–726.

Marx, K. (1970) *Capital, Volume 1*, London: Lawrence and Wishart.

—— (1977) *A Contribution to the Critique of Political Economy*, Moscow: Progress Publishers.

Mayer, C. (1988); 'New issues in corporate finance', *European Economic Review* 1: 167–89.

Mosley, P., Harrigan, J. and Toye, J. (1995) *Aid and Power*, 2nd edn, London: Routledge.

Nelson, R. and Pack, H. (1999) 'The Asian miracle and modern growth theory', *The Economic Journal* 109 (July): 416–36.

Pincus, J. and Ramli, R. (1998) 'Indonesia: from showcase to basket case', *Cambridge Journal of Economics* 22: 723–34.

Radelet, S. and Sachs, J. (1998) 'The East Asian financial crisis: diagnosis, remedies, prospects', *Brookings Papers on Economic Activity*: 1–87.

Rodrik, D. (1995) 'Getting interventions right: how South Korea and Taiwan grew rich', *Economic Policy* 20 (April): 53–97.

—— (1998) 'Who needs capital account convertibility?', *Essays in International Finance* (May): 55–65.

Singer, H. (1995) 'Rethinking Bretton Woods: from an historical perspective', in Griesgraber and Gunter (eds) *Promoting Development*, London: Pluto.

Singh, A. (1998) 'Asian capitalism and the financial crisis', *Centre for Economic Policy Analysis Working Paper Series* III, 10 (August), New York.

Stein, H. (ed.) (1995) *Asian Industrialization and Africa*, New York: Macmillan/St Martin's Press.

Stiglitz, J. (1994) 'The role of the state in financial markets', *Proceedings of the World Bank Annual Conference on Development Economics*, Washington DC: World Bank.

—— (1998a) 'More instruments and broader goals: moving towards the post-Washington Consensus' *The 1998 WIDER Lecture* (Jan), Helsinki. World Bank website: www.worldbank.org/html/extdr/extme/js-010798/wider.htm.

—— (1998b) 'Road to recovery', *Asiaweek*, 17 July. http://www.asiaweek.com/asiaweek/98/0717/cs_13_stiglitz.html.

—— (1998c) 'Responding to economic crises: policy alternatives for equitable recovery and development', *North-South Institute Seminar* (September), Ottawa, Canada. http://www.worldbank.org/html/extdr/extme/jssp092998.htm.

—— (1999) 'Beggar-thyself and beggar-thy-neighbour policies: the dangers of intellectual incoherence in addressing the global financial crisis', *Southern Economic Journal* 66, 1: 1–8.

Stiglitz, J. and Weiss, A. (1981) 'Credit rationing in markets with imperfect information', *American Economic Review*: 393–410.

Thurow, L. (1996) *The Future of Capitalism*, London: Nicholas Brealey.

UNDP (1994) *Human Development Report*, New York: Oxford University Press.

—— (1999) *Human Development Report*, New York: Oxford University Press.

Wade, R. (1990) *Governing the Market: Economic Theory and the Role of Government in East Asian Industrialization*, Princeton: Princeton UP.

Wade, R. and Veneroso, F. (1998) 'The Asian crisis: the high-debt model versus the Wall Street–Treasury–IMF complex', *New Left Review* (March–April): 3–23.

White, G. (ed.) (1988) *Developmental States in East Asia*, New York: Macmillan.

World Bank (1983) *World Development Report*, New York: Oxford University Press.

—— (1993) *The East Asian Miracle, Economic Growth and Public Policy*, Oxford: Oxford University Press.

World Development (1994) Special issue on The East Asian Miracle (see especially articles by Kwon, Lall, Perkins and Yanagihara).

5 The IMF in the Thai economic crisis

Villain or saviour?

Medhi Krongkaew

Introduction

The economic crisis in Thailand, which started in July 1997, is well known for the fact that it was unexpected, as well as for its ferocity. When Thailand turned to Japan and the IMF for help after practically all of its foreign reserves were gone, as a result of a failed defence against speculative attacks on the baht, many people likened this event to a third collapse of the Thai nation.[1] The IMF was looked upon by many in the general public as villainous conqueror who came in with a set of rules and orders otherwise known as 'conditionalities' that the Thais had to follow. The life of many Thais had to change, and so did their behaviour and ways of living and working. The role and involvement of the IMF in the Thai economic crisis was so pervasive in the eyes of many Thais that they have called the period between the end of 1997 and the beginning of 2000 the 'Era of the IMF'.

Negative reactions to the IMF are not new; they have been experienced before in various other countries which have come under the so-called 'IMF-supported programmes' (see, for instance, Lane *et al.* 1999). And it is perhaps an overstatement to say that the public reaction towards the IMF in Thailand as a result of its participation in the crisis solution has been totally negative. Some Thais may have had that kind of reaction, believing that help from the IMF was totally unnecessary. Some have accused the IMF of giving wrong advice or 'wrong medicine' for the Thai economic illness. Many, however, have grudgingly accepted help from the IMF as necessary for the survival of Thailand in its present economic makeup. Perhaps reactions towards the IMF in Thailand are similar to the reactions towards the IMF elsewhere in the world, in policy as well as in intellectual or academic circles.

It is the purpose of this chapter, therefore, to take a look at how the IMF is perceived in the international academic circle – the debate about the role of the IMF in the East Asian economic crisis. Then, the chapter will address the specific issue of how the IMF-supported programmes have helped or hindered the efforts of the Thai government in getting the Thai economy out of its economic crisis. The chapter ends with an observation, and evaluation, of the role and performance of the IMF in the Thai economic crisis.

Why the IMF, and what has gone wrong with its original role?

When a country is having payments difficulties it can use up its own foreign reserve to pay its foreign debts. If this reserve is insufficient it has a choice of borrowing from other friendly governments, private institutions, or international organisations. Or it can go to the IMF, which was set up specifically in 1944 to do exactly this: to help countries with payments problems. By its nature the IMF is a club whose members consist of almost all members of the United Nations. These members pay fees to the club with its own currency plus a proportion in common currencies. These fees form a pool of funds that the IMF can use to help members with payments problems. Contributions to the pool of funds are determined by the economic status of each member: richer members pay more; poorer members pay less. In exchange, members are given voting rights proportional to their contributions. Thus the US, which is the largest contributor, also has the largest number of votes in deciding the policies of the IMF.[2]

Each member has the right to ask for IMF help whenever the need arises, but the kind and conditions of help provided may vary from one country to another. Briefly speaking, the IMF has the following functions:[3]

- To promote international monetary co-operation;
- To facilitate the expansion and balanced growth of international trade;
- To promote exchange stability and orderly exchange arrangements among members without competitive devaluation;
- To eliminate foreign exchange restrictions; and
- To help members adjust their balance of payments without resorting to restrictions in current and capital transactions.

These functions have remained practically unchanged over the past fifty years since the IMF was established, despite the fact that the fixed exchange rate regime which the IMF was set up to work under is no longer the norm of the day. But, to change with the times, the IMF has modified its functions in addition to the primary focus on sound money, prudent fiscal policies, and open markets as preconditions for macroeconomic stability and growth. These modifications include concerns for sound domestic financial systems, improvements in the balance and quality of public expenditure, transparency and accountability in government and corporate affairs, the existence of safety-net provisions for vulnerable members of society who may be affected by economic adjustment and reform, and the deregulation, privatisation or abolition of monopoly practices, in order to benefit society as a whole. Although the IMF can achieve these objectives through its financial assistance, it can also help its members through regular economic surveillance, consultation, monitoring and evaluation.

As a voluntary member of a club or an association, a country can get in and out as it wishes. But once it is a member, a country is obligated to follow the rules of the club. For example, as a member of the IMF, a country must keep other members informed about how it determines the value of its money in relation to the money of other countries, refrain from restricting the exchange of its money for foreign money, and pursue economic policies that will not obstruct standard practices other members have adopted, and so on. At times, some members will not follow the above obligations, in which case the IMF may exert its moral pressure to encourage them to conform to the rules and regulations that they have freely agreed to observe. The IMF will have an even greater leverage (on threat of cutting off assistance or even expulsion from membership) if it has provided financial assistance to those members.

But while member countries have obligations to follow the rules and regulations of the IMF at the risk of losing favour with the IMF, what if the IMF has not done its job properly? Should the IMF be held accountable for its actions, and members be compensated for damages attributable to those actions? Strictly speaking, the accountability issue does not come up if the IMF sticks with the traditional role of lender to countries with payments problems. Since the borrowing countries are obligated to pay back the loans plus necessary interest (the loans are not free), these countries should be fully responsible for their own actions on issues beyond payments problems. But, as mentioned earlier, the modern functions of the IMF have been modified to include the imposition of major structural and institutional reforms in addition to facilitating adjustments in the balance of payments. These additional functions, according to such critics as Martin Feldstein (1998a and 1998b) of Harvard University, could have adverse consequences in the short term and the more distant future. To Feldstein, the IMF should stick to its traditional task of helping countries cope with temporary shortages of foreign exchange and with more sustained trade deficits.

Even if these new-found functions are accepted, there is no guarantee that the staff of the IMF can do their jobs correctly. Perhaps one of the most damaging criticisms of the IMF in its policy prescriptions during the first few months of crisis in Thailand, Korea and Indonesia came from Jeffrey Sachs (1997 and 1998), also of Harvard University (and also together with Steven Radelet in Radelet and Sachs 1999), who argued that the IMF misunderstood the true nature of the problems of these High-Performing AsianEconomies (HPAEs), and thus prescribed the wrong economic medicine. According to Sachs, Thailand, Korea and Indonesia shared the common characteristics of being export-oriented economies with high savings rates, budgets in balance or surplus, and low inflation. The Asian crisis was not a crisis of economic fundamentals but a crisis brought about by the sudden loss of confidence by foreign creditors, whose withdrawal of short-term funds from these economies helped create panic in the financial markets and a severe credit crunch. Similar IMF prescriptions for these countries to cut government expenditures, raise taxes, get rid of bad and unviable financial institutions, and privatise state-owned enterprises brought severe economic contraction to these economies, so much so that the IMF was forced to revert its positions regarding public spending from surplus budget to deficit spending in order to stimulate domestic economies. Similar criticisms were also voiced by such well-known development economists as Joseph Stiglitz, then of the World Bank, and Robert Wade. At the risk of alienating the close relationship between the World Bank and the IMF, Stiglitz was quoted as saying that he disagreed with the IMF's austerity push.[4] Wade (and his co-author, Frank Veneroso, in Wade and Veneroso 1998) added that, unlike in the West, companies in these East Asian countries have high debt-to-equity ratios. Forcing these companies into bankruptcies as part of debt restructuring was likely to generate large social costs through loss of production and unemployment.

Other criticisms include the IMF's failure to give early warnings to members about the impending crisis, the inadequacy of the IMF's financial package to some members, the inability of the IMF to eschew the problems of moral hazard associated with the promise of rescue by the IMF in time of financial troubles, and the inability of the IMF to prevent the contagion effect once a member was afflicted with this economic disease. And despite the transparency that the IMF has asked its members to adopt in their economic decision-making and management, the IMF itself is still a secretive institution whose operations and decision-making procedures are foreign or unknown to outsiders.[5]

Trying to understand the IMF: what it can do and what more can be done

The views above may sound critical of the IMF but at least they are made on the basis that the IMF is still important and needed. Some severer critics (for instance Milton Friedman, see Anna Schwartz 1999, see also Schultz *et al.* 1998) have called for the scrapping of the IMF altogether. It is true that the severity of the Asian crisis has put the IMF on the spot much more starkly than at any other time in history. And the IMF was at pains to explain its position and reasons for its policies wherever and whenever it could (see, for instance, IMF 1999). Probably, no one in the IMF had greater responsibility to explain the positions and reasons of the IMF's role in the Asian crisis than Stanley Fischer (1998 and 1999), the First Deputy Managing Director of the IMF until 2001. Against the above (and other) criticisms, the defence from the IMF could be summarised as follows:[6]

1   The economic surveillance of the IMF on East Asian economies was working fine. Appropriate warnings about certain aspects of macroeconomic problems such as growing current account deficits and large short-term debts were given to East Asian countries in question, especially Thailand, but those warnings were not heeded or acted upon. The IMF could not and would not act alone in sounding these alarms for fear that it might inadvertently cause panic itself.

2   The contagion effect occurred, at least in the short run, because it was rational for investors to pull out their investments in anticipation of a greater crisis. In such a case, competitive devaluation may occur because competing countries have to protect their own export competitiveness.

3   The high-interest regime that the IMF suggested for Thailand, Korea and Indonesia to help stabilise domestic currencies was necessary to stop (or slow down) further devaluation that might bring about competitive devaluation throughout the region, causing deeper crisis. Moreover, if the interest rate action had been delayed, confidence might have continued to erode and might in fact have worsened the crisis.

4   The fiscal tightening which was also suggested in the beginning for all countries in question was based on the thinking that these countries needed to strengthen their fiscal positions, both to make room in their budgets for the future costs of financial restructuring and to reduce the current account deficit. When it was clear that the economic situation in the country had weakened more than expected, the fiscal policy was relaxed to allow greater fiscal deficit.

5   It was obvious that major problems in these East Asian countries were not macroeconomic mismanagement but deficiencies and mismanagement in the financial sector in the forms of weak financial institutions, inadequate bank regulation and supervision, uncontrolled foreign borrowing and unwise investment by the private sector. So the restructuring and reform of this sector should have been the first priority in this crisis management. To delay doing this could only have perpetuated the country's economic problems, as experiences in Japan showed. To Fischer, the best course of action was to recapitalise or close insolvent banks, protect small depositors, require share-holders to take their losses, and take steps to improve banking regulation and supervision.

6   The additional functions of the IMF to look into macroeconomic adjustments and institutional reforms of the countries being assisted were necessary if spending the scarce Fund was to achieve the intended objectives. It would not have been wise to let the troubled country cope with its problems alone when the IMF had a large number of qualified professional staff to help. This should not be construed as intrusion on a sovereign government.

7   The question of moral hazard associated with the IMF lending deserved serious consideration, especially with regard to the behaviour of private-sector lenders. However, moral hazard on the side of· the borrower was likely to be less significant. To Fischer, it was far-fetched to think that policy-makers embarking on a risky course of actions did so because the IMF safety net would save them if things went badly. While it is better for a country to come to the IMF sooner rather than later when it faces payment problems, it should not have too easy access to the Fund without a serious intention (or promise) to keep its economic house in order.

The Asian economic crisis became much more serious than anyone ever anticipated. No one can claim that he or she foresaw a crisis of this magnitude. The IMF has been criticised for its failure to limit the spread of the crisis, for exacerbating the recession in the East Asian economies, and for enforcing Western practices in different Oriental cultures, especially in banking practices and corporate governance. But, as Stanley Fischer tried to explain above, the IMF had its reasons for doing what it did. A fair-minded person must recognise the difficulties the IMF has to face in dealing with real situations in the real world where many interrelated factors must be considered at once. This is much more difficult than looking at the problems from the vantage point of an academic who does not have to weigh up the real situations, or is not accountable for what he or she has recommended. For those critics who would do without the IMF altogether, imagine the much more chaotic situation these countries would have to experience in their struggles in the globalised world. Perhaps the position of such academics as Max Corden (1998) of Johns Hopkins University is more acceptable. Corden argued that there was no easy 'obvious' way out (of the crisis), and certainly not one that could do without the IMF. Furthermore, the IMF was not straightforwardly 'right' or 'wrong'. It was probably now mostly right, after it went off the rails at the beginning. One had to accept the fact that there were trade-offs involved in policy decisions that made it difficult to state categorically who was right and who was wrong.[7]

From this viewpoint, perhaps it is better not to dwell on whether the IMF was right or wrong in its handling of the East Asian economic crisis, but to concentrate on how best to prevent future crises from happening, or how best to respond to crises in the future. The IMF itself is fully aware of its limitations as the world central bank in changing financial situations, and is willing to recommend changes in the international monetary system. This move is now popularly referred to as the architecture of the new international monetary system and it has the following characteristics (see IMF 1998):

1   There will be development, dissemination, and adoption of internationally accepted standards or codes of good practice so that market participants can compare information on country practices against agreed benchmarks of good practices and to make better investment decisions;

2   There will be transparency on the part of members of the IMF in their policy determination, and on the part of the IMF in the openness and clarity of its policies and advice;

3   Financial systems of members need to be strengthened through enhanced technical assistance, better surveillance on the linkages between macroeconomic policies and sound banking systems, more training on bank supervision and other banking problems, and improvement in the IMF's capacity for financial sector analysis;

4   International financial markets will need to be integrated in a more orderly fashion; and

5   The private sector will be induced to get more involved in the prevention and resolution of financial crises, especially in providing liquidity support to countries in times of financial stress, in improving the co-ordination of debtor–creditor relations in voluntary debt-restructuring, and in creating well-functioned corporate bankruptcy systems.

Thailand and the IMF

The year 1997 was not the first time that the Thai government sought the assistance from the IMF in coping with its economic problems. In 1979, Thailand suffered the Second Oil Shock which caused prices to rise over two-digit levels, and caused the twin problems of internal deficits as well as external deficits. The poor performance of exports and high import-demand put enormous burden on the government's macroeconomic management. Pressure on the baht forced the government to make small devaluations twice in the early 1980s, without much effect. The third devaluation in November 1984, of about 15 per cent, brought some good results a year later in the form of a drastic increase in exports. What had led to this third devaluation was that Thailand had experienced difficulties in its external balance in the early 1980s resulting in large drawdown of its foreign reserves. The amount requested was small (285 million US dollars), and the negotiations with the IMF were carried out in an atmosphere of secrecy as the government was afraid that the public might be alarmed by the deteriorating economic situation. The usual IMF conditionalities of course applied, and the government was forced to cut down its spending, increase several taxes, improve tax collections, cut subsidies, and so on.

The experience of working with the IMF during the crisis of 1983–4 must be considered a happy one. The IMF worked closely with the Thai technocrats at the Bank of Thailand and the Ministry of Finance who handled the crisis management. Out of mutual respect for each other, agreements on what needed to be done were reached in an atmosphere of good friendship and cordiality. The outcome of the IMF-supported programme then was also successful, as the Thai economy was able to cope with its economic problems without getting into recession. Of course, the extenuating circumstances surrounding the Thai economy at that time did help Thailand to recover from these economic problems quickly and it went on to grow much faster in the following few years. The three influential factors that are often used to explain the boom in the Thai economy in the late 1980s are (1) the appreciation of the yen as a result of the Plaza Accord, which forced Japan to relocate many of its manufacturing operations outside Japan, and the fact that Thailand was the first country in Southeast Asia that benefited from the new wave of Japanese foreign investment; (2) the increase in exports, thanks in part to the devaluation of 1984; and (3) the increase in the number of foreign tourists visiting Thailand in 1987 (the celebration of the King's sixtieth birthday).

Perhaps this new success was too much, and the private sector in Thailand got carried away. The booming economy created a feeling of euphoria, that Thailand had attained the status of an NIC, and further opening up (or loosening up) of the economy was then called for. The Thai authorities began to liberalise the Thai economy in a big way: foreign exchange controls were quickly lifted, interest ceilings were abolished, more financial facilities both onshore and offshore were established, and so on. But what lay behind these seemingly glowing situations were several weak spots. First, Thailand was spending beyond its means, with its current account in deficit by more than 8 per cent of its GDP. The financial liberalisation which started in 1990 saw an influx of foreign capital due mainly to the high interest rate differentials between Thailand and external sources. These capital inflows, induced mainly by the private sector (commercial banks, finance companies and private firms), were used mainly in the securities and property markets, bidding up stock and real estate prices typical of a bubble economy. Increasingly, these capital inflows changed their nature from long term to short term with maturity within less than one year. The private sector replaced the government as majority foreign debt borrower.[8]

The government's policy of maintaining a fixed exchange rate for the sake of stability in trade and investment, and continued economic growth, created a false sense of security for these foreign capital borrowers, who threw exchange-risk caution into the wind. Moreover, one of the costs of having an influx of foreign currencies into the country was pressure on the local currency to appreciate, which would, in turn, hurt the exports of the country. So the monetary authority had to juggle with the exchange rate policy as well, manipulating the currency weights in the basket of currencies so that the Thai baht remained basically under-valued. In 1995 when the US dollar was depreciating, the Thai baht was able to benefit from this under-valuation because US dollars formed the largest weight. However, in 1997, when the US dollar greatly appreciated against almost all major currencies, the Thai baht was over-valued despite the authority's attempts to adjust the currency basket. This not only hurt Thai exports but also opened up an opportunity for exchange rate speculators to attack the baht because the domestic economy was experiencing strains from problems in several financial institutions and property sectors.

The last straw that broke the back of the Thai economy was, probably, the dismal export performance of 1996. It came as a shock to most people to see a negative growth of exports in 1996 compared to the export growth rate of more than 23 per cent in 1995. Several Thai exports suddenly lost their economic com-petitiveness to lower-cost countries like China and India. With this main source of economic growth of the Thai economy in trouble, it became impossible to defend the baht. Yet the Bank of Thailand maintained its unchanged position regarding fixing the baht to the US dollar, and gambled all the country's foreign exchange reserves trying to defend the attack on the baht. When all the reserves were gone, with no victory in sight, the government had no other choice but to let go of the exchange rate. The baht collapsed, capital started to flow out, and the crisis had begun.

When the Thai government sought help from the IMF in August 1997, both sides (the Thai government and the IMF) expected that when the rescue package was concluded and the IMF money started to come in, the economic downturn would stop and the economy would start to recover quickly. Both were wrong. The recession deepened as the exchange rate fell sharply. The loss of foreign reserves and public funds through financial sector rescue was simply too much for the economy to remain unaffected. After only two months, both had realised that all the economic forecasts made in August 1997 were inaccurate, and a series of adjustments and changes were quickly installed. The projected rate of growth of GDP for 1997 was revised downward from 2.6 per cent, to 0.6 per cent, to –0.4 per cent. Similarly, the forecasted GDP for 1998 was reduced from 2 per cent to between 0 and 1 per cent, to –3 to –3.5 per cent, and eventually to –7 per cent in the succeeding Letters of Intent to the IMF.

It was undeniable that the IMF came to Thailand's aid with a traditional box of tools. Currency devaluation, cuts in government spending, increasing taxes, financial restructuring, and privatisation of state enterprises are some of the standard measures that the IMF had used all over the world, and all of these were used in Thailand. A cut in government spending was certainly a mistake, as the government was not one of the problems. It had in fact enjoyed some fiscal surplus before the crisis, and its spending behaviour was under control. Earlier on in the crisis, it was argued that by cutting government expenditure, the government would not have to compete for scarce funds in the private market, which would enable the private sector to utilise those funds that were available. But the economic contraction was too severe, and the government was deprived of an early opportunity to slow down such contraction through its deficit spending. The raising of the Value Added Tax (VAT) from 7 to 10 per cent was also a mistake. While the government had received an increase in revenue from this tax, this measure had the effect of further suppressing the domestic economy and fuelling inflationary pressure due to domestic price increases. However, both the government and the IMF worked closely to monitor macroeconomic movements during the crisis, and were willing to make necessary adjustments such as the reversal to increased government spending through deficit financing, and introduced measures that would provide social assistance to the rural sector and the unemployed.

Meanwhile, the efforts of the government and the IMF were still concentrated in the financial restructuring of the banking and finance sector in the economy. By the third Letter of Intent to the IMF in February 1998, most planned corrections were in place, and subsequent Letters of Intent simply dwelled on how these planned corrections had progressed. It is now an appropriate time to discuss these planned corrections and how they changed the economic conditions in Thailand.

Financial restructuring

After closing down problem-laden finance companies and setting up the Financial Restructuring Authority (FRA) to auction off good assets to pay back their existing debts, the government went on to recapitalise the remaining commercial banks with a new set of rules concerning capital adequacy and the treatment of non-performing loans. When several small and medium-sized banks failed to raise the required capital, the government took over their operations by forcing the write-down of existing capital before injecting necessary funds into them, with a clear plan that when these newly taken over banks became healthy they would be sold back to private hands. The Financial Institution Development Fund (FIDF), which had already lost a lot of money in its past attempt to rescue finance companies and commercial banks, still needed a lot of money to help out weak commercial banks. Since liquidity had become very tight in the aftermath of the massive loss of foreign reserves and capital outflows, the FIDF needed all the money it could get its hands on. The remaining healthy commercial banks found it convenient to lend to the FIDF rather than lending to private borrowers, especially borrowers in the real sector, as it was safer and had higher returns. This created a short-term distortion in the financial market, in that the FIDF had access to money which was therefore not available to the rest of the economy. To correct this distortion and to help reduce the interest obligations of the FIDF, the government needed to generate domestic credits quickly to relieve the domestic credit crunch. It did this through several emergency decrees enabling the government to issue 500 billion baht-worth of bonds for the FIDF.

In a way, the government decided that it had no choice but to use public money to help prop up commercial banks so that they were able to start lending to the public again. The government realised that without a healthy commercial bank system, there was little hope for the country to recover quickly. Critics of this policy would argue that this was no different from the technique used by the FIDF before the crisis. But according to the government, it was. The new banking rescue operations called for stringent control of new lending, stricter treatment of non-performing loans and a forced corporate debt restructuring. As stated in its fifth Letter of Intent to the IMF, the Thai government, through its comprehensive financial measures announced on 14 August 1998, aimed to do four things. First, it wanted to consolidate commercial banks and finance companies through additional Bank of Thailand interventions and proposed mergers. Second, it continued to encourage private investment and entry (domestic and foreign) into the banking system. Third, it had decided to use public funds to recapitalise all remaining financial institutions but with appropriate safeguards and conditions and with links to progress in corporate debt restructuring. And fourth, it set out a framework for the creation of private asset management companies.

Corporate debt restructuring

The point made in the 14 August comprehensive financial plan on corporate debt restructuring needs further discussion. Despite the government's good intentions, many large commercial banks hesitated to accept financial assistance from the government, because of their own pride as well as a genuine fear of government intervention and control of the bank administration. Private recapitalisation was successful through participation from foreign banks, but still the expansion of new credit was slow and stagnant because there were huge non-performing loans (NPLs) in the banking system. The new loan-loss provisions required that commercial banks with large NPLs maintain large reserves until debts were settled or restructured. Several companies clearly were really unable to service their debts, but some companies deliberately withheld their debt payments and became what is known as 'strategic NPLs'.

Only a forceful application of the bankruptcy and foreclosure law could reduce these strategic NPLs. But for a genuine NPL, the government also provided some help. The Corporate Debt Restructuring Advisory Committee (CDRAC) was created with the aim of promoting market-based corporate debt restructuring. At first, progress on debt restructuring under the supervision of CDRAC was slow, but later the speed of work picked up. At the end of 1999, the level of system-wide NPLs was about 47 per cent of total credits, and about one-third of these NPLs were restructured. The change in bankruptcy law should also help the debt restructuring process: the debtor's position may be strengthened through a chance to put forward his or her business reorganisation plan, while for creditors, the judicial procedure regarding foreclosure and enforcement of security rights may be accelerated.

Exchange rate and monetary policy

One of the hallmarks of the earlier Thai government–IMF policy to cope with economic crisis was the maintenance of high interest rates to stabilise the exchange rate. This policy was subject to acerbic attacks from many quarters but the government persisted. According to the government's thinking, without stability in the exchange rate, no confidence from foreign investors could be forthcoming. And if recovery depended on external sources of funds, this exchange rate policy had to be pursued rigorously and resolutely. The baht stopped sliding and started to recover in February 1998 and remained relatively stable. Starting in late August 1999, however, the baht weakened following exchange rate instability in the region (especially the wide fluctuation of the yen and the US dollar). The government was able to reduce the domestic interest rate around June 1998 to help increase private-sector borrowing.

The Bank of Thailand's monetary policy in maintaining the appropriate level of money supply also paid off in terms of reduced pressure on the price level. It has been shown that inflation hurts the poor and the low-income relatively more than the rich and the high-income. So the fastidious inclination by the Bank of Thailand to keep inflation in check is something not difficult to understand. Since the inflation rate had slowed down, the Bank could then afford to focus more on restoring liquidity, helping to solve NPLs, and being more effective in setting the target for reserve money.

External sector policy

The sharp reduction in imports, with the continuing satisfactory performance in exports (at least in volume terms), helped explain a rapid change in the country's balance of current account from deficit to surplus. This current account surplus continued throughout the first four years of the crisis. The level of foreign reserves at the level of 26–8 billion US dollars at the end of 1999 was considered sufficient for the current level of economic activities. As the recovery gathered pace, the Bank of Thailand reserves could, and did, rise further.

Fiscal policy

One of the major changes in the ways the Thai government coped with the economic crisis is the switch in fiscal policy from fiscal surplus to balanced budget to fiscal deficit. As mentioned earlier, it became obvious three months into the crisis that the austerity programme on the public sector side was not a suitable remedy for the Thai economy. The severe contraction in the domestic economy required the government to stimulate aggregate domestic demand if the economy was to recover quickly. Public sector fiscal deficit had reached 3 per cent of GDP by the end of 1998. There were lingering doubts, of course, that increased public debts would affect the fiscal discipline of the government. However, past experience had shown that the fiscal discipline of the Thai public sector should remain intact despite large public debts.

In order to help facilitate corporate debt restructuring, the government eliminated or temporarily suspended taxes that could hinder debt-restructuring efforts and mergers and acquisitions. To improve fiscal strength and efficiency in the tax system in the future, the government planned several tax reforms including the phasing out of tax exemptions, the introduction of capitalisation rules limiting interest deductibility, and the streamlining of VAT collection and refund procedures. Also included was the appointment of a customs adviser to implement a programme for institutional and procedural improvements in customs administration.

On 30 March 1999, the Thai government announced another major fiscal policy package. The package contained three categories of fiscal measures to stimulate domestic demand and help the economy to recover quickly. The first category was the use of loans from Japan under the Miyazawa Initiative (or Miyazawa Plan) and the World Bank to the tune of some 53 billion baht. This loan money was allocated to every ministry, to be expended quickly with the aim of creating employment, mainly in the rural areas, and so augmenting the income of the people. The second category was the reduction of VAT from 10 per cent to 7 per cent, and the exemption of the first 50,000 baht of personal income from income taxation, with the aim of immediately lowering the prices of most goods and services, and so increasing the purchasing power of the people. And the third was the reduction in the price of oil and gas for industrial as well as household consumption. All things considered, this economic stimulus package added to the recovery attempt of the government to bring the economy back from −10.8 per cent growth rate in 1998 to somewhere between 4.0 to 4.5 per cent at the end of 1999.

Privatisation policy

Finally, the government stepped up the privatisation of several public enterprises. The government recognised that in addition to receiving revenue from the privatisation process, privatisation would also have long-term benefits in the form of more efficient resource allocation and so more efficient economic production. In addition, not forgetting the less well-off, who had suffered particularly from the economic downturn, the government decided to borrow money from the World Bank to provide safety nets for retrenched workers and people in the countryside.

Conclusions: does the IMF help or hurt?

In this chapter I have attempted to explain the role of the IMF in helping member countries with payments and economic problems in general, and in helping Thailand solve its current financial and economic problems in particular. I have referred to contrasting views of the role of the IMF in the crisis situation. Some would find the present role of the IMF irrelevant, even dangerous; but many would still find the role of the IMF useful and important. There is a need to redefine the role of the IMF in the context of new international financial architecture which will make the IMF a more effective international financial institution, including an international banker of last resort.

In its particular involvement with the economic crisis in Thailand, one can see that the IMF worked very closely with the Thai government. Although it is unlikely that the IMF dictated that the Thai authorities follow strictly its policy prescriptions or recommendations, the influence of the IMF is, without a doubt, real. In early

1999, the IMF openly admitted that its austerity programme for Thailand at the beginning of the crisis was wrong, as the cut in public spending and the increase in tax had the effect of squeezing the economy further into recession. However, a few months into the policy implementation, both the IMF and the Thai government saw the same mistake, and they decided to change their policy responses from public sector contraction to public-sector-led economic expansion. This entailed increased government spending through borrowing from domestic sources as well as from overseas. The increase in aggregate demand as a result of this public spending at the end of 1999 showed some signs of leading the economy out of recession, as there were marked increases in manufacturing production and consumption. Investment in the private sector might have been slow, due to the relative lack of credit expansion in the private commercial banks, but the government began to correct this situation by providing several public investment funds for large and small enterprises in the real sector.

While the IMF may have admitted its mistake in fiscal policy, it did not yield to the criticisms made of its monetary and exchange rate policies. For example, it maintained that the high interest rate regime early in the crisis in Thailand helped Thailand regain stability in its exchange rate,[9] and that the high interest rate did not depress the economy further. Jack Boorman, a director of the IMF, for example, attempted to answer two specific criticisms regarding the impact of this high interest rate. One criticism said that the monetary condition had become tight in the context of this interest policy, whereas the other criticism was that the tightening of the monetary conditions contributed to the decline in economic activity. In response to the first criticism, Boorman believed that monetary conditions did not become tightened dramatically in Thailand, as real money and credit growth in Thailand only declined slightly. As for the second criticism, Boorman argued that one could not attribute much of the decline in activities or much of the recession to tight monetary conditions. There were many factors involved, including dynamically unstable factors like unhedged foreign exposure – borrowing short-term loans from foreign sources without insuring against currency devaluation – that weakened the corporate position dramatically (see Boorman 1999).

Other policy recommendations on which the IMF has a firm stand and on which it would not yield to criticism include its suggestion for the governments to carry out the financial restructuring and reform quickly, to observe the best practices in corporate debt restructuring, greater participation of foreign financial institution in such restructuring, and the pursuance of flexible exchange rates and a relatively free capital market. While this 'quick approach' tends to depress prices of both the good and the bad assets of failed finance companies and commercial banks (a 'fire-sales' phenomenon), the IMF argued that the costs of delaying the disposal of these assets might be higher. Strict adherence to the BIS standard of international best practices of defining bad loans and the loan-loss provisioning might also elicit criticism of that governments have to enforce rules that are too tough for struggling institutions.[10] On this point, the government argued that if the overall financial system was serious in its wish to reform, then the strict rules might cause difficulties in the short run, but in the long run the health of these financial institutions would be much stronger. If rules are relaxed, especially when reform is not seriously carried out, the long-term problems of the financial sector are unlikely to be solved. As for the participation of foreign interest and capital, this was in keeping with the acceptance of the principle of globalisation. If Thailand still wants to be an active member of the globalised world, and is willing to reap the benefits of rapid and substantial growth, and accept the ancillary risks, then it must be prepared to live and work in a virtually borderless world. Economic efficiency has known no nationalities.

Almost five years have passed since the Thai economy plunged into its severest crisis. Despite the still-unresolved NPL problems, there have been sufficient signs which show that the worst of the crisis is over, and Thailand has pulled itself out of the recession. While the IMF must take some of the blame for hurting the Thai economy in a certain way, it would be unfair not to give the IMF some of the credit for helping pull the Thai economy out of the crisis. The IMF is not the omnipotent saviour, but neither is it an ignoble villain. As mentioned earlier, it is trying to do the best job it can under circumstances where there is no clear-cut alternative, or the convenient leisure for trial and error. This recognition should obviate the need to debate whether Thailand could do better without the IMF. As long as we are broad-minded and willing to learn from mistakes, the IMF approach is no different from any other approaches tried in an emergency.

Notes

1   The first two collapses were at the hands of the Burmese in 1569 and 1767.
2   For a summary of the historical development of the function of the IMF, see Driscoll (1998).
3   Summarised from Article 1 of the Charter of the IMF.
4   The *Wall Street Journal* on 8 January 1998 reported Stiglitz to have said that: 'You don't want to push these countries into severe recession. One ought to focus ... on things that caused the crisis, not on things that make it more difficult to deal with.'
5   Paul Krugman was among the first ones to make this point. See, for example, Krugman (1998).
6   These views have been collected and summarised from various papers and speeches by Stanley Fischer and other staff of the IMF. Due to the sensitivities and complexities of the issues, it is possible that true views of the IMF may not be totally, truly represented.
7   Similar views may also be found in Dornbusch (1998) and Frankel (1998).
8   There is a vast field of literature on the causes and development of the economic crisis in Thailand. The information contained in this paper came from my own study on the subject. See Medhi, K. (2001).
9   Whereas some critics would still maintain that the exchange rate became stabilised because the massive capital outflows had stopped or reduced substantially to allow for currency appreciation and compensation for exchange rate overshoot. See, for example, Steven Radelet and Jeffrey Sachs (1999).
10 It was likened to the enforcement of correct swimming techniques to a drowning swimmer.

Bibliography

Boorman, J. (1999) 'Asian crisis: world must cooperate to find solutions', *The Straits Times* 4 March.

Corden, W.M. (1998) 'The Asian crisis: is there a way out? Are the IMF prescriptions right?', paper prepared for the lecture delivered in Singapore in September 1998.

Dornbusch, R. (1998) 'After Asia: new directions for the international financial system', http://web.mit.edu/rudi/www/papers.html.

Driscoll, D.D. (1998) 'What is the International Monetary Fund', External Relations Department, IMF, Washington, DC (September). See IMF homepage: http://www.imf.org/external/pubs/ft/exrp/what.htm.

Feldstein, M. (1998a) 'Refocusing the IMF', *Foreign Affairs* 77, 2 (March/April): pp. 20–33.

—— (1998b) 'What the IMF should do', *The Wall Street Journal* 6 October.

Fischer, S. (1998a) 'Reforming world finance: lessons from a crisis', *The Economist* 3 October.

—— (1998b) 'The IMF and the Asian crisis', paper prepared for the Annual Forum Funds Lecture (October).

Frankel, J.A. (1998) 'The Asian model, the miracle, the crisis and the Fund', paper delivered at the US International Trade Commission, 16 April 1998.

IMF (1998) 'Strengthening the architecture of the International Monetary System', report of the Managing Director to the Interim Committee on Strengthening the Architecture of the International Monetary System (October).

—— (1999) 'The IMF's response to the Asian crisis', External Relations Department, IMF (January). See IMF homepage: http://www.imf.org/external/np/exr/facts/asia.htm.

Krugman, P. (1998), 'Will Asia bounce back?', paper prepared for Credit Suisse, First Boston, Hong Kong (March).

Lane, T. Ghosh, A., Hamann, J., Phillips, S., Schulze-Ghattas, M. and Tsikata, T. (1999) 'IMF-supported programs in Indonesia, Korea, and Thailand: a preliminary assessment', *IMF Occasional Paper* 178.

Medhi, K. (2001) 'A tale of an economic crisis', in Y.P Chu and H. Hill (eds) *The Social Impacts of East Asian Financial Crisis*, Cheltenham, UK: Edward Elgar.

Radelet, S. and Sachs, J. (1999) 'What have we learned, so far, from the Asian financial crisis?', paper from the Consulting Assistance on Economic Reform (CAER) II Project (4 January).

Sachs, J. (1997) 'The IMF is a power unto itself', *The Financial Times* 11 December.

—— (1998) 'The IMF and the Asian flu', *The American Prospect* 37 (March–April): 16–21.

Schultz, G.P., Simon, W.E. and Wriston, W.B. (1998) 'Who needs the IMF?', *Wall Street Journal* 3 February.

Schwartz, A.J. (1999) 'Time to terminate the ESF and the IMF', *NBER Discussion Paper* 48 (March).

Wade, R. and Veneroso, F. (1998) 'The Asian crisis: the high debt model vs. the Wall Street–Treasury–IMF complex', paper prepared for the Russell Sage Foundation, 2 March.

Wall Street Journal (1998) 8 January.

6 Economic growth and social development in Malaysia, 1971–98

Does the state still matter in an era of economic globalisation?

Ishak Shari

Introduction

Since July 1997, Malaysia has experienced a drastic change in her economic and political landscape following a serious financial crisis affecting Southeast and East Asia. As her economy plunged into recession in 1998, the worst since Malaysia's independence, it was greatly feared then that the remarkable achievements in social development during the twenty-seven years before the crisis would be significantly eroded. There was concern that the deep recession would expose households to unemployment and poverty, and worse still even trigger racial conflicts and political instability, thus affecting future development prospects in the country. The sporadic ethnic and religious violence occurring in Indonesia during the crisis added further worries to such a possibility in Malaysia. In fact, at one stage, the crisis and its aftermath raised a more fundamental question concerning the possibility of achieving equitable development in developing countries: could the 1997–8 'Asian crisis' signal the end of a development model in which the state had played a significant role in national economic development?

This chapter attempts to address two related questions. First, why is it that Malaysia, having a multi-ethnic society, was able to maintain racial harmony despite her worst economic recession since independence? Second, is it true that the financial and economic crisis entailed minimal social cost to the country, as claimed by government leaders? This chapter attempts to provide some insights into Malaysia's experience in striving towards equitable development in a world where the power and authority of national governments are being reconstituted, and functions of state having to adapt as governments seek coherent strategies of engaging with a globalising world. It is hoped that such an experience can make a small contribution in the search for answers to the question of the appropriate institutional arrangement for organising developing societies, and particularly the complex relationship between market and state, in striving towards human development.

Growth, structural transformation and social progress, 1971–97

It is essential first to describe briefly Malaysia's development experience, particularly in tackling the problems of poverty and income inequality, in an increasingly globalising world during the 1971–97 period. Based on available evidence, there is no doubt that the country enjoyed high export growth, rapid economic growth, increasingly full employment and falling poverty levels during this period.

By using the standard measures, Malaysia's economic performance before the recent crisis was rather impressive. The Malaysian economy grew at an average rate of 6.7 per cent per annum over the 1971–90 period and at a higher average rate of 8.6 per cent per annum during the 1991–7 period. In constant 1978 prices, her per capita GNP increased from RM1937 in 1970 to RM6130 in 1997 (Bank Negara Malaysia 1999: 2).

The rapid overall economic growth in Malaysia during the 1971–97 period was associated with the rapid growth of the export-oriented manufacturing sector. Consequently, the structure of the Malaysian economy was transformed considerably during this period. The share of the primary sector declined from 37.2 per cent in 1970 to 19.6 per cent in 1998 while the manufacturing sector's share increased from 8.7 per cent in 1970 to 35.7 per cent in 1997. The main impetuses for the expansion of the export-oriented manufacturing sector were the electronic and electrical machinery and industrial chemical industries.

The high growth rate of the Malaysian economy during the 1971–97 period was accompanied by generally low inflationary rates. With the exception of the relatively high rates of general price increase in 1973–4 and 1980–1, there was a remarkable record of price stability in Malaysia during this period.

With rapid economic growth, total employment in Malaysia increased from 4.02 million in 1970 to 8.805 million in 1997, i.e. it grew at an average rate of 2.95 per cent per annum. The manufacturing sector was the main sector generating new employment opportunities. Hence its share of total employment increased from 8.7 per cent in 1970 to 27.1 per cent in 1997 while the contribution of the agriculture sector to total employment declined from 53.5 per cent in 1970 to 17.0 per cent in 1997. The rapid expansion of employment opportunities brought down the unemployment rate from 7.8 per cent in 1970 to 5.7 per cent in 1980, before rising again to 8.3 per cent in 1986 due to economic recession. With the recovery of the Malaysian economy from 1987, the unemployment rate was reduced significantly to 6 per cent in 1990 and 2.5 per cent in 1997. In fact, several sub-sectors of the economy were experiencing labour shortages which led to the increasing recruitment of foreign migrant workers.

This rapid economic growth, together with the deliberate government affirmative measures to improve the position of the Bumiputeras and other disadvantaged groups, brought about significant progress in social development. For example, the incidence of absolute poverty in the country dropped significantly. Based on official data, the incidence of absolute poverty in the whole of Malaysia declined from 52.4 per cent in 1970 to 6.8 per cent in 1997. The number of poor households decreased from 1,100,000 to 346,000 during the same period (Malaysia 1991, 1998b).

This remarkable reduction in absolute poverty in Malaysia was accompanied by the reduction in income inequality from the late 1970s till 1990. By using data on the income share going to various income groups and the Gini coefficient, it is found that income disparity in Peninsular Malaysia was relatively high in 1970. The income share of the bottom 40 per cent of households was 11.5 per cent compared with the 55.7 per cent share enjoyed by the top 20 per cent of households. The Gini ratio for the whole of Peninsular Malaysia for that year was 0.513. Income inequality continued to worsen during the 1971–6 period with the Gini coefficient increasing to 0.529.

However, the trend in the income inequalities in Peninsular Malaysia began to change from late 1970s, as shown by the increase in income share of both the bottom and middle 40 per cent of the households and the reduction in the value of the Gini coefficient from 0.529 in 1976 to 0.445 in 1990. The income share for the bottom 40 per cent of households increased from 10.8 per cent in 1976 to 14.5 per cent in 1990 (Ishak 1998, Shireen 1997: p.60). Furthermore, the ratio of urban mean household income to the rural mean household income also narrowed from 2.14:1 in 1970 to 1.7:1 in 1990 while the Chinese–Bumiputera disparity ratio was reduced from 2.29:1 to 1.74:1 (Ishak 1998).

The ability of the Malaysian economy to achieve growth with redistribution enabled the living standards of Malaysians to be improved. There was a wider coverage of basic amenities which contributed to the improvement in the quality of life in the country. For example, the 1991 Population Census reveals that about 86 per cent of total occupied housing units in Malaysia had access to piped water compared to 65 per cent in 1980. Malaysia also recorded a higher literacy rate of 91 per cent in 1997 compared to 72.2 per cent in 1980 (Malaysia 1991, Malaysia 1998b).

The rapid industrialisation in Malaysia, as well as the increased access to education, especially at the secondary and tertiary levels, also brought about a significant increase in the size of the middle class in the Malaysian society. Using the occupational approach in defining the middle class, there were absolute as well as relative increases in the size of the new middle class in the country, particularly among the 'professional and technical', 'administrative and managerial', 'clerical', 'sales' and 'services' occupational categories (Jomo 1999).

Despite these achievements, however, several issues emerged to challenge social policies in the country, even before the crisis. First, despite impressive gains in reducing absolute poverty, some parts of the country continued to register a relatively high incidence of poverty. In 1997, for example, the poverty rate in the states of Sabah, Kelantan and Terengganu were 22.1 per cent, 19.5 per cent, and 17.3 per cent respectively as compared to 6.8 per cent for the whole country (Malaysia 1998b). Second, from 1990, income disparity widened again. While mean household incomes were increasing in both rural and urban areas as well as among the major ethnic groups, the differential rates of income growth among income groups and between strata resulted in a widening of income disparities.

The Gini coefficient for the country increased from 0.445 in 1990 to 0.456 in 1993, 0.462 in 1995 and 0.47 in 1997 (Malaysia 1998b). The urban–rural income disparity ratio increased from 1.7:1 in 1990 to 2:1 in 1997. During the same period, the Chinese–Bumiputera income disparity ratio increased from 1.7:1 to 1.83:1 (Malaysia 1998b). At the same time, income disparity within each ethnic group, particularly among the Bumiputera households, remained relatively high. Third, as in most East and Southeast Asian countries, Malaysian households have few formal mechanisms to protect themselves from risks associated with job losses, disabilities, and ageing. Where such formal mechanisms exist, coverage remains limited though it is increasing over the years. Hence a rather substantial percentage of Malaysian households have to rely primarily on personal savings and informal safety net mechanisms such as family and community links. However, as the country is undergoing a rapid demographic shift with increasing proportions of the population ageing, moving into urban centres, and increasingly working in informal sectors, the informal family-based mechanism will be insufficient to provide the necessary protection. This means that a substantial proportion of the population is exposed to risks such as the economic crisis.

Understanding Malaysian development before the crisis

At a superficial glance, the Malaysian development experience seems to confirm the thesis of orthodox neo-classical writers that her success is owed to liberal, 'market-friendly' regimes and 'open-door' policies towards foreign trade and investment. However, incontrovertible evidence strongly suggests extensive direct state intervention in Malaysia, particularly from 1971 until the mid-1980s.

Industrialisation and rapid economic growth were essential in alleviating poverty and reducing income inequalities in Malaysia during the 1971–90 period. However, industrial policy geared towards expanding the contribution of industry in general, and manufacturing in particular, to GDP and quickening structural transformation, has also been important in Malaysia's achievements towards poverty alleviation and income redistribution. In this respect, extensive government intervention took place to promote certain industries, especially in areas of financial regulations, trade relations and industrial support. Financial institutions in Malaysia faced ownership regulations, primarily to check market power and to direct savings to prioritised areas of investment. Favoured state-sponsored heavy industries enjoyed loans with lower than normal interest rates. Through the credit guarantee scheme and the industrial technical assistance fund series, small- and medium-scale enterprises also enjoyed subsidised credit. However, unlike South Korea and Taiwan, poor mechanisms of control and discipline to direct efficiency gains meant that rents generated as a result were generally squandered (see Jomo 1994).

Another important feature of Malaysia's industrialisation process has been the significant role of foreign direct investment (FDI). Some studies suggest strong incentives, i.e. policies and measures, are introduced to attract foreign capital to Malaysia (Rasiah 1995, Jomo 1996). For example, initial financing and discounted interest rates in export credit refinancing schemes are commonly used incentives.

Tax concessions, including tax holidays, are offered to strategic, export-oriented industries, and for manpower-training and technology-upgrading activities.

Trade policies have been critical to the industrialisation drives in Malaysia. Despite the substantial decline in the average rates of protection, Malaysia still maintains highly differentiated tariff schedules (Rasiah 1995, Jomo and Edwards 1995). In addition, although tariff reforms have continued under the common effective preferential tariff mechanism within the ASEAN Free Trade Area, state-supported heavy industries – such as iron and steel, automobiles and cement – still enjoy high tariffs.

Apart from the significance of industrial policy and trade policy to promote rapid growth, Malaysia has implemented a rather comprehensive package of poverty alleviation and redistribution policies. Although there was no land reform along the line introduced in South Korea and Taiwan, land in Malaysia has been distributed through land development schemes managed by government agencies. Despite various problems, Malaysia deepened its rural development emphasis from 1971 onwards (Ishak 1994). In addition to extensive investments in developing infrastructure in rural areas where Bumiputeras were heavily concentrated, special institutions created by the government (e.g. Majlis Amanah Rakyat (MARA) and Pernas) were given a more direct role in uplifting the socio-economic standing of the Bumiputeras.

With the economy growing rapidly, including the boost from export-oriented manufacturing, poverty continued to decline. The spread of modern farming methods in paddy cultivation also helped raise yields and the income levels of farmers. Other redistributive instruments such as privileged access to education, and special support in business by MARA and Pernas through, for example, captive markets and discounted loans for Bumiputeras were also introduced. Rising commodity prices and agricultural diversification to reduce dependence on particular crops helped smallholders raise household incomes in the late 1970s (Ishak 1994). The government assumed control of rice marketing, and thereby ensured stable prices for farmers and consumers. Marketing cash crop produce through quasi government bodies helped smallholders reduce their dependence on unscrupulous middlemen. The establishment of Permodalan Nasional Berhad (PNB) in 1978, as an additional investment arm through which the Bumiputera trust funds such as Amanah Saham Nasional (ASN) and Amanah Saham Bumiputera (ASB) were administered, enabled the Bumiputera participants of such trust funds to enjoy substantial rents. Other redistributive efforts, as well as the expansion of more remunerative employment, especially the absorption of Bumiputeras in the public sector and wage employment in the manufacturing sector, caused income inequality to decline from the late 1970s until 1990.

Government expenditure on social services has been pertinent to ensure the provision of minimal support for alleviating poverty, reducing inequality and sustaining growth. From the standpoint of externalities involving public goods, government participation has been vital. In this regard, Malaysia has devoted a high share of government expenditure to education and health services. Public expenditure on education and health services as a percentage of total government expenditure remained at about 22 per cent throughout the 1980s.

Investments in human resources – both public and private – in Malaysia also helped reduce poverty and inequality, though the emphasis on secondary and especially tertiary education was not comparable to South Korea. The expansion of education not only helped generate technical and professional labour for industrial upgrading, but also enhanced opportunities for upward social mobility, including skills enhancement and higher remuneration.

Rapid growth, the rise in educational levels and declining unemployment helped push up real wages in these economies despite the weakness of the unions. Real wages in Malaysia grew at an average annual rate of 8.8 per cent in the period 1970–90. Female participation in export-oriented manufacturing grew strongly and hence so did household incomes. The out-migration of rural labour to urban and industrial areas was so extensive that foreign labour became important in low-wage modern agriculture in Malaysia in the early 1980s (see Mehmet 1986).

Hence since export-oriented manufacturing increased the demand for labour, growth in wage employment, enlargement of household incomes and reduction in poverty and inequality, critical interventions stimulated the economy. Thus state intervention has made a significant contribution to Malaysia's progress in attaining rapid economic growth and reducing poverty and income disparities.

Liberalisation measures and financial crisis

Since the mid-1980s, however, Malaysia, as the other newly industrialised economies of East and Southeast Asia, has undergone considerable liberalisation and deregulation. Such moves were first introduced as a temporary response to the severe fiscal and external debt problems facing the country from the early 1980s and the recession of 1985–6. In order to reorientate the Malaysian economy back to the path of sustainable growth, the private sector was encouraged to be the engine of growth through a package of incentives. Thus, the role of the state was restricted to traditional areas of responsibilities such as defence, education and health. Some privatisation in the provision of social services did also take place. Furthermore, provision of subsidies was reduced and more focused, especially for the very poor.

The successful economic recovery from 1987 on encouraged the Malaysian government under Prime Minister Mahathir to continue and consolidate these policies. Hence, with the announcement of the Second Outline Perspective Plan (OPP2) 1991–2000, the economic changes were reiterated and reconfirmed. The continuation of policy changes introduced from the mid-1980s could also be attributed to pressure from the major powers, particularly the United States, and international organisations such as the International Monetary Fund (IMF) and the World Bank. Local elites were also in favour of these policy changes, as they accepted the arguments that liberalisation and deregulation could lead to greater investment and increased trade flows thus contributing to rapid growth, the expansion of employment opportunities and the reduction in poverty incidence. The establishment of the World Trade Organisation has made further liberalisation virtually compulsory.

Hence, increasingly, the policies implemented focussed on making economies more competitive internationally, through freeing of markets and curbing the role of the state, including public expenditure on social welfare, thereby having a major impact on the rural and the urban poor who were unable to fulfil new skill requirements. In addition, from the mid-1980s, the government in Malaysia began liberalising domestic capital markets and foreign investment regimes in its effort to foster rapid economic growth. In the 1990s, the financial liberalisation process was further accelerated. This included among other things moves for greater capital account convertibility and moves to encourage more foreign institutional investors to have greater access to the Malaysian stock market. These moves facilitated a large inflow of funds, particularly in the form of portfolio investment in the local stock markets. For example, out of the massive inflow of capital during the 1990–5 period, portfolio equity finance accounted for 88 per cent of the identified gross capital inflows (Ong 1998).

Thus the sequence of events leading to and worsening the crisis in Malaysia seemed to involve several important developments at both global and national level. Some recent works (Montes 1998) show that the crises in Malaysia were due to the undermining of previous systems of international and national economic governance, due to deregulation and other developments associated with financial liberalisation and globalisation. At the same time, it has been argued that the Asian governments were strongly pushed into financial opening by the US Treasury, multilateral financial institutions (particularly the IMF) and Wall Street fund managers, referred to as the 'Wall Street–Treasury–IMF Complex'.

The financial crisis in Malaysia was further adversely affected by the selective administrative measures – such as declaring all the 100 component stocks of the Composite Index of the Kuala Lumpur Stock Exchange (KLSE) as 'designated securities' ostensibly to check 'short-selling' – introduced by the Malaysian government, which aimed to curb speculation in the currency and stock markets. These measures were motivated by the need to protect the politically-connected business interest. The various contrary statements of Malaysia's Prime Minister (including his tough speech at the joint World Bank–IMF annual meeting in Hong Kong on 20 September 1997) also appeared to adversely affect investors' confidence and contributed further to the fall of the ringgit and the share prices at the KLSE.

The combination of these factors generated contagion effects for Malaysia, where common risk factors were perceived to be present by speculators and genuine investors alike. Furthermore, with the sharp and sudden depreciation of the ringgit, coupled with the reduction of her foreign reserves in initial anti-speculation attempts (estimated to be about US$3.5 billion), the burden of debt servicing rose correspondingly in terms of the local-currency amount required for loan repayment. The fact that a rather significant proportion of the foreign loans was short term became an additional problem. This was followed by the short-term foreign funds starting to pull out sharply, causing reserves to fall further. Hence, despite its relatively stronger initial conditions as compared with other regional economies, Malaysia was not spared from the contagion effect of the crisis.

The social impact of the crisis

After a lag of several months, the financial crisis affecting Malaysia wound its way into the real economy. The Malaysian economy began to experience slow growth in the remaining months of 1997 and registered negative growth in 1998, for the first time since 1985. The contraction of real GDP was rather severe. On a year-on-year basis, real GDP contracted by 6.7 per cent after years of uninterrupted expansion averaging 7.8 per cent per annum.

The contraction of the real economy in turn adversely affected the pace of job creation and led to rising unemployment. Thus, in contrast to the increase by an average of 7.7 per cent experienced during the 1996–7 period, employment in the manufacturing sector registered a decline of 3.6 per cent in 1998. The construction sector experienced the largest decline of 16.9 per cent. However, total employment declined by about 3.0 per cent to 8.537 million in 1998 and the unemployment rate increased to 3.9 per cent of labour force. The number of the unemployed increased from 233,100 in 1997 to 343,200 in 1998. Unemployment was increasing in the country partly as a result of the retrenchment of workers in the major sectors of the economy. According to official statistics, a total of 83,865 workers (about 1 per cent of the total workforce) were retrenched by 4,789 firms in 1998, compared to 18,863 workers reported retrenched in 1997.

However, in a crisis situation, it is difficult to estimate unemployment and retrenchment figures. Allowance, therefore, has to be made for workers unemployed and retrenched but not captured in official figures. A significant number of retrenched workers were foreign labour, and many of them were unregistered (or illegal) workers. This is especially so in the construction sector, where about 80 per cent of the workforce in the late 1990s were migrant workers and a significant percentage is unregistered. According to one estimate, there were 1.7 million foreign workers in Malaysia in 1997, of whom 560,000 were unregistered workers (Bank Negara Malaysia 1998: 63). During this crisis, reverse migration took place among foreign workers in Malaysia, most noticeably among illegal foreign workers, both on an organised basis (repatriation and deportation) as well as on an individual informal basis. Based on official figures, between January and mid-November 1998, at least 383,946 foreign workers and their dependants returned to their countries. In addition, registered foreign workers in the manufacturing industries also faced non-renewal/termination of their contracts by their employers during this crisis. Retrenchment of locals in the informal sector was also taking place and their number most probably was not captured in official statistics. Interviews with various focus groups carried out by a rapid assessment study also revealed that there was considerable under-employment, which most probably was not included in official statistics (Ishak and Abdul 1998).

Some firms reacted to the crisis not by laying off their workers but by cutting wages or lowering (and sometimes freezing) pay increases. For example, in the car assembling industry, workers had to accept a 25 per cent wage cut to avoid retrenchment. There were some employers who imposed excessive pay cuts of 30 to 50 per cent, including for lower-paid workers. The move by firms to cut wages, together with lower or no pay increase agreed upon in collective bargaining nego-tiations between unions and employers as a solution to avoid the retrenchment of workers, contributed to the decline in workers' wages during 1998. In addition, a very high percentage of workers in both the private and public sectors could not work over-time.

Some companies also defaulted or delayed in paying wages and Employment Providence Fund (EPF) contributions on behalf of their workers. For example, during the first six months of 1998, a total of 15,560 employers (or 5.4 per cent of the total registered employers) failed to contribute to the EPF as compared to 13,143 for the whole of 1997. This default by employers would seriously jeopardise the workers' savings for old age.

This changing situation in the labour market resulted in a big drop in workers' income, causing serious difficulties to many of them, especially those having vehicle and housing loans to settle. With the retrenchment of workers and the reduction in wages/salaries experienced by some sectors of the economy, several indicators showed moderating increases in wage rates. It was estimated that wages were increasing at a slower rate of 5.6 per cent in 1998, compared with 10.2 per cent in 1997 (Bank Negara Malaysia 1999: 78). Based on the estimates provided by the *Economic Report 1998/99*, real wages per worker declined by 9.9 per cent during the first seven months of 1998 as compared to an increase of 18.9 per cent during the corresponding period in 1997 (Malaysia 1998a). The fall in real wages was higher in some of the sub-sectors (e.g. the electrical, electronics and machinery industry) of the manufacturing sector.

Although the urban workforce in the formal sector seemed to be the hardest hit by the 1997–8 crisis, those in the informal sector and some sections of the rural working population were not spared either. For example, the livelihood of taxi drivers were adversely affected by the crisis, as people tended to be more cautious with their spending and travelling, and because of falling tourist arrivals. As a result, many taxi drivers had to work long hours, sometimes up to 16 hours per day. The *batik* (traditional textile) cottage industry in Kelantan was also badly affected, due to the rising price of imported white linen and the slump in demand. Hawkers and petty traders were not spared the brunt of the crisis, experiencing big drops in their business. Yet the informal sector provided some sort of safety net for those retrenched and others seeking more income to make ends meet, although this led to an overcrowding problem.

Urban–rural remittances also declined as a result of job losses or a big fall in the worker's income. Many workers interviewed in the rapid assessment study reported that they either had to stop sending money to their parents altogether, or had to reduce the quantum. This could have affected the income of rural people as transfer payments (including remittances from children working in urban areas) form a substantial proportion of their income.

Every section of the community in Malaysia was adversely affected by rising prices of goods and services, including basic essentials, reflecting largely the impact of ringgit depreciation on the prices of imported food. The official consumer price index (CPI) recorded an increase of 5.3 per cent in 1998, as compared to an increase of 2.7 per cent in 1997 and 3.5 per cent in 1996. However, the price increase in a number of essential commodities such as rice, flour, sugar, milk and cooking oil was much higher and affected monthly household expenditures. This is reflected by a significant increase of 8.9 per cent for food items in 1998 as compared to 4.1 per cent increase in 1997 and 5.7 per cent in 1996 (Malaysia 1998b).

It is interesting to note that changes in the Malaysian economy since independence brought about drastic change in the degree to which individuals and households in both the urban and rural sectors are integrated to both domestic and international markets. It is a fact that an increasing percentage of rural households in Malaysia earn much of their income from wage labour. For example, the Household Income Survey 1989 revealed that 45 per cent of heads of rural households in Peninsular Malaysia are classified as 'employees' with another 37.8 per cent classified as 'self-employed' (with most of them being smallholders producing commodities such as oil palm, rubber, cocoa and coconut) (Shireen 1997). This means that a very high percentage of the population have to buy much or all of their food and other consumer goods, and thus are vulnerable to price changes. Therefore with a higher inflation rate as one of the consequences of the crisis, the different groups in both rural and urban areas in Malaysia were exposed to falling real incomes. The burden of rising prices of goods was heavier among some of the rural population as they, too, experienced a big decline in their nominal incomes. For example, unlike the oil palm smallholders who benefited from the sharp increase in the price of palm oil, rubber smallholders' income was badly affected as the price of coagulated rubber was reported to have dropped from RM1.60 per kg to RM0.70–0.80 per kg in 1998.

With increasing unemployment, falling income and rising prices, it was therefore not surprising that the crisis had an adverse impact on poverty and income inequality in the country. According to the official estimate, the incidence of poverty in Malaysia fell to 6.7 per cent in 1997 (Malaysia 1998b). However, in October 1998, the Deputy Minister of the Ministry of Rural Development reported to the Parliament that the incidence of poverty in the country was expected to increase to 8 per cent by the end of 1998. In absolute terms, the number of poor households was expected to increase by 22 per cent from 346,000 in 1997 to 422,100 in 1998 (*Business Times* 1998).

What will be the impact of the crisis on income distribution in Malaysia? Unfortunately, lack of household income data for 1998 does not allow us to answer the question empirically. However, signs seemed to suggest that the urban–rural income imbalances and the overall income inequality improved slightly in 1998, thereby lessening the extent of the widening gap during 1991–7. It is argued that this development could be attributed to the slight fall in the mean income of urban households as well as those in the richest 20 per cent group in 1998. At the same time, the income of households involved in the agriculture sector grew at a slightly faster rate than 1997, owing to higher prices for palm oil and the increased production of food crops in response to the higher costs of imports. It is also argued that the mean income of the bottom 40 per cent of households, especially those in the rural areas, remained stable owing to their ability to diversify their sources of income which helped to cushion the full impact of the economic slowdown.

However, the pattern of income distribution in Malaysia could be adversely affected by the crisis through various other ways. First, an increase in unemployment generated many households with little or zero labour income, thus worsening the overall size distribution of income. Second, the decline in workers' wages, especially among the production workers whose numbers were increasing rapidly with rapid industrialisation in the country, was likely to push down the income share of those in the lower end of wage distribution, thus increasing the income gap between wage earners and asset-holders and worsening income inequality. Third, factors that contributed to increasing differentials between skilled and unskilled workers, and thus contributed to greater income inequality during the 1991–7 period, still prevailed. As argued in Ishak Shari (1998), one of the factors contributing to growing income inequality had been the sharp wage differentials between skilled and unskilled categories, as the government was working towards technological deepening in the manufacturing sector. Due to a mismatch between the demand and supply of skilled and unskilled labour, unskilled wages lagged behind, and the bottom of the income distribution suffered: hence the worsening of income inequalities. This problem appeared to persist despite the crisis.

The financial and economic crisis also seemed to have a negative impact on household investments in human development, particularly in education, health and nutrition, and fertility for several reasons. First, although social services were subsidised, households still incurred direct or associated costs in trying to get access to these services. With reduced income and higher prices, including medicines and schooling expenses, poor and low-income households tended to consume less than what is individually and socially optimal. Second, human capital investment takes time, which becomes scarcer as household members work longer hours to cope with falling incomes. Third, the quality and quantity of certain public services was likely to be affected owing to budget constraints and big shifts of clients from private to public providers. Fourth, as households tried to maintain current levels of consumption, they were most likely to reduce human capital investment or even deplete existing stocks. It is therefore important to conduct further research on the welfare declines and falling investment in human development induced by the crisis.

The initial tight fiscal policy measures implemented by the Malaysian government, among other things, are affecting some programmes for the poor in some parts of the country. Although the big budget cut has been compensated for by an additional allocation of RM3.7 billion to be made available as assistance to vulnerable groups adversely affected by the crisis, and while the government has expanded programmes to improve the livelihood of the poorest households, some government-supported NGOs have had to reduce their activities significantly, thus affecting their programmes to help the poor and the vulnerable groups.

The fall in the value of the ringgit and the rising cost of overseas education have resulted in a reduction in the number of students sent overseas. For example, the number of Malaysian students undertaking tertiary education in Britain dropped by about 44 per cent, from 18,000 in 1997 to 10,000 in 1998. The pressure on local institutions of higher learning to accept more students is greater. However, given the limited resources available, not all students can receive tertiary education. For example, in 1998, from a total of 112,000 high-school students who applied to enter public tertiary education, only 40,220 or 35.9 per cent managed to secure a place in public tertiary institutions. Some of them managed to join private universities and colleges. However, while students who secure places in state and private universities can apply for government study loans, those joining private colleges have to depend on their own resources, or some private funding institutions/foundations. Though private college education is about two-thirds cheaper than going overseas, their fees are still high, and well beyond the reach of students from most middle- and lower-income groups. In 1999, the number of applicants for tertiary education was bigger. At the same time, due to various reasons, universities had to increase the fees for their post-graduate programmes, thus creating a disincentive to potential applicants. These trends, if unchecked, will eventually affect the ability of the country to produce the needed manpower for R & D activities to propel the economy forward in the future.

A brutal crisis?

The above discussion, which admittedly is based on very limited data, seems to suggest that the social impact of the financial and economic crisis in Malaysia, as in other affected countries, is both widespread and may be potentially long-lasting. In fact, if the adverse impact of the crisis on foreign workers is taken into consideration, it is misleading to argue that the social cost of the crisis is minimal. Furthermore, it is important to remember that the social impact of any financial and economic crisis may take some time to overcome.

Nonetheless, based on available information, it is evident that the intensity of the social impact of the financial and economic crisis in Malaysia is relatively less severe compared to those experienced by other countries in Asia affected by the crisis. It is also interesting to note that while the crisis triggered unprecedented political development in Malaysia, it was of a much smaller magnitude compared with Indonesia. There were street protests and discontent at the grassroots, especially among the young, after the dramatic dismissal of the Deputy Prime Minister in September 1998. However, unlike in Indonesia, there is relative peace, and inter-ethnic relations have not been affected in Malaysia. How is it that the multi-ethnic society in Malaysia has not been torn apart with the worsening of the crisis as was the case in Indonesia? While this question begs further investigation, the different circumstances existing in the two countries may provide some initial explanations.

First, as mentioned above, the Malaysian state has given high priority to distributional issues, particularly in eradicating poverty and reducing economic disparities among major ethnic groups since the implementation of the NEP in 1971. In addition to its long-term objective of preserving and building on the country's social progress, the Malaysian state was also committed to mitigating the short-term adverse effects of the economic slow-down on vulnerable groups in Malaysian society. Thus the government ensured that budget shares for social services, particularly health and education, in 1998 would remain approximately at their 1997 levels and that public expenditure on major anti-poverty programmes would be protected in real terms despite the reduction of its total development expenditure. The programmes of support for key social sector services include: the construction of additional classrooms for primary and secondary schools in rural areas and upgrading of rural school facilities; the expansion of education facilities for skill development, including retrenched workers; the enhancement of the Higher Education Loan Fund to increase accessibility to higher education, especially among low-income groups; the construction and equipping of health clinics, particularly in rural areas; and the provision of adequate funds for medicine and other essentials in public health services to cater for the needs of the population.

Second, Malaysia's rapid economic growth during the twenty-seven years prior to the crisis produced a large and expanding middle class that is multi-ethnic in composition, with the Bumiputera middle class becoming very conspicuous and important. It has been argued that the characteristics of this growing middle class in Malaysia, particularly the attitude of acceptance and acquiescence vis-à-vis the state and political leadership among the significant section of them, have contributed to the maintenance of the status quo (Abdul 1999). This is not to deny that there is an increasing resentment among the middle class, particularly among the Bumiputeras middle class, with the way liberalisation and deregulation measures have reversed some of the restructuring achievements of the NEP. Furthermore, the government's pursuance of a policy of widespread privatisation of public assets, which created opportunities to politically-connected corporate leaders to make huge profits while burdening the people, including the middle class (for example, through increased toll charges on privatised roads), has led to further discontents among the middle class. The manner with which the ruling elite ejected the former Deputy Prime Minister and the subsequent events after his arrest further angered the middle class. However, while resenting the government, especially after the burst of the 'wealth-creating' bubbles, their opposition has not been along ethnic lines, and thus does not adversely affect the inter-ethnic relations in the country.

Third, the rather long period of rapid growth which resulted in labour shortages and the employment of a large number of foreign workers, both legal and illegal, in the economy before the crisis also played a fairly important role. With the unemployment rate of 2.6 per cent and the presence of more than one million foreign workers in the country, the impact of the crisis on employment opportunities has been relatively moderate. At the same time, by sending back retrenched foreign labour, Malaysia was able to 'export back' the social cost of the crisis. The restrained attitude of the unions and workers' willingness to suffer a decline in real wages rather than facing retrenchment also contributed to this situation. Furthermore, the enforcement of legal provisions protecting workers' interests during the crisis, ensuring that any retrenchment exercise was undertaken in accordance with the law, is also a very important factor. According to the Employment Act 1955 (Section 69), retrenched workers must be paid lay-off benefits or compensation.

Fourth, while the medium- and long-term impact of the measures introduced in early September 1998 need further detailed study, the short-term macroeconomic impact of the measures seems to be favourable in mitigating the adverse impact of the crisis. With the introduction of the selective capital control measures on 2 September 1998, the monetary authorities lost no time in sharply reducing the interest rate. For example, the base-lending rate (BLR) of commercial banks, which rose from 10.33 per cent at the end of 1997 to 12.27 per cent at the end of June 1998 – thus exacerbating the contraction of economic activities during the first half of 1998 – was reduced to a maximum rate of 8.92 per cent by end of September and to 8.05 per cent as at 10 November 1998, which is below the level prevailing before the financial crisis, i.e. 8.93 per cent at end of June 1997. This development has helped many firms to get access to cheaper loans and avoid going bankrupt, thus putting a brake on further retrenchment.

Furthermore, Malaysia's refusal to seek an IMF bail-out package is another possible explanation for the different adverse social impact in the country. IMF intervention required the governments in the receiving countries to cut domestic expenditures and raise interest rates to a high level through fiscal and monetary tightening measures. These policy adjustments invariably led to further contraction of the economy, and worsening of the social impact of the crisis. In addition, they also had to undertake substantial reforms in areas such as corporate governance, labour markets and their trade regimes. Malaysia, on the other hand, as mentioned above, introduced selective capital control on 2 September 1998. Although Malaysia's exchange controls were described by IMF Managing Director as 'dangerous and indeed harmful', the short-term macroeconomic impact of the measures seems to be favourable in lessening the adverse impact of the crisis. With the introduction of the selective capital control measures, the monetary authority in Malaysia was able to sharply reduce the interest rate and so enabled many firms to get access to cheaper loans and avoid going bankrupt. At the same time, it enabled the government to adopt an expansionary fiscal policy.

Conclusion

The causes and consequences of the recent financial and economic crisis in East and Southeast Asia are quite complicated and many of us have yet to understand it in any great depth. Furthermore, available information does not allow a carefully considered assessment of the welfare consequences of the crisis for different socio-economic groups, including the poor and vulnerable groups. While some analysts are quick to jump to the conclusion that the crisis has proven the failure of the 'Asian development model', the discussion above has shown that the issue is more complex. It must be admitted that the crisis has shown the truth of the allegation that such a development model encourages corruption and nepotism, particularly in the case of Indonesia. However, there may be a larger truth that still needs to be discovered.

The IMF and the World Bank have long been advocating the liberalisation of capital markets, including the establishment of stock markets, as well as markets for other derivative financial instruments. They have, therefore, largely ignored the arguments for financial repression and restraint advocated by some new developments in information economics (e.g. Stiglitz 1999), and the actual success of directed credit (only reluctantly acknowledged in the Bank's Miracle study). There is a significant body of persuasive contrary literature (e.g. Singh 1995) raising serious doubts about the nature and contribution of equity financing to late industrialisation. As the financial crisis experience shows, unregulated finance capital will end up largely in short-term and speculative ventures, which will in the long run debilitate growth and efforts to eradicate poverty and reduce income inequality. Consequently, there is now greater appreciation among governments of the dangers of exposing their financial system to fast liberalisation, especially when they lack experience in dealing with the international capital market, and when banking regulation and supervision are still insufficient. Governments are also now more willing to discipline not only labour but also finance.

The discussion in this chapter therefore challenges the common assertions that, with globalisation, the state is increasingly irrelevant (Ohmae 1992) or that the power of the state is being transcended and is increasingly becoming hollow and defective (Strange 1995). The development experience in Malaysia (as in other newly industrialised economies in East and Southeast Asia) demonstrates the possibility of different trajectories, despite being increasingly integrated in the globalised world economy, due to variations in the role of markets and the state as co-ordinating mechanisms. Furthermore, the experience of the financial crisis of the late 1990s in Malaysia as well as in other affected countries (particularly Indonesia) demonstrates that the implementation of the neo-liberal version of globalisation, particularly financial liberalisation, has brought about widespread hardship among the disadvantaged groups in these countries and has caused political as well as social turmoil. Policy prescriptions from the IMF, which involved tight monetary and fiscal policies, worsened the suffering of those adversely affected by the crisis. The aims of IMF policies appeared to ensure the maintenance of the domestic currency's convertibility and free capital flows, and guarantee repayment to foreign lenders. According to UNCTAD's *Trade and Development Report 1997*, foreign lenders emerged from the crisis without substantial loss, even though they accepted exposure to risk just as other lenders had done. Hence, a stronger role of the state in developing countries in order to promote equitable and sustainable human development during the present phase of globalisation seems important.

While recognising the importance of a stronger role of the state to ensure the attainment of equitable and sustainable human development, it is of utmost importance to recognise two convincing arguments against the state. First, the experience of this century (including the recent developments in those countries affected by the crisis) reveals a propensity and a capacity of the state for totalitarian regulation and repression, not only of people but also of institutions, social practices and the very fabric of normal life. Second, the state is a strikingly inefficient economic actor. In addition, today's world is characterised by the erosion of the sovereign state system.

Therefore, in a world in which powerful international organisations and trans-national corporations, as well as the states in the advanced industrial countries, are devoted to maximising the freedom of financial capital around the globe, and in the absence of any new international financial architecture, the states in developing countries need to assert social control and to continue to pursue redistributive policies that could change the impact of the globalisation process on their people. In this regard, however, a fundamentally different alternative, involving the democratisation of the state and the economy, would have to be considered. This would require a challenge to the national and international structures of power. Higgot's proposal for an alternative is worthy of further consideration:

> We may be seeing a trend away from 'automatic pilot' types of market strategy towards more active policies of the types enshrined in the Asian 'development state' model ... [T]he impact of the global economic crisis has created a space for the opinion that there are more than the traditional two economic policy agendas available to governments. A third way would involve some sort of 'middle' ground; in which the regulatory role of governments might be revitalised, greater attention might be given to social issues, and the emergence of a more 'national' or possibly post-crisis 'regional' approaches to economic management might be facilitated.
>
> Higgot 1999: 12–13

This means that the need to develop a balanced relationship between state, market and civil society is crucial in the attainment of equitable and sustainable human development in the rapidly globalising world. A balanced relationship between these three institutions would certainly be an uneasy one and more often than not saddled with contradictions. However, using humanitarianism as its basis, a desirable reconfiguration of the interests of the state, market and civil society is still possible. Unorthodox measures may even be necessary to meet the needs of the new relationship.

Bibliography

Abdul, E.R. (1999) 'The political dimensions of the economic crisis in Malaysia', paper presented at the ASEAN Inter-University Seminar on Social Development, Pattani, Thailand, 16–18 June.

Bank Negara Malaysia (1998) *Quarterly Bulletin*, Third Quarter 1998, 13, 3, Kuala Lumpur: Bank Negara, Malaysia.

—— (1999) *Annual Report 1998*, Kuala Lumpur: Bank Negara Malaysia.

Business Times (1998) 30 October.

Higgott, R. (1999) 'Bank from the brink? The theory and practice of globalization at century's end', paper presented at 13th Asia-Pacific Roundtable, Kuala Lumpur.

Ishak, S. (1994) 'Rural development and rural poverty in Malaysia: the experience during the New Economic Policy (1971–1990)', in J. Ariffin (ed.) *Poverty Amidst Plenty*, Kuala Lumpur: Pelanduk Publications.

—— (1998) 'Economic growth and income inequality in Malaysia 1971–1995', paper presented at Workshop on Economic Growth, Poverty and Income Distribution in Asia-Pacific Region, University of New South Wales, Sydney, 18–20 March.

Ishak, S. and Abdul, E.R. (1998) 'Rapid participatory assessments of the social impact of the financial crisis in Malaysia', draft final report presented for UNDP Regional Bureau for Asia and the Pacific.

Jomo K.S. (ed.) (1994) *Privatizing Malaysia: Rents, Rhetoric and Realities*, Boulder, CO: Westview Press.

—— (1996) *The Southeast Asian Misunderstood Miracle?*, Boulder, CO: Westview Press.

—— (1999) 'A Malaysian middle class?: some preliminary analytical considerations', in K.S. Jomo (ed.) *Rethinking Malaysia*, Kuala Lumpur: Malaysian Social Science Association.

Jomo K.S. and Edwards, C.B. (1995) 'Malaysian industrialization: policy, prospects and performance', paper presented at the seminar on Governance Mechanisms and Technical Change in Malaysian Industrialization, Bangi, 15–16 July.

Malaysia (1991) *The Second Outline Perspective Plan 1970–1990*, Kuala Lumpur: Percetakan Nasional Malaysia Berhad.

—— (1998a) *Economic Report 1998/99*, Kuala Lumpur: Ministry of Finance.

—— (1998b) *Social Statistics Bulletin, Malaysia*, Kuala Lumpur: Department of Statistics.

Mehmet, O. (1986) *Development in Malaysia: Poverty, Wealth and Trusteeship*, London: Croom Helm.

Montes, M.F. (1998) *The Currency Crisis in Southeast Asia*, Singapore: Institute for Southeast Asian Studies.

Ohmae, K. (1992) *The Borderless World*, London: Fontana.

Ong, H.C. (1998) 'Coping with capital flows and the role of monetary policy: the Malaysian experience, 1990–1995', in C.H. Kwan, D. Vandenbrink and S.Y. Chia (eds) *Coping with Capital Flow in East Asia*, Singapore: Institute of Southeast Asian Studies.

Rasiah, R. (1995) *Foreign Capital and Industrialization in Malaysia*, London and New York: Macmillan and St Martins Press.

Shireen, M.H. (1997) *Income Inequality and Poverty in Malaysia*, Lanham: Rowman and Littlefield.

Singh, A. (1995) 'How did East Asia grow so fast?: Slow progress towards an analytical consensus', *UNCTAD Discussion Papers* 97 (February).

Stiglitz, J. (1999) 'More instruments and broader goals: moving towards the post-Washington Consensus', the WIDER Annual Lecture, Helsinki.

Strange, S. (1995) 'The defective state', *Daedalus* 124, 2: 55–74.

UNCTAD (1997) *World Development Report 1997*, Geneva: United Nations.

Part II

Divergent development paths among the Asian miracles

7 Beyond policy explanations

Towards an alternative analysis of economic development in the Asia-Pacific region

Martin Andersson and Christer Gunnarsson

Introduction

The so-called miracle economies of the Asia-Pacific region are characterised not only by exceptionally high growth rates and successful industrialisation programmes, but also by their relatively equitable distribution of income. It is this combination of growth, structural transformation and equity that makes the Asia-Pacific experience unique. In fact, it is the combination that makes the miracle and makes it worthwhile studying whether there are policy lessons to be learned. Is there an Asia-Pacific model of economic development? On the one hand, there are major differences among the countries of the region, especially in terms of equity and the extent of structural change. These differences may be due to the fact that the countries have reached different stages or levels of economic development, but they may also indicate that an identical development model has not been applied throughout the region, or that the conditions for development in the countries have varied greatly in time as well. On the other hand, in comparison with other developing regions the combination of growth, structural change and equity appears to be peculiar to the Asia-Pacific region. Then, one important question is what makes this unique combination come about in this particular region, and another equally important question is why this combination is far more manifest in some countries than in others. A related question is whether the financial crisis revealed weaknesses in an Asian model proper, or whether the crisis exposed the fact that the conditions for economic growth in the region had changed in the 1990s. [1]

Two seemingly incompatible explanations have dominated the debate on the economic miracle, explanations that we prefer to categorise as the market-friendly (MF) approach and the state-led (SL) approach. Both purport to account for the combination of growth, structural transformation and equity. The familiar story is that the MF approach emphasises openness, market mechanisms and private initiative, whereas the SL approach emphasises selective state intervention and guidance of the market. The controversy has had three focal points: (1) how to account for the remarkable export performance, (2) what role should be attributed to government policies and (3) what is the significance of the relatively equitable distribution of income? These themes correspond to three concepts that have been used to characterise the economic miracle: *export-led growth, developmental state* and *growth with equity*, concepts that are all included in the dominant explanations for the miracle, albeit in different ways. In the MF explanation, openness was the key to export-led growth, granted prudent governance, and equity resulted from full employment and the non-discriminatory role of policies. In the SL explanation, government intervention was the very engine that guided the economies towards export-led growth, and equity was maintained as a consequence of a conscious choice of development strategies.

The purpose of this chapter is to highlight some theoretical and empirical weaknesses in the two explanations. A major problem is their implicit *policy-choice perspective*, which means that the miracle is explained in terms of a set of policy choices made by governments. It is based on a view of economic growth as determined by a series of choices, largely unconstrained by either history or context. This is not to say that policies, or scope for policies, are by any means futile or negligible. On the contrary, policy choices may have an enormous impact on economic performance, but when a policy-choice perspective is employed to explain historical development it may overstate the capacity of policy-makers to bring about change and underestimate the processes and structures under which these policy choices are made. To be convincing, the policy-choice perspective must not only provide evidence that implemented policies have been effective, but also be able to show that identical policies are likely to result in similar effects in different historical and circumstantial contexts.

However, an even more serious problem is that the key issue, to identify the causal mechanism behind the economic miracle in Asia-Pacific, is anticipated when the analysis focuses on policies. Since the revealed growth is assumed to have been the outcome of a specific policy choice, the analysis is focused upon why and how this policy was implemented to become so efficient. If instead the aim is to identify the dynamics behind the combination of growth, structural change and equity, the causal analysis has to focus on the context in which policies were implemented. It has to take into account the interaction of a number of factors that may have influenced the growth process, and among which policy measures are but one, albeit important, aspect. And if it is settled that specific policies have in actual fact mattered, it should be possible to demonstrate under what circumstances they have done so. This implies that a study of the role of policies in the process of economic growth is different from a policy-choice analysis.

To use concepts such as export-led growth, developmental state and growth with equity does not *necessarily* imply a policy-choice perspective. In a causal explanation, they may have important functions if they are placed into a spatial and time-bound context. However, in this chapter we shall critically analyse the use of the three concepts in typical analyses of the Asia-Pacific economic miracle.[2] The critique is partly theoretical and methodological and partly empirical. A primary aim is to suggest an alternative way to explain the economic miracle that goes beyond the explanations offered by the MF and SL approaches. It will be argued that, since the concepts of export-led growth and developmental state are used in policy-choice analyses, they tend to conceal more than they reveal about the dynamics of industrialisation in the market economies of the region. We propose a different perspective that focuses on the institutional arrangements needed for the rise of the domestic market economy, and in particular on the arrangements that eliminate the roots of economic backwardness in the agrarian economy. We shall argue that the policy interventions made may have been effective, but perhaps not always in the ways the policy-makers intended.

Export-led growth

Let us begin with a key concept in typical accounts of the Asia-Pacific success-story: *export-led growth*. The thesis that Asia's economic miracle is export-led appears to be common knowledge among laymen and experts alike. There is no doubt that the concept has a striking appeal, and the reason is clearly the obvious and remark-able export performance since the early 1960s. Export-led growth can be taken to mean the export performance per se, but it can also refer to the gradual embracing of export-promotion policies throughout the region. The term export-led growth is, therefore, often used as synonymous with export-oriented policies and the concepts are employed interchangeably.[3] This is due to the fact that the focus, from the very beginning, is on policy. In this perspective it is a priori decided that exports constitute the engine of growth and the policy controversy is about what policy measures have been decisive in promoting the export sector, openness and general economic policies or more selective and *dirigiste* measures.

The plea for openness is a typical market-friendly argument, upon which there is much disagreement with proponents of the state-led approach. However, in one important sense the two schools of thought come down on the same side, namely in the conclusion that the miracle can be explained with the concept of export-led growth (Balassa 1981 and 1988, Krueger 1981, Kuznets 1988, Little 1981, Riedel 1975 and 1988, Haggard 1990, Weiss and Hobson 1995).

Proponents of the MF approach argue that free markets combined with prudent macroeconomic management, non-distorted prices and public investments in education, infrastructure and institutional arrangements formed the underpinnings of the miracle. Openness is the key word here. The policy employed strove towards an allocation according to free trade principles. Government involvement was minimised and the policies implemented were of general character and non-discriminatory. Flexible exchange rates, flexible labour markets, neutral tax systems and free entry contributed to the miracle.

In contrast, the SL approach holds that the miracle was achieved by means of strong policy interventions that distorted the relative price structure in ways that favoured the export sector. Seminal studies by Amsden and Wade have shown that promotion of certain sectors by means of protectionist trade regimes and inter-ventionist industrial policies has been a key element in the export-promotion strategy. Selective measures such as state ownership, quotas, prohibitions, controls, tariffs, allocation of foreign currency, investment credits, export credits and rebates on imported inputs were undertaken within this policy (Amsden 1989, Wade 1990).

The economies of the Asia-Pacific region are all relatively open capitalist market economies, in which trade historically has served as an important contribution to growth, and continues to do so. It is also undeniable that the export share of GDP has increased since the 1960s. However, to argue that growth is export-led is more than to say that an economy has benefited from a relatively high degree of openness, or from selective trade-promoting policies. To establish the advantages of relative outwardness is one thing, to argue that exports have functioned as the prime, or sole, engine of growth is quite another. In general, historical evidence suggests that the MF case is clearly overstated and that the SL approach comes closer to describing the real conditions prevailing in the region, at least from the 1960s up to the mid-1980s. However, our concern is with the explanatory value of the underlying concept of export-led growth. From a methodological point of view the concept is imprecise and problematic. A fundamental problem is the implicit assumption that exports have played a leading role in the process of industrialisation. Thereby, it overemphasises external factors, while internal mechanisms of change are disregarded or considered only if they are important on the supply side for creating suitable or necessary conditions for the export expansion.

The counterfactual hypothesis is that the economic miracle in Asia-Pacific would not have materialised without the rising export economy. The question is how this came about, i.e. how the export expansion preceded the growth process and got it going. In the MF approach the export-led economy is contrasted against import substitution regimes (ISI), and the major concern is to show that the switch in policy from ISI to export-oriented regimes (EO) made all the difference. The argument is that when the economies opened up to trade the industrialisation process gained momentum, resulting in the long period of high and sustained economic growth.

One problem with this analysis is that it is basically a proposal about policies to encourage exports. It may well be that these measures to promote exports have been effective in bringing about the export expansion as such, but the causal relationship between export-promotion policies and the dynamics of industrial-isation remains unclear. So, the policy-choice perspective jumps from identifying export-promotion policies to inferring dynamic effects measured as growth of GDP per capita. What possible mechanism could make the growth of the export sector trigger off GDP growth? The SL approach is extremely vague on this point, basically because it has no theory of development for the internal market economy. It puts forward convincing evidence of export success stories that have been created by means of selective industrial policies (Amsden 1989, Wade 1990), but it does not demonstrate how export industries have led the way in inducing a growth mechanism in the home market. The problem is that the SL approach does not concern itself with this issue. In fact, economic performance is measured in terms of export performance per se and by the capturing of international market shares. The successful export performance *is* the miracle, not a factor that explains it.

The MF approach is clearly more sophisticated on this particular point. The theory postulates that the rise of labour-intensive export industries brought about growth in the domestic economy, basically via an employment- and income-generating mechanism. One assumption of this analysis is that export industries can be established by means of a steady transfer of cheap labour from the agricultural sector and that this can be achieved without a prior technological revolution in the agricultural sector. A second assumption is that since the domestic market is initially small, due to small populations and low purchasing power, the drive towards industrialisation logically has to be export-oriented. In the longer run the domestic market will catch up as an increasing number of workers are employed in the industrial sector, but initially it is export demand that leads the industrialisation process. A third assumption is that there is no capital scarcity. In the open economy, capital is available through FDI and portfolio investments so that all the capital required for industrial investments does not have to be raised domestically.

How realistic is this export-led model in the case of the Asia-Pacific region? The critique of the export-led thesis is not a new one. Empirically the export-led model has been questioned by, among others, Adelman (1984), Oshima (1987), Ranis (1996) and Rodrik (1994). Rodrik suggests that the investment boom of the 1960s is the core explanation of the Asian miracle. It was launched by a successful co-ordination of investment decisions by the state and facilitated through a combination of a well-educated population and relative equality of income. The export-era in the Taiwanese and Korean development was the result of the growth record rather than its cause. According to Rodrik, the export boom came too late to be able to work as the engine of growth. Although a reasonable account, and indeed one that concurs with our analysis, this says nothing about where the sources of home market growth may have come from, let alone how it may be causally linked to growth in agricultural productivity and rising rural per capita incomes. In particular, the causal relationship between growth and equity remains unexplained.

In fact, the empirical evidence in favour of the export-led growth model is not strong at all. The SL version is flawed because it lacks theoretical content and the MF version seems to be at odds with historical evidence. The latter's assumption that major technological improvements in the agricultural sector were uncalled-for does not hold water. In the first-tier miracles Taiwan and South Korea, the export expansion was clearly preceded by institutional and technological improvements in the agricultural sector, which made possible a transfer of labour to the industrial sector (Oshima 1987, Ranis 1996, Burmeister, Ranis and Wang 2001). In the Southeast Asian economies, the early attempts towards industrialisation in the 1950s (the Philippines) and 1960s (Malaysia, Thailand and Indonesia) were basically inward-oriented and capital-intensive. With the exception of Malaysia, technological and institutional improvements in agriculture remained insufficient and had few substantial positive effects on the industrial economy during this period. So in the beginning there was already an apparent difference between the countries in Northeast Asia and Southeast Asia in the extent to which agricultural modernisation preceded or coincided with the process of industrialisation. Where technological improvements remained inadequate, as in Southeast Asia before the 1970s, little surplus labour was made available and the industrialisation process took on a more substitutive and capital-intensive form. In contrast, technological change played a decisive role in the first phase of industrialisation in Taiwan and Korea, even to the extent that industrialisation was agriculture-led (with emphasis on the domestic market) rather than export-led (Adelman 1984). Whether the same mechanism applied to Southeast Asia in the 1980s and 1990s is debatable.

The second assumption, that the domestic market was insufficient because of low purchasing power, appears equally problematic. The export-oriented economies of Taiwan and Korea had much larger domestic markets in terms of purchasing power than the more inward-oriented economies of Southeast Asia. Did this follow from the export-orientation or from the modernisation of agriculture? Exports may generate increasing incomes through the employment mechanism, whereas growing agricultural incomes are derived from productivity growth. In the case of Taiwan and Korea it is quite clear that the income-generating effects of agricultural modernisation preceded the effect of increasing employment in export industries. Thus market deepening, i.e. the growth of purchasing power in the home market, originated in agricultural productivity and was only later to be driven by the industrial employment effect.

The third assumption, i.e. access to FDI, is largely irrelevant, since the early industrial development in Korea and Taiwan during the 1960s and 1970s relied on FDI to an almost negligible extent.[4] It seems obvious, then, that the capital resources employed in the industrial economy had to be raised domestically and most likely from the agricultural sector, the productive and income-generating capacity of which was put to the test, a test it was obviously capable of standing up to, especially in Taiwan. In the industrialisation of Southeast Asia since the mid-1980s conditions are clearly different. The industrialisation boom that followed after the abandoning of the ISI model was largely built upon access to FDI and portfolio investments. In these cases it might be that the growth process is, in fact, more export-led, which also means that the other two assumptions of the export-led growth model apply as well. It might be that the growth of the export sector has preceded the growth of the agricultural sector and that domestic demand is, in fact, lagging behind the demand derived from the export sector. If this is so, the export-led model would be a better account of the industrialisation of the ASEAN countries than of the earlier cases of industrialisation in Northeast Asia. It remains unlikely, however, that this is an effect of policy changes. It is more likely to be a direct consequence of changing global conditions, including the liberalisation of financial markets and the shift in comparative cost structures after the Plaza Accord of 1985. However, even if this industrialisation is more export-led, one should not under-value the importance of institutional and technological changes in the agricultural sector that were undertaken in Thailand and Indonesia during the 1970s and 1980s. Considerable productivity growth and rising per capita incomes in agriculture may have played important roles in the industrialisation process under these new conditions as well. It is a noteworthy fact that the Philippines is the least successful export economy among the ASEAN four, and that this same country remains the economy with the most troublesome agrarian conditions. Hence there has been limited scope for a transfer of labour to the industrial sector in the Philippines.

The most important objection to the thesis of export-led growth is, thus, the fact that it grossly underestimates the role of demand in the domestic market and in particular the demand that is derived from agricultural modernisation. Export-expansion is taken to be necessary due to the limited size of the home market, which in turn is due to low purchasing power. As an alternative we suggest that the transformation of agriculture with considerable productivity improvements after (but also before) land reforms, and the green revolution in large parts of the Asia-Pacific region, gradually from the beginning of the 1950s onwards, had manifest effects on the growth potential of the domestic market. This is a factor that accounts for the uniqueness of the region in comparison with other regions, while at the same time indicating an explanation for the differences in terms of structural change and equity among countries in the region. So, in line with Kravis (1970), we suggest that foreign trade is more likely to have functioned as a handmaiden of growth, as an extra stimulus, but not as the engine of growth in the Asia-Pacific region.

The developmental state

The controversy about how to account for the Asia-Pacific growth story has to a large degree been centred around the issue of the role that should be attributed to the state, whether in the form of policies (e.g. trade regimes and industrial policy), institutional and organisational arrangements (e.g. the financial system or bureaucratic capacities) or more fundamental institutions (e.g. legal arrangements and forms of governance). Advocates of the SL approach have argued that omnipotent and highly competent Asia-Pacific governments and bureaucrats have been deeply involved in shaping the economic miracle, whereas proponents of the MF approach have gone to great lengths in attempts to depreciate the (positive) influence of government interventions.

In the World Bank assessment of the miracle, *The East Asian Miracle* (World Bank 1993), it was argued that the growth stories could be explained as a result of a successful mix of market forces and government policies. Investments in infrastructure and human capital were important contributions, and the governments created prerequisites for the market by setting up regulatory frameworks favourable to private investments, by developing new forms of co-operation and by maintaining macroeconomic stability. In contrast, the role of industrial policy, accorded decisive importance by the SL approach, was seriously downplayed. At this precise point the divergences between the two approaches become crystal clear. The World Bank study emphasised the importance of a *regulatory state* in a market economy. This was decidedly not what was meant by a *developmental state*. Chalmers Johnson's study of the Japanese miracle, in which the concept was coined, takes as a point of departure exactly this difference between a regulatory state (Western style) and a developmental state (Asian style). In the latter the state itself leads the drive towards industrialisation, whereas in the Western type the state concerns itself with forms and procedures (rules), but not with substantive matters (Johnson 1982). So either the Asian miracle should be associated with a Western-style regulatory state or with an Asian-style developmental and plan-rational state.

The MF case for the regulatory state may be illustrated by a study published by the Asian Development Bank only weeks before the 1997 crisis blew open (*Emerging Asia*, Asian Development Bank 1997). In this study the Asian governments are praised for adhering to the principle of rule of law. 'Sound policies and effective government institutions helped nurture and support markets in East Asia ... governments generally made good choices and backed their policies by strenuous efforts to foster sound institutions and implementation capacity' (ADB 1997: 62). In contrast to most other LDCs, Asian governments 'got things done' and 'quickly corrected mistakes'. This is exactly why East Asia can be held up as a model to the world, namely that the state stood up to its regulatory task and abstained from interfering with the market. In fact, like in the World Bank miracle study, the Southeast Asian more market-led model is held up as preferable to the Northeast Asian more interventionist model and there is no mention of inadequacies in market regulation, let alone of cases of cronyism. In one sense, this is a thoughtful approach in that it recognises the obvious differences between forerunners and followers with respect to both policy experience and pre-conditions for growth. In another sense it is totally ahistorical. It arrives at conclusions based on normative theory and takes no account of differences in political-economy conditions between the Northeast and the Southeast. The underlying proposition is that the policy packages pursued in the ASEAN region after 1985 had also been available in Korea and Taiwan some twenty years earlier and that the difference was a matter of choice.[5]

A typical SL view before the crisis was that the miracle could be explained by the 'unusual combination of bureaucratic autonomy and collaborative linkaging with the economic sector' (Weiss and Hobson 1995: 162). In their view a decisive factor has been the organisation of the governing apparatus and its relation to both the domestic economy and the international environment. Collaboration and coordination are then the key to the miracle. 'The stronger the collaboration, the stronger the infrastructural power and consequently the capacity for effective co-ordination' (Weiss and Hobson 1995: 168). The fundamental content of this argument is that the Asian collaborative and organised form of capitalism is superior to the Anglo-American rule-governed type of market economy, the close government–business ties being the cardinal advantage of the model. Nothing is said about possible problems associated with this 'embeddedness' of the state, or about any observed changes in state–business relations during the period of financial deregulation and increasing openness since the late 1980s.

The concept of the developmental state has two components: one *ideological*, one *structural*, and it is this ideology–structure nexus that distinguishes developmental states from other forms of states. In terms of the ideology component, a developmental state is essentially one whose ideological underpinning is 'developmentalist', which means that it is assumed to conceive its 'mission' as engaging and promoting actions that foster economic development, by which is usually meant promoting industrialisation. Thus, such a state is assumed to have different *motives* to other states and establishes as its principle of power and legitimacy its revealed *ability* to promote sustained development.

In terms of structure, the developmental state is defined according to its ability and capacity to implement and carry out its intentions in the form of policies and institutional arrangements to the extent that these have a bearing on the functioning of the economic system. The state-holding elites must be able to establish a state-structure that provides them with a capacity to implement economic policies prudently and effectively. Whether such a capacity exists will depend on a number of circumstances – political, institutional, administrative and technical. A fundamental condition for such a capacity to exist is the *autonomy* of the state from social forces, so that it can use these capacities to devise long-term economic policies unhindered by the claims and actions of special interests.

So a developmental state differs from other states in that it is assumed to have both different motives (economic development) and different means and opportunities to carry out activities in accordance with formulated goals. Methodologically there are fundamental problems with this definition of the developmental state. First, it runs the risk of being *tautological* since evidence that the state is developmental is often drawn deductively from the performance of the economy. This produces a definition of a state as developmental if the economy is developing, and equates economic success to state strength while measuring the latter by the presumed outcomes of its policies. The problem here is that such a definition leaves no space for alternative outcomes, i.e. failures. All unsuccessful cases of state intervention are assumed away as non-developmental. We are not told whether the failures were due to ideological or structural factors, whether government intervention was ever intended to be growth-enhancing, or whether the failures were due to insufficient means of control, wrong policies or simply bad luck.

Second, for the very same reason, the concept has a *taxonomic* content rather than an explanatory value. It describes a condition under which motives, means and opportunities coincide favourably to produce happy endings. Typically, it classifies Asian state intervention as developmental and African as non-developmental according to outcomes, but it does not provide a theory that explains the differences in outcome although at a glance the policies would appear to have been roughly similar.

Thirdly, the developmental state concept leans towards *teleology* in that it assumes an intentional relationship between policies and outcomes. Successful outcomes are identified as signs of goal-attainment, as the fulfilling of the intentions and policies of the state. Likewise, in non-developmental states failures are taken to be associated with specific purposes, with goals and actions of a state that is non-developmental in its orientation and structure. In sum, the developmental state is not a theory of economic development; it is a classification of a phenomenon that begs explanation.

In terms of empirical content there are other problematic aspects of the developmental state concept. First, the assumption that developmental states are guided by motives and ideologies that are different from those of other states is highly dubious. It assumes that Asian governments and bureaucracies have a clear vision of development and that they are not intertwined with special interests. This is a problem that follows from the tautological definition of the developmental state. Normally, the developmental mission formulated by the state takes the shape of economic nationalism, i.e. nations seek to 'catch up' with countries that are considered more developed. They can do so for a variety of reasons, and the fundamental motive may indeed be national defence and security rather than the enhancement of prosperity of its people. Still, it does remain a fact that nationalism was a strong or even leading factor in most Third World attempts towards industrialisation in the 1950s and 1960s under the rubric of import-substitution policies (ISI), i.e. the antithesis of export-led growth. There is no doubt that ISI was basically a nationalist development strategy, which means that the many failures associated with ISI have to be accounted for by other factors than a non-developmental ideology.[6]

Second, the assumption is made that state capacities are crucial for the carrying through of development-enhancing policies. A 'strong', 'autonomous' state, largely 'insulated' from societal pressures has had the capacity to implement growth-enhancing policies. Why is this autonomous state not predatory? In the case of the Asian developmental state, autonomy and insulation are often determined in terms of bureaucratic capacities. The state apparatus is governed by a segment of highly competent and development-oriented technocrats, who have not let themselves become affected by political movements or economic interest groups. Although the politicians might 'reign', it is the bureaucrats who 'rule'. This obsession with bureaucratic competencies is somewhat curious. Clearly, the existence or absence of administrative capacities and means of control may be decisive for the success or failure of policy implementation. Still, since the emphasis is on the necessary combination of national developmental motives and administrative capacities, one has to assume that these insulated and apolitical bureaucrats are the actual carriers of the national development vision. This technocracy is supposed to carry out policies that are good for the nation, and they do so for no apparent reason, not even self-serving ones, since they are, by definition, not allowed to enrich or empower themselves. In fact, to argue that growth is technocracy-led would only be logical if we ascribe a less interventionist and more regulatory role to the state. This means that a technocracy-led economy would be best associated with a MF approach.

Third, how could discretionary and discriminatory interventions avoid harming the functioning of the market economy? One suggestion would be that state powers are not exactly autonomous in a top-down sense but rather 'embedded' in society (Evans 1995). This means that policies are formulated and carried out through close collaboration between the state and leading industrial actors in a corporatist or even neo-mercantilist partnership. The problem is of course that state embeddedness might just as well be reformulated in terms of 'rent-seeking', i.e. as evidence of weakness and lack of independence of the state.

The Asia-Pacific economies have another characteristic feature, however, namely that they are trade-oriented, and for that reason they should not be associated with ISI regimes. The concept of *mercantilism* was introduced by Chalmers Johnson to depict the unique government–business partnership in the East Asian model. In Johnson's analysis mercantilism is identified in terms of the specific forms of collaboration between government and industry in combination with a unique type of ideology. Plan rationality is the code word used for this combination of administrative organisation and ideology.

However, mercantilism ought to be given a more precise economic content. Mercantilist regimes are extremely trade-orientated (as suggested by the term itself), but opposed to the idea of free trade. The dogma that a positive trade surplus serves the interest of the national economy appears to have had great impact on the miracle countries of Asia-Pacific. One unique feature of the Asia-Pacific developmental states is indeed their trade-orientation. Their own exports have been favoured and fostered, and selective efforts have been made by the governments to encourage exports. Taiwan's huge trade surpluses were no accident but largely a conscious mercantilist strategy for the purpose of financing investments necessary for the industrial development of the country. In such a strategy the state does take a leading role, sometimes as in Taiwan by relying heavily on state-owned industries, but more often by supporting and promoting sections of private industry. Mercantilism, thus, does rely strongly on partnership relations with sections of industry, especially large export-oriented companies. But mercantilist policies cannot only be characterised in terms of collaborative arrangements between policy-makers and industry under the umbrella of an export-led development strategy. More important is to identify the instruments applied in the attempt to foster national economic development. One aspect is what types of instruments are used to direct and allocate capital to export industries; the second aspect is the extent to which any efforts are made to create institutions that facilitate the integration of the domestic economy. The first aspect has to do with *dirigiste* 'developmental' policies, whereas the latter aspect concerns institution-building in the home market. If the focus is on explaining the outward orientation of the economy, i.e. choice of policies, the national economy can be likened to a firm, which functions as a hierarchy (i.e. market adverse) within its own borders and competes in foreign arenas (markets). Again, the problem with this approach is that in its analysis there is no such thing as an internal market. If the focus is on identifying the mechanisms of development in the domestic economy, one should rather raise questions about what arrangements have been set up to integrate and foster the functioning of the internal market, also within this mercantilist policy framework. Such interventions can be part and parcel of a mercantilist trade strategy, but they may also be made in a different context.

If we wish to evaluate the role of the state we have to be distinct in identifying the mechanisms of state control and leadership. Loose concepts such as 'collaboration' will not suffice and to assume away the political instruments and focus on bureaucratic structures is to miss the point. Fundamentally, one has to determine what instruments of control have been available to and used by the governments in their attempts to guide the structural transformation of the economy. So we need to consider not only the devices that have favoured the export sector as such, since these are time-specific and often employed after the early phase of industrialisation, but also the extent to which interventions have had the function of encouraging and helping to build market-supporting institutions.

Making functional sense of the developmental state

The economic essence of the developmental state is its control, or even socialisation, of national savings and its instruments of resource allocation via the financial system. This may be of particular importance under conditions of capital scarcity. In this sense the developmental state is not Asia-specific. In some respects it is specific to policies of industrialisation under conditions of underdeveloped market institutions but, in fact, state intervention in the form of the socialisation of savings can also be identified in developed economies up to the 1980s. So in one sense the developmental state is time-specific in that its mechanisms of control are largely removed during the process of financial deregulation and globalisation of capital.

So a more precise definition of the developmental state can be given: *a developmental state is a vehicle of industrialisation that uses control over the financial system to direct national savings into productive investments.* This definition has the advantage that the developmental state is not defined by outcomes but by the instruments of intervention. Interventions may be substitutive to the extent that market institutions are done away with, or are damaged, but they may also be instrumental in building market institutions. A developmental state may indeed produce development failures as well as success stories. In backward economies success or failure is likely to depend on the degree to which the interventions made have an effect on the creation of market institutions. Fundamentally, such mechanisms relate to the modernisation of the agricultural sector.

What does this tell us about the role of the state in the Asia-Pacific economic miracle? Was state intervention basically carried out to substitute for missing market institutions, or were interventions that helped, intentionally or unintentionally, to build market-supporting institutions more instrumental? In the process of industrialisation from the 1950s onwards in Taiwan and Korea, and from the 1960s and 1970s in Southeast Asia, there is not a lot of evidence of a directly harmful effect of the substitutions made by the state. Cases in point are the Philippines under Marcos and the excesses of the Suharto regime in Indonesia. So either there was a parallel development of strong market institutions, or the state interventions spilled over to the market. If the Asia-Pacific region is compared to the extreme cases of substitution in Africa, it is clear that in the latter continent the agricultural sector was largely strangulated by surplus capital extraction and little was transferred back to agriculture in terms of productive resources. Heavy taxation and price controls kept the agricultural sector backward and no linkage effects developed from the state-substitutive form of industrialisation. If market institutions did develop they had to do so informally, as 'guerrilla' institutions. Thus the failure of African state-led industrialisation is best explained not by the absence of a developmental state in either ideological or structural terms, but by policies that destroyed rather than engendered the rise of market.

The Asia-Pacific case has few resemblances with Africa. State intervention was motivated for nationalist purposes and the instruments used served the purpose of fostering industrialisation. Many interventions were clearly substitutive in that the aim was to build national industrial capacities. In those cases the economy worked under conditions of capital scarcity and the state took on the task of socialising savings and allocating them to productive investments. Government control over the financial system, basically the banking system, was the fundamental instrument in this strategy, a strategy that was followed all over the Asia-Pacific region. However, this may explain the allocation of funds to export industries, but it does not account for the dynamics of the home market. A case in point is Taiwan. Mercantilist policies to foster export industries may be identified and accounted for, but they do not explain the emergence of the large sector of small and medium-size firms (SMEs), which is a typical feature of the Taiwanese economy. The SME sector has developed largely without any state support; in fact, even to the point of active discrimination. If there exists a causal and functional connection between inter-ventionist policies and the rise of SMEs, we should be able to deduce an explanation for the fact that such a connection appears to be missing in other countries with developmental states. Thus institutions may be fostered by state interventions, but they may also emerge in informal ways outside the range of the state, in guerrilla forms (Lam and Clark 1994).

For the home market to develop, it was necessary that some interventions helped to set up institutions that reduced the degree of backwardness in the rural economy. Land reforms are often brought up as an underlying precondition (background) for the economic miracle in Taiwan and Korea. From our perspective, the important aspect is that the land reforms were part and parcel of a process of institution-building and technological change in the agrarian economy. The introduction of high-yielding varieties, fertiliser programmes, credit systems, and marketing systems were important aspects of such interventions, and were introduced even during the colonial period in Taiwan and Korea. Combined with other government investments in infrastructure and education, these measures surely helped in transforming the agricultural economy in ways that stimulated the growth of the home market. These interventions may have had other intentions, and basically most interventions were for the purpose of extracting and transferring capital from agriculture to industry (to the Japanese economy during the first half of the twentieth century), but the outcomes worked to stimulate market growth from below and the rise of SMEs.

In Southeast Asia similar consequences of government intervention are not easily identified in the domestic economy. Except for the case of Malaysia, little was done to promote productivity in agriculture by means of technological or institutional investments until the 1970s.[7] In addition, the industrial export boom since 1985 has certainly involved government participation, but one should bear in mind that the conditions for government intervention have been drastically altered. With the liberalisation and globalisation of financial systems, the old instruments of control and regulation are no longer available to the governments. The pre-1980s period was typified by socialised savings, the rationing of capital, and selective controls in an economy characterised by capital scarcity. From the mid-1980s onwards, the private capital markets were strengthened, controls were eased, dependency on exports magnified, protectionism was dismantled, and the prices were set 'right'. In fact, and this is an important point, in an increasingly open economy, interventions of a mercantilist type may no longer be needed to foster the export economy.

Thus the mercantilist state is unlikely to have played any role in the financial crisis, since its means of control had gradually been done away with or made non-existent during the 1990s. In fact, deregulation of national financial systems was a major ingredient in the emerging integration of the Asia-Pacific region after the mid-1980s. Deregulation removed the capital scarcity restriction and made it possible for ASEAN countries to industrialise by means of access to foreign capital, a formula that had remained largely unavailable in Korea and Taiwan during their early phases of industrialisation. The state therefore played a distinctly different role in the industrialisation in Southeast Asia after 1985 as compared to Northeast Asia in the 1960s and 1970s, and this divergence was not due primarily to differences in initial conditions in terms of resource endowment and institutions, but rather to greatly altered global conditions. Thus it was not the crisis that marked the weakening of the developmental state, since the latter had already gradually ceased to exist, but rather the weakening of the developmental state that made a development possible that led up to the crisis.

Growth with equity

The economic miracle in Asia-Pacific is often cited as a case of relatively even distribution of income, although questions have, for good reasons, been raised about the credence of this proposition in the case of Southeast Asia. Indonesia, Malaysia, Thailand and especially the Philippines show much larger income disparities than Korea and Taiwan. Nevertheless, the region is clearly more egalitarian than most other developing regions, in particular in comparison with Latin America. Therefore, it is not fair to characterise the growth experience of Asia-Pacific as 'growth without development', the term 'growth with equity' surely being more accurate. The problem, then, is to account for the relatively equal distribution of income in the region, as well as for the revealed differences between countries with respect to income distribution. Of particular importance is the need to clarify how equity may be causally related to the growth process, including institutional arrangements and policy interventions.

We have argued so far that the concept of export-led growth is built upon assumptions that fail to tally with a factual course of events, and that the SL approach that a capable, foresighted and omnipotent state has been paving the way for growth through a continuous implementation of development-promoting policies is flawed because it assumes away the dynamics of the home market. Equal distribution of income is often ascribed to either the workings of an export-led growth model, or to certain conscious policy interventions. In the MF view, equity comes about as a likely result of the labour-intensive production organisation that follows from reliance on comparative advantages in an open trade regime. In the SL view, the state is thought to have actively intervened to level out income disparities in order to gain legitimacy for the maintenance of an authoritarian 'developmentalist' system. From both perspectives, the land reforms of the early 1950s in Korea and Taiwan are put forward as important events.

For the MF approach, the land reforms contributed to an equalisation of opportunities and to a freeing of the labour force. This was later to become an advantage in the labour-intensive export-led industrialisation. Fei, Ranis and Kuo – the inventors of the term 'growth with equity' – saw the equitable growth pattern in Taiwan as the outcome of market forces, given the crucial job done by the state in setting up a proper institutional environment. Two policy shifts are emphasised as central conditional factors for growth with equity – the land reform and the switch to export-orientation in the early 1960s. This is a reasonable account, although it has a teleological slant towards assuming a policy purpose behind the equitable growth pattern. With respect to the dynamism of 'growth with equity', this perspective is a variant of export-led growth. It is the export-orientation that accounts for the growth and the land reform that made it become equitable. By this logic export-expansion without land reform would foster inequalities, and land reform without a switch to export-orientation would provide equity but no growth.[8]

In the SL view, the sale of public land and land transfers to the tillers were taken to be 'autonomy enhancing devices' for the state (Weiss and Hobson 1995: 164) and factors that were 'critical in buttressing state power' (Amsden 1990: 14). Equalisation of land was done for political reasons. Not only did the state need to have the rural population on its side, but the government also needed to curtail the power of the landed elite in order to improve its autonomy. This was, in fact, an implicit feature in the politics of the developmental state. Wade (1990) refers in passing to the land reforms that the government in Taiwan launched to equalise land ownership so as to build legitimacy and to avoid a peasant revolt as had been the experience of the ruling KMT party in mainland China. For Wade, there was a deliberate quest on the part of the state to create a more egalitarian society in order to 'build support'. The KMT had to make efforts to include the island's population into the nationalistic project. To distribute land to the landless was then an appropriate strategy, since the government with this action could kill two birds with one stone: the peasants became owner-cultivators and the demise of landlords erased any concentration of wealth (and hence power) in the rural areas.

In other studies some stress is laid on governmental policies in maintaining equal income distribution (Johnson 1987), but adjacent to the land reform, the policy shift to export-oriented industrialisation is the focal point in explaining growth with equity in both the MF and SL explanations (Fei *et al.* 1979, Deyo 1987). For the former, this shift constituted a market-friendly change that led to a rapid absorption of surplus labour in the industrial sector producing for international markets. When this surplus vanished, real wages rose to the benefit of the unskilled and hence equality increased. For the latter, the same shift created a homogenous labour market without unemployment through the government's inclination and alertness to bet on the right horse, the labour-intensive export industries. The story for South Korea is similar although the inequalities began to rise after the government's push for heavy industry after 1973 (Adelman 1998).

Thus this policy perspective on equity relates either to a debatable economic explanation or to a political explanation without real economic content. Basically, the experience of growth with equity in the region has been used to question the view that there exists a Kuznetsian trade-off between growth and equality (Fei *et al.* 1979, Birdsall *et al.* 1998). The equity discussion is sometimes somewhat deceptive, since it makes one think of deliberate and concrete policies aimed at *distributive policies*. If the focus is on policies the matter is quite straightforward; it is basically a question of measuring the effectiveness of different policy alternatives. But if we wish to find a causal connection between equity on the one hand and economic growth and structural change on the other hand, the matter clearly becomes more complicated.

The concept of 'growth with equity' is different from the other two concepts dealt with here, 'export-led growth' and 'developmental state', in the sense that it is merely descriptive. It describes a state of affairs and it says little or nothing about any causal relationship between growth and equity. So the divergence of the Asia-Pacific experience from the Kuznetsian trade-off can be interpreted in three ways: (1) export-led growth based on labour-intensive technology maintained equality through a full employment mechanism, (2) the state mediated inequalities by means of interventions in the market mechanism and (3) equity and growth are interrelated and mutually re-enforcing in the process of structural transformation. Since we have already questioned the theoretical assumptions underlying the first two propositions, we have to elaborate on the third possibility. This means that we complicate the story by noting that equality was decreasing before the policy shift towards export-promotion, and that the first steps of the process of industrialisation were taken even before the land reforms. The picture becomes even more complicated when we introduce Southeast Asia into the story.

When criticising the notion of export-led growth our purpose was not just to underplay its contribution to the growth of GDP. Rather, the purpose was to suggest that, if the mechanism by which the export sector is supposed to have led the growth of the domestic economy remains unclear, there must be some other dynamism at work. In fact, the existence of such a mechanism would suggest a different type of socio-economic change from that in an export-led economy. In such an analysis particular attention should be given to the role and type of *agricultural modernisation*, not the reform policies as such. In most policy studies such aspects are neglected.

The case of Taiwan can be taken to be an ideal type – in the Weberian sense – of this type of agricultural modernisation. During the colonial period the Japanese Empire used Taiwan as a source from which to extract primary products, mostly rice and sugar (Ho 1979). But, unlike most colonial experiences, a number of modernising projects were undertaken, such as the development of irrigation systems, and the introduction of new seeds, fertilisers and infrastructure. As a result, productivity in Taiwanese agriculture rose substantially. Thus the domestic market seems to have played a crucial role in Taiwan before the shift towards export-orientation. It is important to bear in mind that this was hardly intentional. Government policies vis-à-vis the rural society focused on land reforms for political reasons and to secure a transfer of surplus resources to the urban sector. Investments in infrastructure, education, rural credit, fertilisers, marketing and farmers' cooperatives contributed to the building of an institutional structure that was greatly supportive for the domestic market economy. It is highly unlikely, however, that the full extent to which these interventions were to shape the course of development of the economy was to any greater extent foreseen in the early 1950s. This means that the institution-building effects of the policy interventions in agriculture were perhaps more important than the interventions per se.

Taiwan is of course a special case in many respects. Clearly, the equitable distribution of income was not an effect of redistributive policy measures – other than the land reform – and the export economy emerged under conditions of equity; it was not the originator of equity. Income distribution in Taiwan is also much more even than in other economies in the region. However, since relative equity is a characteristic of the Asia-Pacific region at large and we assume that this has something to do with the ways in which the domestic market economy has emerged, the equity issue has to be related to the question of structural change in the agrarian sector in some way or another. Technological improvements in general and, in some cases, land reforms, are likely to have provided important contributions to change in several countries. Reforms and technological improvements have made productivity and incomes rise on larger and middle-sized production units (Adelman 1984).

Most scholars would perhaps agree on the importance of agricultural modern-isation in general, but what is of importance is the actual type of modernisation. Insufficient domestic purchasing power, i.e. the assumption in the export-led model, is associated with one particular type of agrarian modernisation where the agrarian sector supplies the industrial sector with low-cost labour and capital, whereas its role as a market for manufactured goods is negligible. This means that the demand-generating effects of production and income growth in the agrarian sector are taken to be low. Thus, in an export-led economy, industrialisation can take place in a state of agricultural stagnation or even with the agricultural surplus being taxed away. In the Lewis model, the agricultural sector functions as a source of capital accumulation and as a supplier of redundant labour. The growth of the modern sector attracts underemployed labour from the agrarian sector at a low price. Because of low incomes within the agricultural sector, the total income-generating capacity will be insufficient for the sector to serve as a market for manu-factured consumption goods. In consequence, the export sector will have to function as a prime engine and as a leading sector. Growth of domestic demand will occur via multiplier effects only.

The conclusion from this is that growth with equity might be something more than just a descriptive concept. In fact, we suggest that it represents a specific type of economic growth, which may have its roots in the way backwardness in the agricultural sector is reduced in the early phase of industrialisation. If agriculture is left relatively backward, the process of industrialisation is likely to be of a more substitutive type with large income disparities between industry and agriculture. The Philippines is a case in point, but generally it would be fair to say that industrialisation in Southeast Asia has relied far less on agricultural modernisation than was the case in Taiwan, in particular, and Korea. We have already noted that industrialisation in Southeast Asia relies more on exports and the urban–rural income gap remains large, even though there has been a modernisation of agriculture.

If we acknowledge that agriculture was in a state of progress before the land reform, and the rise of domestic purchasing power was a consequence of both these phenomena, then the mechanisms of change are altered in comparison with the standard explanations. The exports then became the engine of growth after the domestic market had matured. One corollary of this reasoning is that an egalitarian society based on a declining agricultural sector (due to its increasing productivity) perhaps is an agent of growth, i.e. growth *because of* equity.

Conclusion

In this chapter we have called into question the use of the concepts of 'export-led growth', 'developmental state' and 'growth with equity' when applied in a policy-choice perspective. While acknowledging the importance of policies, we believe that historical processes cannot be understood by highlighting policy decisions alone. Any causal explanation based on a policy-choice perspective needs to be supplemented by studies of the context of development and change, in which policy decisions are made and policies implemented. Unless that is done, the emphasis on policy choices will be unable to explain fundamental elements in the socio-economic transformation. Outcomes are sometimes *unintended consequences*, and implemented policies are not always as pioneering as policy-makers foresee. Sometimes, good policy intentions produce disasters and, sometimes, unwise choices do not make much difference. At any rate, one cannot judge history from a snapshot without understanding how the picture has evolved. Therefore our critique has centred on some of the methodological and empirical implications of much of the miracle literature (be it either the market-friendly or state-led approach). The methodological objection to the SL approach in its use of the three concepts is that it runs the risk of becoming tautological as well as both taxonomic and teleological. The dynamics and causality of economic change are, in short, missing in this school of thought. The shortcomings of the MF approach are just as serious. They are mostly due to a denial and ignorance of historical evidence. In particular, state interventions, in spite of clear documentation, are simply not accepted and agricultural change and domestic demand are largely disregarded. Hence none of the dominant modes of explanations is able to show how equity, state interventions and export performance are inter-linked causally in the development process.

Without providing a thorough alternative answer ourselves, we suggest that in Northeast Asia, the agricultural transformation, and its equitable implications, formed the basis for subsequent development. When industrialisation deepened and capital scarcity became evident, the state, by controlling national savings, played an important role in channelling capital to investments in the export industries. The rise of SMEs in Taiwan is, however, a sober reminder that these policy measures have their limits. It is also debatable if the Taiwanese and Korean industrialisations actually were export-led, if we by this term mean that exports were the engine of growth. Export-led growth is easier to say than to show. The economies in Southeast Asia have followed another path, partly because they lagged behind in modernising the agricultural sector and partly because other means for industrialisation were available in their take-off period. Changing world market conditions – meaning an easing of the capital constraint – and a relatively weak agricultural transformation – meaning a less developed domestic market – made the developmental state less prominent. The inflow of foreign capital and dependence on export markets thus signified the Southeast Asian story.

The rise of Asia-Pacific is perhaps the most encouraging change in post-World War Two history, not least for the current Third World. But in order to take advantage of these events and learn a useful lesson that can be employed in the formulation of development policies elsewhere, one should be careful not to toss around catchy concepts. The key to success is to be found somewhere out there, but if the policy-choice perspective continues to reign, our search will remain a random walk.

Notes

1 There are alternative ways to characterise the different schools. For instance, the market-friendly approach is sometimes referred to as the 'neoclassical' explanation and the state-led approach is alluded to as the 'revisionist' school. For an overview of the controversy, see Chapter 1.
2 Our aim is not historiographic, i.e. we shall not examine extensive accounts of examples of studies within the different schools of thought. The studies referred to are taken to be leading and representative examples of the two types of explanations. Many of these studies are excellent in their own right, but we shall demonstrate that their explanatory powers are weighed down by their policy-choice perspective.
3 A somewhat less strict expression is export-oriented industrialisation, which, however, also indicates that exports have been a leading sector in the process of industrialisation.
4 Less than 5 per cent of the capital formation emanated from foreign sources throughout the period 1955–85 in both Korea and Taiwan.
5 The revolution in the international financial system since the mid-1980s is totally overlooked and it is not recognised that the ASEAN industrial boom is largely driven by FDI from Northeast Asia. The authors, Jeffrey Sachs and Steven Radelet, must however be given credit for consistency. After the crisis, Sachs and Radelet maintained that there was nothing wrong with the institutional foundation of the Asian economies. This may be at odds with facts, but it is surely consistent with their previous analysis (Radelet and Sachs 1998).
6 The fact that the interventionist structures and policy instruments set up under ISI were captured by non-productive or non-developmental groups is another matter, but this was basically an effect of the ISI strategy, not its source.
7 Productivity rose markedly in the post-1970 period in Malaysia but started from a decidedly higher level than other economies in SEA due to improvements in the pre-1970 period.
8 In recent writings Ranis has taken a different view on this point. He now sides with those who have questioned the notion of export-led growth and suggests that the early phase of industrialisation in Taiwan was agriculture-led (Ranis 1996).

Bibliography

Adelman, I. (1984) 'Beyond export-led growth', *World Development* 12, 9: 937–49.

—— (1998) *Social Development in Korea, 1953–1993* http://are.berkeley.edu/~adelman. Also in Dong-se Cha, Kwang Suk Kim and Dwight H. Perkins (eds) (1997) *The Korean Economy 1945–1995: Performances and Vision for the 21st Century*, Seoul: Korean Development Institute.

Ahuja, V., Bibani, B., Ferreira, F. and Walton, M. (1997) *Everyone's Miracle? – Revisiting Poverty and Inequality in East Asia*, Washington DC: World Bank.

Amsden, A.H. (1989) *Asia's Next Giant: South Korea and Late Industrialization*, New York: Oxford University Press.

—— (1990) 'Third world industrialisation: "Global Fordism" or a new model?', *New Left Review* 182: 5–31.

Asian Development Bank (1997) *Emerging Asia – Changes and Challenges*, Manila: ADB.

Balassa, B. (ed.) (1981) *The Newly Industrializing Countries in The World Economy*, New York: Pergamon Press.

—— (1988) 'The lessons of East Asian development', *Economic Development and Cultural Change* 36, 3: 273–90.

Birdsall, N., Graham, C. and Sabot, R.H. (eds) (1998) *Beyond tradeoffs: market reform and equitable growth in Latin America*, Washington, DC: Brooking Institution Press.

Burmeister, L., Ranis, G. and Wang, M. (2001) 'Group behavior and development: a comparison of farmers' organisations in South Korea and Taiwan', *Economic Growth Center Discussion Paper* No 828, Yale University, New Haven.

Deyo, F. (1987) *The Political Economy of the New Asian Industrialization*, Ithaca: Cornell University Press.

Evans, P. (1995) *Embedded Autonomy: States and Industrial Transformation*, Princeton, NJ: Princeton University Press.

Fei, J.C.H., Ranis, G. and Kuo, S.W.Y. (1979) *Growth With Equity: The Taiwan Case*, Washington, DC: Oxford University Press.

Haggard, S. (1990) *Pathways from the Periphery: The Politics of Growth in the Newly Industrializing Countries*, Ithaca and London: Cornell University Press.

Ho, S.P.S. (1979) *Economic Development of Taiwan 1860–1970*, New Haven: Yale University Press.

Johnson, C. (1982) *MITI and the Japanese Miracle: The Growth of Industrial Policy 1925–1975*, Stanford: Stanford University Press.

—— (1987) 'Political institutions and economic performance: the government–business relationship in Japan, South Korea and Taiwan', in Deyo, F. (ed.) *The Political Economy of the New Asian Industrialism*, Ithaca: Cornell University Press.

Kravis, I. (1970) 'Trade as a handmaiden of growth: similarities between the 19th and 20th centuries', *Economic Journal* 80, 323 (December): 850–72.

Krueger, A. O. (1981) 'Export-led industrial development reconsidered', in Hong, W. and Krause, L. (eds) *Trade and Growth of the Advanced Developing Countries in the Pacific Basin*, Seoul: Korea Development Institute.

Kuznets, P.W. (1988) 'An East Asian model of economic development: Japan, Taiwan, and South Korea', *Economic Development and Cultural Change* 36, 3: 11–43.

Lam, D. and Clark, C. (1994) 'Beyond the developmental state: the cultural roots of "guerrilla capitalism" in Taiwan', *Governance: An International Journal of Policy and Administration* 7, 4: 412–30.

Little, I.M.D (1981) 'The experience and causes of rapid labour-intensive development in Korea, Taiwan Province, Hong Kong, and Singapore and the possibilities of emulation', in Lee, E. (ed.) *Export-Led Industrialisation and Development*, Singapore: Maruzen Asia.

Oshima, H.T. (1987) *Economic Growth in Monsoon Asia*, Tokyo: Tokyo University Press.

Radelet, S. and Sachs, J. (1998) 'The East Asian Financial Crisis: Diagnosis Remedies, Prospects', mimeo, Harvard Institute for International Development.

Ranis, G. (1996) 'The trade–growth nexus in Taiwan's development', Center Discussion Paper No. 758. Economic Growth Center, Yale University.

Riedel, J. (1975) 'The nature and determinants of export-oriented direct foreign investment in a developing country: a case study of Taiwan', *Weltwirtshaftliches Archiv* 111, 3: 505–28.

—— (1988) 'Economic development in East Asia: Doing what comes naturally?', in Hughes (ed.) *Achieving Industrialization in East Asia*, Cambridge: Cambridge University Press.

Rodrik, D. (1994) 'Getting interventions right: how South Korea and Taiwan grew rich', working Paper. NBER Working Paper Series No. 4964.

Wade, R. (1990) *Governing the Market: Economic Theory and the Role of Government in East Asian Industrialization*, Princeton: Princeton University Press.

Weiss, L. and Hobson, J.M. (1995) *States and Economic Development: A Comparative Historical Analysis*, Cambridge: Polity Press.

World Bank (1993) *The East Asian Miracle: Economic Growth and Public Policy*, Washington, DC: Oxford University Press.

8 Education, equality and economic development in Asia-Pacific economies[1]

Anne Booth

Introduction

The literature on the 'Asian miracle' which proliferated in the mid-1990s offered a range of explanations for the remarkable growth record of the Asian 'high performers', (or HPAEs as they have become known) but almost all the contributions agreed on the importance of education (World Bank 1993: 43, Birdsall *et al.* 1995: 481, Campos and Root 1996: 56). These authors pointed to the virtuous circle, which they claimed was found in much of East Asia, where education stimulated growth and growth stimulated education. In addition, they claimed that high rates of investment in education lowered inequality, which in turn further stimulated both economic growth and more investment in education. Furthermore, rapid growth in the HPAEs speeded up the demographic transition which allowed governments greatly to increase the educational budget per student, thereby improving quality of instruction.

There can be little doubt that these views have now become orthodoxy, a canonical tradition which many writers on East Asia (at least until 1997) followed uncritically. Indeed it is now frequently asserted in the literature on educational development that the Asian tigers created a 'new model' a key component of which is 'forging newer, closer links between education, training, and economic growth' (Ashton and Sung 1997: 207). In contrast with the mature industrial economies, especially the UK and the USA, where the educational system is claimed to have developed independently of the needs of the economy, it is argued that in the so-called Asian tigers, 'the relationship between education and economic growth has been much stronger, with the educational system and its output exhibiting a very strong and much closer linkage to the requirements of the economy' (ibid. 207). Cummings (1995: 67) goes so far as to argue that 'the Asian state in seeking to coordinate not only the development but also the utilisation of human resources involves itself in manpower planning and job placement and increasingly in the coordination of science and technology'.

It is not the intention of this chapter to argue that all these assertions are wrong for all the countries categorised by the World Bank as HPAEs, but rather to point out that much of the 'Asian miracle' literature suffers from gross over-generalisation. Findings from a very small number of countries (especially Japan, South Korea and Taiwan) have been assumed also to hold in most of South East Asia, and frequently China as well, often with only the most cursory examination of the statistical record in these countries. Nowhere is this more true than in the discussion of education and its role in the growth process. Because Taiwan and South Korea undeniably 'educated ahead of demand', even at the risk of substantial educated unemployment, it is widely assumed that the fast-growing economies of South East Asia (Singapore, Malaysia, Thailand and Indonesia) did the same.[2] In fact it is very clear that the course of educational development in these four countries has been very different from that in Taiwan and South Korea. Partly this reflects very different colonial legacies, but it also reflects very different government policies towards the role of education in the growth process in the post-independence era, both within South East Asia and between South East and North East Asia.

This chapter reviews these policies for Singapore, Malaysia, Thailand, Indonesia and Vietnam. The first four countries were among the HPAEs whose record has been examined by the World Bank (1993), and by numerous other analysts as well. Vietnam is one of the South East Asian 'transitional' economies which has now largely abandoned central planning and is moving towards market capitalism, with some important consequences for its educational sector. It has joined the Association of Southeast Asian Nations (ASEAN), and, at least until 1997, viewed its more successful ASEAN partner economies as offering useful lessons for its own development strategies. It will be argued below that the accelerated economic growth which has occurred in Vietnam under transition has affected the educational sector in ways which are not entirely positive, and the Vietnamese government would be wise to learn from the mistakes of some of its ASEAN partners before its education system deteriorates to a point which jeopardises its future growth.

But before we examine country case studies, it is useful to look at the data on secondary and tertiary enrolments, and on educational expenditure, for a group of Asian economies (Table 8.1). It is clear that there is no strong relationship between per capita GDP and enrolments; although Singapore had a higher per capita GDP in 1996 than either South Korea or Taiwan, both secondary and tertiary enrolments were lower.[3] Thailand stands out as having a rather low secondary enrolment ratio for its level of income; it was lower than China's in 1996. Thailand, Malaysia, and Indonesia all had lower secondary enrolments in 1996 than Taiwan and South Korea had achieved in 1980, although both Malaysia's and Thailand's per capita GDP in the mid-1990s was higher than that of South Korea in 1980.[4] Vietnam stands out as the only country to experience a fall in secondary enrolment rates over the 1980s. There is also a wide variation in government expenditure as a proportion of GDP with Indonesia, China and Vietnam all having markedly lower ratios than the other countries in 1995.

Singapore

Singapore is often considered, along with South Korea and Taiwan, to exemplify the model of the densely populated, resource-poor Asian economy which achieves rapid and sustained economic growth through heavy investment in education and

Table 8.1 Educational indicators for fast-growing Asian economies, 1980–96

Country[a]	Gross secondary enrolment ratio		Tertiary students per 100,000 people		Government education expenditures as % GDP	
	1980	1996	1980	1996	1980	1995
Singapore	58	72	963	2,722	2.8	3.0
Taiwan	80	96[b]	2,035	3,160	3.6	5.5
South Korea	78	102	1,698	5,609	3.7	3.7
Malaysia	48	62	419	971[c]	6.0	5.2
Thailand	29	57	1,284	2,096[d]	3.4	4.1
Indonesia	29	48[c]	367	1,167[d]	n.a	2.8[e]
China	46	71	166	473	2.5	2.3
Vietnam	42	41[c]	214	404[d]	n.a	2.7[f]

Sources: *UNESCO Statistical Yearbook 1998*; with additional data on Taiwan from the *Taiwan Statistical Yearbook*, 1995, Tables 47, 53, and *Taiwan Statistical Data Book*, various issues.

Notes:
a Ranked in order of per capita GDP, 1992
b Data refer to 1992
c Data refer to 1994
d Data refer to 1995
e Data are taken from World Bank (1998)
f Data refer to 1993

training. The Singapore government over the years has done much to foster this image, and the official rhetoric about the Singapore model is replete with references to the importance of human resource development, and the pursuit of excellence in education. But at the same time, government ministers have always been aware of the formidable challenges which education policy in the island republic must confront. A government report published in 1979 stated the key problems as follows:

> Most school children are taught in two languages – English and Mandarin. 85 per cent of them do not speak either of these languages at home. Our system is largely modelled on the British pattern but the social and demographic background could hardly be more dissimilar. If, as a result of a world calamity, children in England were taught Russian and Mandarin, while they continued to speak English at home, the British education system would run into some of the problems which have been plaguing the schools in Singapore and the Ministry of Education.
>
> Goh 1979: 1-1

The report went on to emphasise that the decades of the 1960s and 1970s had seen a steady decline in numbers of children enrolled in the Chinese stream schools in Singapore and an increase in numbers enrolled in schools where English was the medium of instruction. This reflected widespread parental conviction that fluency in English was crucial in gaining access to well paying jobs. However, many children from backgrounds where English was not spoken faced enormous difficulties in the English stream schools, difficulties which were aggravated by teachers who were themselves often inadequately trained and faced large classes. Surveys carried out by the Ministry of Defence in the mid-1970s found that, of those recruits who had been to English medium schools but who had not passed O levels, only 11 per cent had retained reasonable fluency in English. The majority of students were not successful in passing O level examinations. Some 65 per cent of children entering first year primary school did not succeed in passing at least three O levels, and over one-third did not pass the primary school leaving examination. Out of each cohort of 1,000 entering primary school in the early 1970s, only 137 succeeded in completing senior high school; in Taiwan the comparable figure was 514 while in Japan it was 926 (Goh 1979: Annex 3).

Of course it could be argued that in ethnically homogeneous countries such as Taiwan and Japan, children progressed through a school system where they were taught in the language they used at home, and where they did not have to grapple with instruction in a foreign language. But the consequences of the Singapore system, with its high failure and low continuation rates, for the skill level of the labour force were by the 1970s already serious. In 1974, less than 30 per cent of the labour force had completed secondary schooling; for males the percentage was slightly lower (Booth 1999b: Table 2). This could be compared with South Korea where in 1974 well over 40 per cent of the male labour force had completed secondary schooling (Table 2). In 1974 per capita GDP was over twice as high in Singapore as in South Korea. Part of the explanation for the poor educational level of the Singapore labour force in the 1970s was the extremely limited access to education provided by the colonial government. But since self-government was achieved in 1959, the pace of educational expansion, especially at the post-primary levels, was slow. Partly this reflected the government's preoccupation with physical infrastructure development, including ambitious housing development schemes. But in addition, education development was dominated by a narrow preoccupation with manpower-planning projections, underlying which was a fear of the politically destabilising effects of unemployed high school and college graduates.[5]

The recommendations of the Goh report included a compulsory nine-year cycle for all children, and streaming of children so that the groups of differing ability could be taught at a pace which suited their abilities. High drop-out rates among the less bright children were to be addressed by providing a vocational route through the system (Ashton, Green, James and Sung 1999: 38). But the government continued to be concerned about the links between education and the needs of the labour market, especially after the economy slowed sharply in the mid-1980s. Enrolment growth over the 1970s at both the lower secondary and the academic upper secondary levels was very slow in comparison with most other parts of the region (Table 8.3). Although part of this slow growth could be attributed to demographic change, low continuation rates were also to blame. A government report on future options for the economy published in 1986 stressed the continuing low level of education among the Singapore workforce; in 1979 it was still the case that 60 per cent had at most completed primary school, and only 3 per cent had tertiary qualifications (Republic of Singapore 1986: 113). Attention was drawn to the sharp disparities between Singaporean educational achievement and that of Japan, the USA and Taiwan. An academic analysis of policy options for the Singapore economy published in 1988 also drew attention to the failings of the education system and argued that improving both the quality and quantity of educated people in the Singapore workforce was 'now an urgent task because there has been an underinvestment in both formal and informal education' (Lim *et al.* 1988: 167).

The Singapore government was not slow to grasp the lessons of these and other studies, and educational opportunities have certainly expanded in Singapore since the mid-1980s, especially at the upper secondary, vocational and tertiary levels (Table 8.3). In addition the rapid demographic transition in the island republic has meant lower numbers of children coming into the school system, especially over the 1980s, so more resources can be spent per pupil. Yet secondary enrolment rates by the early 1990s were still well below those in South Korea and Taiwan (Table 8.1), and as late as 1997, almost 25 per cent of the labour force still had, at most, only completed primary education (Booth 1999b: Table 2). The 2000 Population Census reported that 31.7 per cent of the resident non-student population over the age of 15 had either no educational qualifications or at most primary schooling (Lee 2001: 38).

In the mid-1990s, academic studies were still drawing attention to the very low level of educational attainment in the population compared with Western countries with similar levels of per capita GDP (Chen 1996: 84–5). Cheah (1997: 131–2) pointed out that the 'bias against tertiary education was sustained for too long' and that only in the 1990s was a second university formally established. In the mid-1990s Singapore still lagged well behind Japan, the USA and much of West Europe in terms of numbers of research scientists and engineers per capita and per member of the labour force. Most workers with low educational attainment were in low-paying jobs with limited opportunity for job progression. Many were in the older age groups, and there are now fears that if they are made redundant from manufacturing employment, they will find it difficult to get alternative employment, except at very low rates of pay. This implies that when they retire they will have inadequate savings and pensions entitlements to finance their old age.[6] The consequences of this for social inequalities are examined further below.

It can of course be pointed out that Singapore's relatively weak educational achievement has not stopped the economy growing very rapidly over almost four decades. This is obviously true, but in the early phase of Singapore's economic development, much of the industrial development was labour-intensive and demanded relatively unskilled workers.[7] Industrial technology and often the skilled labour to manage it were provided by multinational companies locating in Singapore. Many dropouts from the education system were absorbed in unskilled service sector jobs. Both the government and academic analysts are now acutely aware that this type of economic growth is not sustainable, and that heavy investment in human resource development will be crucial for Singapore's future. But this awareness has developed slowly, many would argue far too slowly, in response to changes in the labour market, and to a growing appreciation on the part of the authorities of the experience of other fast-growing Asian economies. It certainly cannot be argued that the Singapore government has led the market in investing in the development of human resources.[8] In that sense it has clearly played a very different role from governments in South Korea and Taiwan; indeed I will argue below that it has played a very different role from the government of its near neighbour, Malaysia.

Malaysia

Rudner (1994: 285) has characterised British colonial educational policy in the Federated Malay States (FMS) as seeking 'to strike a balance between the provision of sufficient English schooling to satisfy urban manpower and colonial administrative needs, while avoiding unwanted social changes among the local population'. Both the British colonial authorities and the Malay aristocratic elites were concerned that exposing the mass of the Malay peasantry to English education would make them discontent with their traditional rural lifestyles, and encourage them to drift to the cities where they would inevitably form an economic underclass. While urban schools catering largely for Chinese, Indian and Eurasian children expanded with both government and private finance, rural education for the Malays was

Table 8.2 Percentage distribution of the labour force by educational attainment

	Male	Female
South Korea 1974		
No schooling	12.9	28.5
Primary	41.0	49.9
Secondary	38.5	20.0
College/University	7.6	1.6
Total	100.0	100.0
Thailand 1981		
No schooling	5.6	10.4
Primary	82.4	82.4
Secondary	8.3	4.2
College/University	3.8	2.9
Total	100.0	100.0
Indonesia 1994		
No schooling	7.5	16.4
Primary	59.6	59.9
Secondary	29.7	21.1
College/University	3.2	2.6
Total	100.0	100.0

Source: South Korea: *1974 Special Labour Force Survey Report* (Bureau of Statistics, Economic Planning Board); Thailand: *Report of the Labour Force Survey Round 2* (Bangkok: National Statsitical Office); Indonesia: *Labour Force Situation in Indonesia 1994* (Jakarta: Central Bureau of Statistics).

Table 8.3 Annual average rates of growth of lower and upper secondary enrolments, 1970–92

Country	Lower secondary		Academic upper secondary		Vocational upper secondary	
	1970–80	1980–92	1970–80	1980–92	1970–80	1980–92
Thailand	9.4	3.6	9.4	−0.3	n.a	0.4
Malaysia	6.9	1.4	9.9	3.2	13.7	7.8
Singapore	0.8	n.a	0.8	5.3	6.6	5.4
Indonesia	9.8	4.0 (4.5)	11.0	6.7 (6.9)	n.a	−5.4
Vietnam	n.a	−0.5	n.a	−2.9	n.a	−5.4
China	7.1	−0.4	10.7	−0.4	35.5	6.3
Taiwan	3.0	0.8	−0.5	1.8	6.6	2.4
South Korea	5.8	−1.2	12.2	3.5	9.5	−0.1

Sources: Thailand: Data from Bureau of Educational Policy and Planning, Ministry of Education. Estimates refer to 1972–81 and 1981–93 respectively. For 1972–81 data refer to all secondary schools. Malaysia: Data from *Mid-term Reviews* of the Second, Third, Fourth, Fifth and Sixth Malaysia Plans. There are gaps for some years which were filled by interpolation. After 1980 data were also taken from *Education Statistics of Malaysia* (annual; Educational Planning and Research Division, Ministry of Education).
Singapore: Data from *Economic and Social Statistics of Singapore, 1960-82, Statistical Yearbooks of Singapore*, various issues. Up to 1980 data refer to all academic high schools; from 1981 to 1991 academic high schools and pre-university high schools are combined. Data for 1992 not available.
Indonesia: Data from *Lampiran Pidato Kenegaraan*, various issues. They refer to government and government-assisted schools only; Islamic schools are omitted. Figures in brackets for 1980–92 refer to both government and private, including religious, schools.
Vietnam. Data are from World Bank (1997), Table 2.3 and refer to 1984/5 to 1994/5.
China: Data from *China Statistical Yearbook*, various issues.
Taiwan: Data from *Educational Statistics of the Republic of China, 1993*.
South Korea: *Education in Korea*, various issues.

Notes:
In most cases growth rates are estimated by fitting a semi-log function to the data. Unless othrewise noted data refer to both government and private schools.

restricted to vernacular instruction designed to make them better farmers and fishermen, more aware of the world around them but still content with their rural way of life. Although enrolments in Malay vernacular schools increased rapidly, by the late 1930s only about 20 per cent of eligible children were attending school; many parents could not see the point of education which did not lead to social mobility (Snodgrass 1980: 237–43, Rudner 1994: 289–90).

When the Federation of Malaysia was formed and granted full independence from Britain in 1963, the educational legacy was thus highly inequitable in terms of race, class and place of residence. Although, in the post-war years, primary schooling for Malays in the vernacular had greatly expanded, it remained very much second-class education, and it was often very difficult for a Malay primary graduate to continue to secondary and tertiary education. The influential Razak Report of 1956 advocated universal primary education and unification of the education system, with Malay/English bilingualism as the ultimate goal (Snodgrass

1980: 245). Universal primary education was seen as the easier of these two objectives, and considerable progress was made in the 1960s; bilingualism required more resources and was opposed by both Chinese and Indian minorities. The result was that English remained the medium of instruction in many secondary schools and in the universities, and in 1970 when the New Economic Policy (NEP) was adopted, Malays were still only a minority in higher education.[9] A crucial aim of the NEP was to sever the link between ethnicity and post-primary education and make access to secondary schools and universities available to all on the basis of ability.

Affirmative action was needed to accelerate Malay enrolments at upper secondary and tertiary levels and, after the 1969 riots, the government made it clear that a number of measures would be adopted to facilitate increased Malay progression through the education system. The most controversial was the adoption of Malay language instruction at all levels as this inevitably discriminated against non-Malays. The more affluent sent their children to Western Europe, the USA, Canada and Australia for secondary and tertiary education, but many non-Malays from less wealthy families found their progress blocked both by the language requirements and by stringent ethnic quotas. They had little choice but to drop out or seek tertiary qualifications in low-cost countries such as India or Taiwan, although degrees from these countries were often not recognised in Malaysia (Snodgrass 1998: 176).

Enrolments of Malays at the secondary and tertiary levels did increase rapidly and, by 1985, 68 per cent of upper secondary and 63 per cent of degree enrolments were Malay, slightly higher figures than the population share (Government of Malaysia 1989: Table 13.2). Although rates of growth of enrolments at the lower and upper secondary levels slowed in the 1980s, compared with the rapid growth of the 1970s, gross secondary enrolments had reached 62 per cent in 1996, which was a higher percentage than that attained by Singapore in 1980, although real per capita GDP in Malaysia in the mid-1990s was still below that reached in Singapore in 1980 (Tables 8.1 and 8.3). But gross secondary enrolment ratios in 1996 were still below those in Taiwan and South Korea in 1980, although by the mid-1990s Malaysia's per capita national income was well above that of both South Korea and Taiwan in 1980. Government expenditure on education was over 5 per cent of GDP in Malaysia from the early 1970s right through until the late 1990s, a higher percentage than in most other parts of Asia (Table 8.1, see also Khoman 1993: 344).

By the latter part of the 1980s, the impact of the expansion in education on the labour force data was very obvious. In 1988 when per capita GDP was still rather lower than the level Singapore had attained in 1974, the proportion of the labour force with, at most, primary schooling was substantially lower (Booth 1999b: Table 5). For male workers the proportion with, at most, primary education was lower than in South Korea in 1974. The proportion of women in the labour force with, at most, primary education was considerably higher than for men, but still much lower than in Singapore in 1974 (Booth 1999b: Table 5). A comparison of Malaysian educational progress from 1970 to 1990 with that of Singapore does not, in my view, support the rather simplistic argument that resource-rich countries such as Malaysia neglect human resource development, and do not invest in education to the same extent as the resource-poor countries.[10] After 1970 the Malaysian government was determined to increase Malay enrolments in secondary and tertiary education, even if the economic rationale for increased investment in education, especially at the tertiary level, did not at the time appear compelling.[11] Over the years from 1970 to 1995, government expenditure on education seldom fell below 5 per cent of GNP, and in the mid-1980s was over 6 per cent.[12]

But doubts have been expressed about the cost-effectiveness of such high levels of government expenditure on education. Foreign observers such as Snodgrass (1998: 178) have pointed out that although the Malaysian government has consistently spent a high percentage of GDP on education since the early 1970s, this 'has not necessarily led to superior educational outcomes' compared to countries such as South Korea and Taiwan. Very large amounts of money have been spent on institutions which are targeted entirely to the Malay population and are intended to allow them to overcome perceived disadvantages in the educational system. Yet secondary and tertiary enrolments are not exceptionally high, even by ASEAN standards, and there is little evidence that student learning outcomes are high in international terms. While the Malaysian experiment in affirmative action can be defended on the grounds that, without it, social tensions would have become dangerously high and could even have led to violence and civil war, there can be little doubt that, from an educational point of view, it has been an expensive experiment, and the results have been achieved at high cost.

There was also concern that the rapid expansion of educational opportunities for the Malay population would not be matched by a commensurate growth in job opportunities outside agriculture, leading to the creation of an unemployed under-class. In fact, over the boom years from the mid-1980s to 1996, the Malaysian economy was able to absorb almost all the educated people which the expanded secondary and tertiary system turned out. Government expenditure on education was consistently higher than in many other Asian countries until the mid-1990s. The reasons for this emphasis on education could be found in the determination of the Malay-dominated ruling coalition to erase the sharp distinctions in educational attainment and employment by ethnic group which were a legacy of colonial policies and which remained a potent source of discontent for the Malay majority in the post-independence era. By the early 1990s, 'the identification of race or ethnicity with economic function or occupation and sectoral activity had been generally reduced', although not completely eliminated (Gomez and Jomo 1997: 166). Indigenous Malays were still under-represented, and Chinese over-represented, in administrative and managerial occupations in 1995, which demonstrates the lags that exist between changes in educational achievement and changes in labour force structure.

In spite of the expansion in numbers in the secondary system, which has continued right up until the latter part of the 1990s, gross secondary enrolment ratios in 1996 were still below those attained by South Korea and Taiwan in 1980. In addition, tertiary enrolments were low in comparison with many other Asian countries. In 1996 there were fewer than 1,000 tertiary students per 100,000 people in Malaysia compared with over 2,000 in Thailand (Table 8.1). It can be argued that these comparative figures are distorted in that a much larger proportion of young Malaysians study abroad. That is certainly true; if we allow for the 50,000 or so Malaysian students studying abroad in 1995 and the smaller number (about 6,100) in private tertiary institutions in Malaysia, there were 1,143 students enrolled in tertiary institutions per 100,000 people in 1995 (Government of Malaysia 1999: Table 4-5). But even this figure is still well below those reached in Thailand, Taiwan and South Korea in 1980, although the Thai figures are inflated by the high enrolments in the two open universities.

The Malaysian government is now aware of the need to expand domestic provision of tertiary education, especially as the sharp depreciation of the ringgit in 1997–8 greatly increased the cost of studying abroad. Government projections indicate that numbers studying for diploma courses in domestic tertiary institutions will almost double between 1995 and 2000, while those studying for degree courses will increase by 127 per cent (Government of Malaysia 1999: Table 4-5). In the past the government could justify its cautious approach to the expansion of tertiary numbers, especially in the private sector, by the need to maintain quality. Certainly it can be argued that the Malaysian tertiary sector has not experienced the rapid expansion of low-quality diploma mills of the type which are found in Thailand, the Philippines and Indonesia, and indeed in Japan and South Korea as well. But the expansion planned for the next decade can probably only be achieved at the cost of some decline in quality, as qualified teachers are in short supply, as are other facilities including libraries and laboratories.

Thailand

Although Thailand was never colonised by a Western power, the Thai government was slow to expand access to education and in the early years of the twentieth century the vast majority of the population was illiterate (Feeny 1998: Table 13.1). Universal primary education was adopted as an ideal in the 1920s, and after the 1932 revolution pursued with some vigour by the government, although little progress was made in rural areas (Phongpaichit and Baker 1995: 368). But literacy rates did increase, especially for males, who had access to some education in monasteries, and by 1947 it was estimated that about two-thirds of the male population and 40 per cent of women were literate. After 1950 primary enrolments in the secular education system increased rapidly, and by 1970, the great majority of children in the 7–12 cohort were in school (Wilson 1983: Table V-2, World Bank 1994: 217). But at the secondary level, enrolments were extremely low; there were virtually no secondary schools outside Bangkok and a few large provincial towns until the 1960s, and even when provision expanded in the 1970s and 1980s, 'cost and location still made it difficult for a villager to climb the educational pyramid any higher than the primary level' (Phongpaichit and Baker 1995: 369). The rapid growth in enrolments over the 1970s was almost entirely in urban areas. The effect on the educational attainment of the labour force was obvious; in 1981, while only 6 per cent of the male labour force and 10 per cent of the female labour force had had no formal education, only a meagre 12 per cent (7 per cent for female workers) had post-primary education (Table 8.2). The contrast with South Korea in 1974 was stark (in 1981 Thai per capita GDP was about the same as in South Korea in 1974).

Over the 1980s, secondary enrolment growth fell sharply compared with the 1970s, and by the latter part of the 1980s, access to education had become a highly controversial issue in discussions of public policy in Thailand. Academics and independent think-tanks such as the Thai Development Research Institute stressed the very low level of educational attainment of the labour force, in comparison not just with Taiwan and South Korea but also with Thailand's poorer neighbours such as the Philippines and Indonesia (Myers and Sussangkarn 1992: 14, Khoman 1993: 329–30). Cross-country regressions showed that Thailand was well below the trend line relating per capita GDP to post-primary enrolments; in other words, enrolments were much lower than for other countries at similar levels of per capita GDP. By the early 1990s there were growing signs that the poor level of education, especially among new entrants to the labour force, was creating serious economic problems (Bello *et al.* 1998: 56–7). Employers in both manufacturing industry and the modern service sector complained that new recruits had to be given substantial remedial training, especially in numeracy and technical skills, before they could operate modern equipment. In the increasingly tight labour market of the early 1990s, workers who had acquired basic skills were often poached by rivals, making firms increasingly reluctant to invest in on-the-job training. As a result of skill shortages, industries which were being priced out of markets for labour-intensive manufactures, such as garments and footwear, found it difficult to move into medium-technology sectors, especially for export. In 1996 after a decade of rapid growth, exports hardly expanded at all (Warr 1998: 50–8).

Since the early 1990s, the issue of education and its contribution to the development process has been the subject of considerable national debate in Thailand. The need for Thailand to develop into a more knowledge-based economy with a more skilled and adaptable labour force is stressed in a number of official government statements. The low continuation rates into upper secondary and tertiary education, especially in scientific and technical disciplines, and the poor rating of Thai students in international achievement tests in science and mathematics is emphasised by academic commentators, as is the need for better pay and conditions for teachers (Parkay *et al.* 1999). Certainly there has been a marked increase in the proportion of young people in the lower secondary and upper secondary age groups who are staying on in school, and the government seems determined to bring about further increases in secondary enrolment ratios (Table 8.4). Since the crisis, government educational expenditure has increased as a share of the total government budget, and in 2000 it amounted to 4 per cent of GDP, a much higher percentage than in any year between 1991 and 1996 (Ministry of Education 1999: 81).

It is likely that the severe economic downturn in 1997–8 has made many parents in Thailand more aware of the importance of educating their children so that they can compete successfully in a much tougher labour market. When jobs for

Table 8.4 Secondary enrolments in Thailand, 1983–96 (thousands)

Year	Lower secondary		Upper secondary	
1987	1,217	(32.6)	893	(24.2)
1988	1,221	(32.8)	862	(23.4)
1989	1,282	(34.4)	837	(22.7)
1990	1,394	(37.2)	834	(22.5)
1991	1,570	(41.4)	879	(23.6)
1992	1,772	(46.8)	945	(25.3)
1993	1,991	(53.4)	1,056	(28.2)
1994	2,200	(59.7)	1,185	(31.5)
1995	2,363	(64.4)	1,321	(35.3)
1996	2,445	(66.0)	1,482	(40.2)
1997	2,463	(66.4)	1,635	(44.7)
1998	2,427	(66.8)	1,680	(45.9)

Source: Bureau of Educational Policy and Planning, Office of the Permanent Secretary, Ministry of Education.

Note:
Figures in brackets refer to enrolments as a percentage of the numbers of children in the relevant age cohorts.

young school leavers with only a primary certificate were plentiful, there was little incentive for parents to keep children in school to complete the secondary cycle. But now there are fewer employment opportunities for new entrants to the labour force and employers are more demanding in terms of educational qualifications. At the same time, the more difficult economic climate has encouraged many in government and in the NGO community to see the education system as a means of inculcating 'Thai' values in order to preserve national unity (Witte 2000). The old laissez-faire approach to educational expansion now has few supporters, either among politicians or in the wider community.

Indonesia

Indonesia emerged into the post-independence era with probably the poorest educational legacy of any country in South East Asia. The Dutch had expanded vernacular schooling for the indigenous population in the inter-war years, but for many children their only educational experience was in an Islamic school where almost all the teaching was religious. Access to secondary and tertiary education was extremely limited for indigenous Indonesians (Booth 1998: 268ff.). In spite of the efforts made in the early post-independence years to increase enrolments at all levels, by the late 1960s it was estimated that only about 50 per cent of children between 7 and 12 were in primary schools, and enrolments rates at the post-primary level were much lower.

It was only in the early 1970s, when the oil boom led to greatly expanded government revenues, that the government increased the allocation of resources to the educational sector. From the early 1970s to the latter part of the 1980s, enrolments at both the primary and the secondary levels increased rapidly; indeed, over the 1970s enrolment growth in Indonesia at both the lower and the upper secondary levels was among the fastest in Asia (Table 8.3). By the latter part of the 1980s, the government was able to claim universal primary education, and gross enrolment rates at the lower secondary level of around 55 per cent (in 1987–8). Gross enrolment rates at the upper secondary level in 1987–8 were around 35 per cent (Government of Indonesia 1993: Chapter XVI). Government expenditure on education also increased rapidly in the decade until 1985; it amounted to 4.1 per cent of GDP in 1985–6, although it fell thereafter (World Bank 1998: 148).

In quantitative terms the achievements of the 1970s and 1980s were certainly impressive and, as in the case of Malaysia, do not confirm the argument that resource-rich countries neglect education. In fact it was the increasing revenues from petroleum exports which permitted the rapid growth in government expenditures on education during the fifteen years from 1974 to 1989. But by the early 1990s there was much evidence of serious problems in the Indonesian education sector. Over the fifth five-year plan (1989–94), numbers enrolled in both lower secondary and academic upper secondary schools actually contracted, so that enrolment ratios were lower by 1993 than they had been in the late 1980s (Booth 1994: Table 14). In addition, it was clear by 1990 that universal primary education had not been attained; in 1990 it was estimated officially that only about 90 per cent of children between 7 and 12 were attending school. In more remote parts of the archipelago the percentage was much lower (Booth 1994: 26–36).

The government reacted to the disappointing figures of the early 1990s with a pledge to achieve universal education over a nine-year cycle by the end of the first decade of the twenty-first century. Crude participation rates in the lower secondary system were to increase by steps until they reached 87 per cent by 2004 (Jones and Hagul 2001: 213). This would involve an expansion in numbers at the lower secondary level of close to two million students. To accommodate an increase of this magnitide it was estimated that some 45,000 new classrooms would be needed, and tens of thousands of new teachers would have to be recruited and trained. Unfortunately the Soeharto government in its final phase proved unwilling to increase budgetary expenditure on education; in fact it had fallen somewhat as a percentage of GDP since the mid-1980s, and by 1991–2 was 2.7 per cent of GDP (World Bank 1998: 148). Although enrolment rates did increase after 1993 at both the lower and upper secondary levels, by 1997–8 it was estimated that only about 45 per cent of youths aged between 13 and 15 were in lower secondary education (Government of Indonesia 1998: Table XVIII-3).

As in Thailand, there was much evidence that in Indonesia in the early 1990s many parents either could not afford the paid-out costs of keeping a child in secondary education, or if they could, they were unwilling to incur the expenditure because they did not see the benefits in terms of entry into better remunerated or more prestigious occupations.[13] Many young people with completed primary education were able to find employment in jobs such as construction and manufacturing, and staying on to complete the lower, or even upper, secondary cycle did not necessarily mean that they would be able to get more highly prized jobs as white collar workers. But at the same time, social rates of return estimates for Indonesia indicated that investment in lower secondary education yielded high returns (14 per cent in 1989), and indeed some experts were arguing that the government was underinvesting in education and devoting a disproportionate share of the government investment budget to physical infrastructure (MacMahon and Boediono 1992: Table 7, Boediono 1994).

Numbers in higher education in Indonesia have been growing rapidly since the 1980s, with much of the expansion coming from enrolments in private institutions. There has been much criticism that this expansion has been at the expense of quality and that many of the private universities are simply low-quality diploma mills, catering to the demand for paper qualifications so that graduates can get at least a place in the queue for white collar employment. The evidence from labour force surveys shows that, even before the financial crisis and severe economic downturn of 1997–8, unemployment rates for men and women in urban areas between the ages of 20 and 30 with tertiary qualifications were very high (Manning and Junankar 1998: 60–1). This was in part attributed to rather rigid and inflexible markets for white collar workers; once people find such jobs they tend to stick in them. But in addition there was much criticism from the employer side that the quality of university graduates in Indonesia was extremely poor and that most of them required months or even years of on-the-job training before they could contribute much to output. In addition, as the labour market for particular categories of skilled worker tightened, there was evidence of increased poaching which made employers reluctant to invest in long periods of on-the-job training.

Given the magnitude of the growth collapse in Indonesia in 1998–9, it was to be expected that the problem of unemployment among young upper secondary and tertiary graduates would worsen. In 1999, there were almost three million people with upper secondary and tertiary qualifications between the ages of 15 and 30 who reported themselves as currently unemployed and seeking work; by 2001 the number had dropped only slightly to 2.9 million (Central Board of Statistics 2000: Table 29.9 and 2002: Table 29.5). But in spite of dire predictions that the economic crisis would lead to mass withdrawals of pupils from schools, the available evidence indicates that age-specific enrolment rates do not appear to have declined between 1996–7 and 1998–9 even for the poorest quintile of the population (Jones and Hagul 2001: Table 2). The efforts of the government to provide financial support for schools and students seemed to have prevented large-scale dropouts, although there can be little doubt that the economic crisis has delayed the achievement of universal nine-year education.

The problem of poor quality remains serious.[14] Indonesian teachers are often poorly trained, especially in maths and science subjects. The curriculum is overloaded and unintegrated. There is very little funding for non-salary costs, and many schools suffer from a serious shortage of textbooks and other teaching aids. Especially at the lower levels, many children spend only two or three hours in school per day. Assessment procedures are often unsatisfactory, and fail to encourage individual initiative and clear oral and written expression. A sustained improvement in quality can only be achieved with a much greater commitment of government funding. This would allow higher salaries to be paid to teachers, school buildings to be repaired and extended, and more teaching aids to be provided. Under the new decentralisation reforms, primary and secondary education will be the responsibility of districts. How they will cope with, and fund, the education sector remains to be seen.

Vietnam

In French Indochina, even more than in most other parts of South East Asia in the era of European colonialism, only a very small number of children were given access to post-primary education in the language of the colonial power (Furnivall 1943: 111). After the country was partitioned in 1954, the northern economy was centrally planned, with a minimal role for the market in allocating resources. This model was imposed on the south after reunification in 1975 with, at best, partial success, and by the mid-1980s the government, motivated in part by the Chinese example, decided to abandon central planning and move towards a market economy while at the same time opening the economy to foreign investment and to greater participation in international trade.

In 1980, after reunification but before the implementation of market reforms, primary and secondary enrolments were very high in Vietnam, indeed amazingly high given the country's low per capita GDP. At the primary level, 95 per cent of children aged between 7 and 12 were in primary school, a higher ratio than, for example, Brunei, although per capita income was vastly higher there (UNESCO 1996: 132). At the secondary level, gross enrolment ratios in 1980 were considerably higher than in Indonesia or Thailand (Table 8.1). These data of course may well have been overstated, but it does seem clear that in the latter part of the 1980s and early 1990s, enrolments at the lower and upper secondary levels declined in absolute terms (Table 8.3, see also World Bank 1997: 14). Given that numbers of children in school-age groups were growing rapidly, the enrolment ratios fell at the secondary level, and although there was some recovery in enrolments by the mid-1990s, the gross secondary enrolment ratio in 1994 was still below that achieved in 1980. Why did this happen? Certainly the economic restructuring which began in the mid-1980s under the rubric 'doi moi' did lead to increases in the costs of school attendance, while at the same time many teachers, especialy those with degrees in foreign languages, maths and science found that they could get far more lucrative employment in the burgeoning private sector. In addition, many teachers were forced into moonlighting in other occupations to supplement inadequate official salaries (Fforde and de Vylder 1996: 230–3).

As in other parts of the region, parents saw little point in making a financial sacrifice to keep their children in poorly staffed and equipped secondary schools when the rewards in terms of access to better jobs appeared so uncertain.[15] In addition, the return to family farming meant that most rural households needed the labour of their teenage children on the farm (Booth 1997: 245–7, Glewwe and Jacoby 1998: 226). Moock (1999: 97) points out that the restructuring of the education system which took place in 1989 added an extra year to the lower secondary cycle in the north, and this 'probably dampened demand for upper secondary level education'. In addition the government ended its automatic, guarantee of public sector jobs for upper secondary and tertiary graduates, which would have deterred households from investing in these levels of education for their offspring.

In spite of the high enrolment ratios of the late 1970s and early 1980s, the Vietnamese labour force at the end of the 1980s was not especially skilled. The 1989 census data for Vietnam indicated that 48.5 per cent of the labour force in Vietnam had either no education or, at most, incomplete primary schooling. A further 28.7 per cent had completed primary and only 23 per cent secondary education or above. Even this level of education was greater than would be expected given the low per capita GDP, and if we compare the Vietnamese data with those from Thailand in 1990 we see that an even lower proportion of the Thai labour force had more than primary education, although a much greater proportion had completed primary school (Booth 1997: Table 6). In 1990 per capita GDP in Thailand was several times that of Vietnam. But at the same time it was clear that by the early 1990s the Vietnamese education system was under enormous strain, and massive resources would be required to improve both the quantity and the quality of its output.

The investigation by Glewwe and Jacoby (1998) into the causes of the enrolment decline in Vietnam after the transition found that the decline occurred across all five income quintiles, although by 1992 enrolments of young people in the 12–17 age group in the highest two income quintiles appeared to be on the upturn, while enrolments in the poorest three income quintiles were still on a downward trend. It is clear from recent studies that in Vietnam, as in many other parts of Asia, household income is an important determinant of the probability that a child will enter secondary school and complete the cycle. Behrman and Knowles (1999: 225) in their analysis of data from a 1996 household survey found that 'children from higher income households have a considerable advantage in schooling over children from lower income households'. They point out that although the government policy was to reduce or abolish fees for children from lower-income households, these exemptions appeared to be more effective at the primary level, where in fact they applied to all children. In addition fees were only a small fraction (around 7 per cent) of all school-related household expenses. This point was also stressed by Glewwe and Jacoby (1998: 216) who conclude that reducing or abolishing fees will not necessarily make a large difference to the total costs of schooling for many households.

By the mid-1990s, the Vietnamese government was wrestling with the same problems of achieving both greater equality and greater efficiency in the education system as were several of its ASEAN neighbours, but with fewer budgetary resources to devote to their solution. In 1993, public expenditure on education amounted to less than 3 per cent of GDP (Table 8.1). In addition, Vietnam has not yet achieved fertility declines of similar magnitudes to those experienced in Thailand and in many parts of Indonesia, so that numbers of children entering the educational system will continue to grow for some years to come. It seems inevitable that reliance on private finance, already high by the early 1990s, will continue to grow, especially at the upper secondary and tertiary levels (Moock 1999: 103). This of course means that unless the government can target scholarships to bright children from poorer backgrounds, the education system in Vietnam will become a vehicle for perpetuating social inequalities rather than ameliorating them.

Future challenges for education policies in ASEAN

The main purpose of this chapter has been to argue that the four HPAEs in South East Asia, and Vietnam, the largest of the ASEAN transitional economies, have all followed different education policies over the decades of rapid growth since the 1960s. These reflect in part their different colonial legacies, and in part the different attitudes of their governments to the role of education in the growth process. Although both the Taiwanese and South Korean experiences have been influential in South East Asia, as in other parts of the world, there is little evidence that educational development in Indonesia, Thailand, Malaysia and Singapore has followed either the Taiwanese or the South Korean path. Certainly the experience of these two countries has been much cited, especially by educational reformers, but usually in order to point out the lower level of educational attainment prevailing in, for example, Singapore or Thailand compared with either South Korea or Taiwan when these countries had similar levels of per capita GDP. Several countries in South East Asia, including Vietnam after the transition began in the mid-1980s, have experienced periods of stagnant or falling enrolments at the secondary level and often these periods have coincided with rapid economic growth and rapid growth in the demand for labour. There is plenty of evidence that at the secondary level parents weigh up the costs and benefits of continuing education very carefully and often decide against keeping children in school.

Some analysts have argued that the equity outcomes of rapid growth in the HPAEs have been unusually favourable, and that this is in large part due to their human resource development strategy. There is again often a tendency to generalise the experience of Taiwan and South Korea to other parts of the East Asian region with scant regard for the facts. Elsewhere (Booth 1999a: 315–16) I have pointed out that the available evidence shows that the distribution of income in several fast-growing South East Asian countries is not especially egalitarian, and indeed government policies which in effect restricted access to secondary and tertiary education have aggravated inequalities. The case of Singapore is especially instructive. Rao (1996: Table 18.2) has demonstrated that the Gini coefficient of personal income accruing to resident taxpayers in Singapore has increased somewhat between 1970 and the early 1990s, by which time it was 0.47 indicating a fairly skewed distribution. Rao attributed at least part of the increase in earnings inequality to the growth in demand for skilled workers with tertiary qualifications over the 1980s and 1990s, especially in sectors such as finance. In other parts of South East Asia, such as Thailand and Indonesia, attempts by government to increase educational enrolments at the secondary level could, in the short run at least, aggravate existing income inequalities as those households who benefit from the increased expenditure will probably not come from the bottom deciles of the income distribution.[16] The very poor will be increasingly marginalised in the race for better jobs and higher incomes.

Given that in most parts of South East Asia enrolments in the higher levels of education are much higher in the upper income groups, and given the evidence of a tight link between level of education and lifetime earnings, there can be little doubt that restricted access to higher education is a powerful reason for the transmission of relative deprivation across generations. Khoman (1993: 330) has argued for Thailand that 'this inter-generational perpetuation of inequality is likely to accelerate in future as production technology becomes increasingly more complex and employment shifts increasingly out of agriculture and into industry'. Certainly the successful implementation of the nine-year cycle in both Thailand and Indonesia could potentially be a vehicle for greater equality, especially if at the same time a generous scholarship programme is available to permit bright children from less affluent homes to progress to upper secondary and tertiary levels. But that will involve a sharp increase in government educational expenditure relative to GDP, especially in Indonesia, where in the latter part of the 1990s it was below 3 per cent of GDP.

To conclude, the argument that heavy investment in education has led to equitable economic growth in several of the fast-growing economies of South East Asia since the 1960s seems to me to be for the most part unconvincing and unsupported by the evidence. Neither do I think that their governments have been especially astute at planning educational development in order to meet the demands of a fast-changing labour market. Indeed in several cases it is very clear that educational and skills bottlenecks have forced governments into relying on expatriate labour, and in some cases have retarded economic growth. This has probably been less true in Malaysia and Singapore than in Thailand and Indonesia, but even in these economies there was clear evidence of skill shortages by the mid-1990s which were in turn due to the limited expansion in tertiary provision. The advantage conferred on the Thai, Indonesian and Malaysian export sectors by the substantial real devaluations of 1997–8 can only give a short-term breathing space; in the medium term, if these countries do not educate more of their young people to a higher standard, then the goal of catching up with the developed economies is unlikely to be achieved.

Notes

1   This is a revised and updated version of Booth (1999b).
2   Ahuja, Bidani, Ferreira and Walton (1997: 53) argue that 'in most East Asian economies educational expansion took place ahead of demand, delivering new cohorts of appropriately skilled workers for each phase of industrialisation'. I would argue that in several South East Asian economies the process has been far from smooth; the Philippines has had to export its large surplus of skilled workers while Thailand and Indonesia suffered from skills shortages in the early 1990s.
3   The data in Table 8.2 exclude students enrolled abroad; the implications of this for Malaysia are discussed further below.
4   Behrman and Schneider (1994: 21) stress that per capita income does not appear to be closely correlated with enrolment rates and years of schooling for a cross-section of Asian countries in 1965 and 1987. They also point out that the seven Asian

economies with high growth rates 'as a group do not appear to have had unusually great schooling investments, although some individual countries within this group did have relatively high enrolment rates at some school levels'.

5 Goh (1979: Chapter 11) discusses the problems of implementing manpower-planning in Singapore with characteristic candour; however, he stresses the importance of this type of planning for Singapore's economic future. Cheah (1997) and Ashton, Green, James and Sung (1999: Chapter 3) give more recent analyses of how the system of education and skills training has changed in Singapore over the 1980s and 1990s in response to changes in trade patterns and economic structure.

6 See Ben Dolven (2000).

7 Huff (1995: 740) quotes Dr Goh Keng Swee's comment made in 1970 that 'the electronic components we make in Singapore probably require less skill than that required by barbers or cooks, consisting mostly of repetitive manual operations'. Ashton, Green, James and Sung (1999: 32–3) claim that from 1965 to 1979 'the main demand from employers was for semi-skilled labour'. It was only in the 1980s that the demand for more skilled labour in both manufacturing and the modern service sector began to grow rapidly; this was in large part due to the government policy of increasing wages and encouraging the traditional labour-intensive sectors of manufacturing to relocate elsewhere.

8 The Singapore economy remains very dependent on expatriate labour in both manufacturing and the service sector; it is estimated that around 450,000 expatriates worked in Singapore in the latter part of the 1990s.

9 Snodgrass (1998: 175) points out that in the 1960s 60 per cent of the student body at the University of Malaya was Chinese and only around 20–25 per cent Malay.

10 See for example Ashton and Green (1998) for a statement of this view.

11 A study carried out in the early 1970s argued that social returns to tertiary education expenditures were quite low, and that the Malaysian government was probably over-investing in education across the board (Hoerr 1973: 302). There is no evidence that the Malaysian government took such warnings seriously, which was just as well as the analysis on which they were based was certainly flawed. Had investment in post-primary education slowed in the 1970s and 1980s, skill bottlenecks would have emerged by the early 1990s which would have retarded growth.

12 These data are taken from the annual publication, *Educational Statistics of Malaysia*, published by the Educational Planning and Research Division, Ministry of Education, Kuala Lumpur.

13 Survey data indicated that in Indonesia in 1992, paid-out costs of lower secondary education amounted to almost 22 per cent of average annual per capita household expenditures. The comparative data assembled by Tan and Mingat (1992: 190) show that 27 per cent of operating costs in public secondary education in Indonesia in the mid-1980s were covered by fees, a higher ratio than elsewhere in East Asia except for South Korea.

14 International comparative tests suggest that achievement of 9–10 year olds in Indonesian schools is below the international mean (World Bank 1997: 120).

15 Fforde and de Vylder (1996: 232) argue that by the early 1990s 'it was no longer true that education in Vietnam was free'. As in Indonesia, by the early 1990s, paid-out costs of education at the lower secondary level amounted to a considerable proportion of average per capita household consumption expenditures in Vietnam (Booth 1997: Table 8).

16 See Ahuja, Bidani, Ferreira and Walton (1997), Table 2.5 for data on the distribution of enrolment rates across income groups. In Indonesia and Vietnam, the differences at the primary level are not great but they become far more pronounced at the higher secondary and post-secondary levels. See King (1997) and Glewwe and Jacoby (1998) for further discussions of Indonesia and Vietnam respectively.

Bibliography

Ahuja, V., Bidani, B., Ferreira, F. and Walton, M. (1997) *Everyone's Miracle? Revisiting Poverty and Inequality in East Asia*, Washington: World Bank.

Ashton, D. and Sung, J. (1997) 'Education, skill formation and economic development: the Singaporean approach', in A. Halsey, H. Lauder, P. Brown and A. Wells (eds) *Education: Culture, Economy and Society*, Oxford: Oxford University Press.

Ashton, D. and Green, F. (1998) 'The evolution of education and training strategies in Singapore, Taiwan and South Korea: a development model of skill formation', paper presented to the ESRC Pacific Asia Programme Conference, Recovery and Beyond in Pacific Asia, London, Foreign and Commonwealth Office, November.

Ashton, D., Green, F., James, D. and Sung, J. (1999) *Education and Training for Development in East Asia*, London: Routledge.

Behrman, J.R. and Knowles, J.C. (1999) 'Household income and child schooling in Vietnam', *World Bank Economic Review* 13, 2: 211–56.

Behrman, J.R. and Schneider, R. (1994) 'An international perspective on schooling investments in the last quarter century in some fast-growing East and Southeast Asian countries', *Asian Development Review* 12, 2: 1–50.

Bello, W., Cunningham, S. and Po, L.K. (1998) *A Siamese Tragedy*, London: Zed Books.

Birdsall, N., Ross, D. and Sabot, R. (1995) 'Inequality and growth reconsidered: lessons from East Asia', *World Bank Economic Review* 9, 3: 477–508.

Boediono, (1994) 'Pendidikan, perubahan struktural dan investasi di Indonesia', *Prisma* XXIII, 5 (May): 21–38.

Booth, A. (1994) 'Repelita VI and the second long-term development plan', *Bulletin of Indonesian Economic Studies* 30, 3 (December): 3–40.

——(1997) 'Vietnam and ASEAN: how far apart', in B. Beckman, E. Hansson and L. Roman (eds) *Vietnam: Reform and Transformation*, Stockholm: Centre for Pacific Asia Studies, University of Stockholm.

—— (1998) *The Indonesian Economy in the Nineteenth and Twentieth Centuries: A History of Missed Opportunities*, London: Macmillan.

—— (1999a) 'Initial conditions and miraculous growth: why is South East Asia different from Taiwan and South Korea?', *World Development* 27, 2: 301–22.

—— (1999b) 'Education and economic development in Southeast Asia: myths and realities', *ASEAN Economic Bulletin* 16, 3: 290–306.

Bureau of Educational Policy and Planning (Thailand), Office of the Permanent Secretary: Ministry of Education.

Campos, J.E. and Root, H.J. (1996) *The Key to the Asian Miracle: Making Shared Growth Credible*, Washington, DC: Brookings Institution.

Central Board of Statistics (2000) *Keadaan Angkatan Kerja di Indonesia (Labor Force Situation in Indonesia) August 1999*, Jakarta: Central Board of Statistics (February).

—— (2002) *Keadaan Angkatan Kerja di Indonesia (Labor Force Situation in Indonesia) August 2001*, Jakarta: Central Board of Statistics (February).

Cheah H.B. (1997) 'Can governments engineer the transition from cheap labour to skill-based competitiveness? The case of Singapore', in M. Godfrey (ed.) *Skill Development for International Competitiveness*, Cheltenham: Edward Elgar.

Chen, G. (1996) 'The graduate and skills labour markets: dimensions of manpower management', in C.Y. Lim (ed.) *Economic Policy Management in Singapore*, Singapore: Addison-Wesley Publishing Company.

China Statistical Yearbook (various issues).

Cummings, W.K. (1995) 'The Asian human resource approach in global perspective', *Oxford Review of Education* 21, 1: 67–81.

Dolven, B. (2000) 'Old dogs, new tricks', *Far Eastern Economic Review* 27: 68–9.

Economic and Social Statistics of Singapore, 1960–82, Singapore: Department of Statistics (1983).

Education in Korea (various issues) Seoul: Ministry of Education and Human Resources.

Education Statistics of Malaysia (annual), Kuala Lumpur: Educational Planning and Research Division, Ministry of Education.

Educational Statistics of the Republic of China (1993) Taipei: Ministry of Education.

Feeny, D. (1998) 'Thailand versus Japan: why was Japan first?', in Y. Hayami and M. Aoki (eds) *The Institutional Foundations of East Asian Development*, London: Macmillan.

Fforde, A. and de Vylder, S. (1996) *From Plan to Market: The Economic Transition in Vietnam*, Boulder: Westview Press.

Furnivall, J.S. (1943) *Educational Progress in Southeast Asia*, New York: Institute of Pacific Relations.

Glewwe, P. and Jacoby, H. (1998) 'School enrolment and completion in Vietnam; an investigation of recent trends', in D. Dollar, P. Glewwe and J. Litvack (eds) *Household Welfare and Vietnam's Transformation*, Washington, DC: World Bank.

Goh, K.S. (1979) *Report on the Ministry of Education 1978*, Singapore: Office of the Deputy Prime Minister.

Gomez, E.T. and Jomo K.S. (1997) *Malaysia's Political Economy: Politics, Patronage and Profits*, Cambridge: Cambridge University Press.

Government of Indonesia (1993) *Lampiran Pidato Pertanggungjawaban Presiden/Mandataris MPR Republik Indonesia, 1 Maret 1993*, Jakarta: Department of Information.

—— (1998) *Lampiran Pidato Kenegaraan Presiden Republik Indonesia, 15 Augustus 1998*, Jakarta: Department of Information.

Government of Malaysia (1989) *Mid-term Review of the Fifth Malaysia Plan 1986–1990*, Kuala Lumpur: National Printing Department.

—— (1999) *Mid-term Review of the Seventh Malaysia Plan 1996–2000*, Kuala Lumpur: National Printing Department.

Hoerr, O.D. (1973) 'Education, income and equity in Malaysia', *Economic Development and Cultural Change* 21, 2: 247–73.

Huff, W.G. (1995) 'What is the Singapore model of economic development?', *Cambridge Journal of Economics* 19: 735–59.

Jones, G.W. and Hagul, P. (2001) 'Schooling in Indonesia: crisis-related and longer-term issues', *Bulletin of Indonesian Economic Studies* 37, 2: 207–32.

King, E.M. (1997) 'Who really pays for education? The roles of government and families in Indonesia', in C. Colclough (ed.) *Marketizing Education and Health in Developing Countries*, Oxford: Clarendon Press.

Khoman, S. (1993) 'Education policy', in P. Warr (ed.) *The Thai Economy in Transition*, Cambridge: Cambridge University Press.

Labour Force Situation in Indonesia (1994), Jakarta: Central Bureau of Statistics.

Lampiran Pidato Kenegaraan (various issues).

Lee B.G. (2001) *Census of Population 2000: Education, Language and Religion*, Singapore: Department of Statistics (June).

Lim, C.Y. *et al.* (1988) *Policy Options for the Singapore Economy*, Singapore: McGraw-Hill.

MacMahon, W.W. and Boediono (1992) 'Universal basic education: an overall strategy of investment priorities for economic growth', *Economics of Education Review* 11, 2: 137–51.

Manning, C. and Junankar, P.N. (1998) 'Choosy youth or unwanted youth? A survey of unemployment', *Bulletin of Indonesian Economic Studies* 34, 1: 55–93.

Ministry of Education (1999) *1999 Educational Statistics in Brief*, Bangkok: Bureau of Policy and Planning, Office of the Permanent Secretary, Ministry of Education.

Moock, P.R. (1999) 'Improving eduction in a transforming country', in J.L. Litvack and D.A. Rondinelli (eds) *Market Reform in Vietnam: Building Institutions for Development*, Westport: Quorum Books.

Myers, C. and Sussangkarn, C. (1992) *Educational Options for the Future of Thailand*, Bangkok: Thai Development Research Institute.

Parkay, F.W., Potisook, P., Chantharasakul, A. and Chunsakorn, P. (1999) 'Transforming the profession of teaching in Thailand', *International Journal of Educational Reform* 8, 1: 60–73.

Phongpaichit, P. and Baker, C. (1995) *Thailand: Economy and Politics*, Kuala Lumpur: Oxford University Press.

Rao, V.V.B. (1996) 'Income distribution in Singapore: facts and policies', in C.Y. Lim (ed.) *Economic Policy Management in Singapore*, Singapore: Addison-Wesley Publishing Company.

Report of the Labour Force Survey Round 2, Bangkok: National Statistical Office.

Republic of Singapore (1986) *The Singapore Economy: New Directions, Report of the Economic Committee*, Singapore: Ministry of Trade and Industry (February).

Rudner, M. (1994) 'Colonial education policy and manpower underdevelopment in British Malaya' in *Malaysian Development: A Retrospective*, Ottawa: Carleton University Press.

Snodgrass, D.R. (1980) *Inequality and Economic Development in Malaysia*, Kuala Lumpur: Oxford University Press.

—— (1998) 'Education in Korea and Malaysia', in H.S. Rowen (ed.) *Behind East Asian Growth: The Political and Social Foundations of Prosperity*, London: Routledge.

Special Labour Force Survey Report (1974) Bureau of Statistics: Economic Planning Board.

Statistical Yearbooks of Singapore (various issues), Singapore: Department of Statistics.

Taiwan Statistical Data Book (various years), Taipei: Council for Economic Planning and Development.

Taiwan Statistical Yearbook (1995), Taipei: Directorate-General of Budget, Accounting and Statistics.

Tan, J.P. and Mingat, A. (1992) *Education in Asia: A Comparative Study of Cost and Financing*, Washington: World Bank.

UNESCO (1996) *World Education Report 1995*, Oxford: UNESCO Publishing.

—— (1998) *Statistical Yearbook*, Oxford: UNESCO Publishing.

Warr, P.G. (1998) 'Thailand', in R. McLeod and R. Garnaut (eds) *East Asia in Crisis: from Being a Miracle to Needing One*, London: Routledge.

Wilson, C.M. (1983) *Thailand: A Handbook of Historical Statistics*, Boston: G.K. Hall and Co.

Witte, J. (2000) 'Education in Thailand after the crisis: a balancing act between globalization and national self-contemplation', *International Journal of Educational Development* 20: 223–45.

World Bank (1993) *The East Asian Miracle: Economic Growth and Public Policy*, Washington, DC: The World Bank.

—— (1994) *World Development Report 1994*, New York: Oxford University Press.

—— (1997) *Vietnam: Education Financing*, Washington: World Bank.

—— (1998) *Indonesia: Education in Indonesia from Crisis to Recovery*, Report 18651-IND, Washington: World Bank (December).

9 Growth and vulnerability before and after the Asian crisis

The fallacy of the universal model[1]

Jomo K.S.

Introduction

From the 1980s onwards, and especially in the early and mid-1990s, there has been growing international recognition of the sustained rapid economic growth, structural change and industrialisation of the East Asian region. There has also been a tendency to see East Asia as much more of an economically integrated region than it actually is, and a corresponding tendency to see economic progress in the region as being similar in origin and nature. Terms such as the 'Far East', 'Asia-Pacific', 'Pacific Asia', 'East Asia', 'yen bloc', 'flying geese', 'tigers', 'mini-dragons', and so on, have tended to encourage this perception of the region as far more economically integrated and similar than it actually is.

The World Bank (1993) argued that of the eight highly performing (East) Asian economies (HPAEs) identified in its study *The East Asian Miracle*,[2] three Southeast HPAEs – namely Indonesia, Malaysia and Thailand – provided the preferred models for emulation by other developing countries. Yoshihara (1988) had earlier argued that Southeast Asian economies were characterised by ersatz capitalism because of the compromised and inferior roles of their states, their discriminatory treatment of ethnic Chinese and their failure to develop better technological capabilities. Jomo *et al.* (1997) criticised the World Bank's claims that the Southeast Asian highly performing economies were superior models for emulation.

The East Asian currency and financial crises of 1997–8 radically transformed international perceptions and opinion about the East Asian experiences, with earlier praise quickly changing into severe condemnation. This was most obvious with regard to the issue of business–government relations, which had previously been characterised as key to the East Asian success story. Instead, these often intimate relations have since been denounced as 'crony capitalism' responsible for the onset as well as the severity of the crisis (Backman 1999, Clifford and Engardio 2000). Various accounts (Jomo 1998, Furman and Stiglitz 1998, Radelet and Sachs 1998, Krugman 1999, Bhagwati 1998) have since characterised the crises as the consequence of international financial liberalisation and related increases in easily reversible international capital flows. These accounts have also emphasised the role of the International Monetary Fund (IMF), particularly its policy prescriptions and conditionalities, in exacerbating the crises.

This chapter consists of two parts. In the first, the so-called East Asian model, especially as presented by the World Bank (1993), will be critically examined. Subsequently, the variety of East Asian experiences will be emphasised (Perkins 1994). The second-tier Southeast Asian experiences will then be shown to be distinct from and inferior to those of the first-generation newly industrialised economies (NIEs), especially the Republic of Korea and Taiwan Province of China (elaborated in Jomo 2001b and 2002). The last sections of part one will review the circumstances leading to the onset of the East Asian crises of 1997–8, and examine whether and how the East Asian 'models' may have contributed to the crises.

The second part considers the implications of pre-crisis developments and more recent challenges. In particular, it reviews some exchange rate dilemmas, limited technological capabilities and new investment-promotion strategies. The concluding remarks consider the likelihood of convergence – and the viability of distinct development models – in the face of continued globalisation and Anglo-American inspired liberalisation.

The rise and fall of the Asian model

The East Asian miracle[3]

The most important and influential document which attempted to explain the rapid growth, structural change and industrialisation of much of East Asia in the last three decades or more has been *The East Asian Miracle* study (EAM) published by the World Bank in 1993.

In EAM, the World Bank identified eight high-performing Asian economies: Japan; the four first-generation NIEs or NICs, dragons or tigers, namely the Republic of Korea, Taiwan Province of China, Hong Kong (China) and Singapore; and the three second-generation Southeast Asian NICs, namely Malaysia, Indonesia and Thailand. Interestingly, China was left out, perhaps because the Chinese experience would upset the Bank's analysis and conclusions in very fundamental ways. EAM recognises that the likelihood of eight relatively contiguous economies growing so rapidly for such a sustained period of time is less than one in 60,000. Yet it does not acknowledge the significance of geography – unlike the later 1997 *Emerging Asia* study led by the Harvard Institute of International Development for the Asian Development Bank (ADB 1997). With the publication and release of EAM, the Bank seemed to be shifting its position from the neo-liberalism, or extreme economic liberalism of the 1980s, to acknowledging an important developmental role for the state in the 1990s. EAM appeared to have had something to do with this shift. This impression has been reflected in other Bank activities and publications, especially the *1997 World Development Report* which seemed to advocate effective, rather than minimalist, states (World Bank 1997).

In EAM, the Bank identified at least six types of state interventions, which it saw as having been very important for East Asian development. It approved of the first four, deemed to be functional interventions, but was more sceptical of the last two, deemed to be strategic interventions. Functional interventions are said to compensate for market failures, and are hence necessary and less distorting of markets, while strategic interventions are considered to be more market-distorting. The two types of strategic interventions considered are in the areas of finance, specifically what it calls directed (i.e. subsidised) credit, and international trade, while the four functional interventions the Bank approved of are:

1   Ensuring *macroeconomic* discipline and macroeconomic balances;
2   Providing physical and social *infrastructure*;
3   Providing good *governance* more generally; and
4   Raising *savings* and investment rates.

It is very important to compare what has actually happened in East Asia with the way the World Bank has presented this. Beginning with the importance of macro-economic discipline, there is very little dispute that maintaining macroeconomic balances has been important in East Asia. But what the Bank considers to be the acceptable parameters of macroeconomic discipline may be disputed. One finds, for instance, that inflation was generally kept under 20 per cent in the HPAEs, but it was certainly not always kept below 10 per cent in all the economies. In other words, single-digit inflation was neither a policy priority nor always ensured in some East Asian countries during their high-growth periods.

Similarly, when considering other macroeconomic balances such as the fiscal balance and the current account of the balance of payments, one finds that the balances were not always strictly maintained in the way the Fund and the Bank now seem to require of much of the developing world. Malaysia and Thailand have had relatively high current account deficits throughout the 1990s, while other countries with much lower deficits were not spared the recent currency attacks and massive depreciations.

On physical and social infrastructure, until the 1980s, the Bank would probably have gone along with what the East Asians have done. However, since the 1980s, the Bank has increasingly seemed to recommend privatisation and the private provision of physical infrastructure. With the exception of Hong Kong (China), most physical infrastructure in East Asia had previously been provided by governments. Fairly recently, there have been the beginnings of privatisation in the provision of physical infrastructure, which has become the basis for powerful private monopolies associated with 'crony capitalism'.

The role of government has been extremely important in providing so-called social infrastructure and services in East Asia. In some of its other documents, the Bank seems to acknowledge this, but nonetheless it recommends a more modest role for government in the provision of social infrastructure. For instance, the Bank recommends universal and free primary education, but does not recommend the subsidisation of education beyond the primary level, when the 'user/consumer' (student) should bear the full costs of education as far as the World Bank is concerned. This would have had very serious consequences in terms of human resource development, if one contrasts that recommendation with the actual experience of East Asia. To give some sense of how important government support for education has been beyond the primary level, in the Republic of Korea today, over 40 per cent of young people attend universities. Thailand has a percentage of close to 20 per cent, Indonesia has 10 per cent, and most of the first-generation East Asian NIEs have well over 25 per cent, generally over 30 per cent.

The notion of good governance is somewhat ambiguous and often used rather tautologically. When things are going well, it is assumed that there must be good governance, and conversely, if things are not going well. So one does not really have much of an explanation of good economic performance by simply invoking good governance, although it is widely touted these days, sometimes ad nauseam. There have, however, been important efforts to try to understand the factors contributing to good governance. In this regard, the *1997 World Development Report* has been important and useful. It seems from the East Asian experience that what was called 'strong government' (in Gunnar Myrdal's sense) has been an important notion, though one often misunderstood and wrongly associated with authoritarian government.

What is called 'embedded autonomy' has become a useful way to try to understand what the conditions of good governance are. Here, embeddedness refers to the institutional capacity and capability of the governments concerned to effectively provide the co-ordination necessary for rapid capital accumulation and economic transformation. Autonomy is primarily understood to be from 'vested interests', 'special-interest groups', 'distribution coalitions' and 'rent-seekers' who, in more favourable or conducive circumstances, would be able to influence public policy to their own advantage. Embedded autonomy is therefore considered to have been very crucial in ensuring that regimes in East Asia could effectively serve as developmental states.

The role of the state in encouraging savings and promoting investments is also generally accepted. However, much of East Asia's large savings is actually comprised of corporate or firm savings, rather than just household savings. Household savings in East Asia are not spectacularly higher than in the rest of the world, except in Malaysia and Singapore. The difference in Malaysia and Singapore is due to the mandatory or forced savings schemes introduced in the late colonial period and the relatively high proportion of the working class or wage owners as a proportion of the labour force. The latter is particularly true in the case of Singapore, but is also not insignificant in the case of Malaysia. The significance of coerced savings should be noted because of the popular view that the high savings and investment rates in the region exist because East Asians are culturally, if not congenitally, thrifty.

The large contribution of high corporate savings implies that firms have often been able to enjoy very high profit rates due to government interventions, subsidies, tax breaks and other incentives for particular types of investments favoured by the governments, enabling the firms concerned to enjoy higher 'rents'. But more important is the fact that attractive conditions (e.g. tax incentives and other inducements), largely created by governments, have induced high rates of reinvestment of the huge profits of firms. How have such high rates of reinvestment been secured? In some East Asian countries they have been assured by the very strict controls on foreign exchange outflows. Capital flight was made very difficult in certain East Asian economies, especially in the Republic of Korea and Taiwan Province of China, during their high-growth periods. High levels of reinvestment have also been successfully induced by structuring laws so that the reinvestment of profits is subject to little or no tax, or by offering other incentives to undertake state-favoured investments.

In pursuing these supposedly functional interventions, the East Asian governments were not just market-conforming, but instead played important roles, which have been more than simply market-augmenting, as suggested by EAM. On the more controversial, so-called strategic interventions in finance and international trade, the Bank almost grudgingly concedes that financial interventions have been important and successful in East Asia, particularly in Northeast Asia – i.e. in Japan, the Republic of Korea and Taiwan Province of China. However, the Bank implies that nobody else is capable of successfully pursuing the types of policies that the Northeast Asians successfully implemented, because state capabilities in Northeast Asia have been almost unique and are non-replicable.

Creating the conditions for attracting investment, both domestic private investment as well as foreign investment, has had much more to do with reforming incentives and governance more generally to attract particular types of investments to generate specific sources of economic growth, rather than liberalising financial markets as such. Southeast Asian governments, notably Singapore and Malaysia, have especially sought to attract FDI into areas where indigenous industrial capabilities were not expected to become internationally competitive. Venture capital markets, rather than the usual stock markets, tend to be more supportive of developing new industrial and technological capabilities.

In many cases, infant industries were generally provided with effective protection conditional on export-promotion, which had the effect of forcing the firms and industries concerned to quickly become internationally competitive. By giving firms protection for certain periods, depending on the product, and by also requiring that they begin exporting certain shares of output within similarly specified periods, strict discipline was imposed on the firms in return for the temporary trade protection they enjoyed. Quantitatively, such policies forced firms to push down their own production costs as quickly as possible; for example, by trying to achieve greater economies of scale and accelerating progress up learning curves. Requiring exports has also meant that producers had to achieve international quality standards quickly, which technologically imposed pressures for progress in terms of products as well as processes. With strict discipline imposed, but also some flexibility in enforcement, many firms managed to rapidly achieve international competitiveness.

EAM and its supporting studies have implied and argued that Southeast Asia began to take off after it reversed such trade interventions. Hence, the mid-1980s are portrayed by the Bank as a period of economic liberalisation and deregulation leading to economic recovery and rapid growth and industrialisation. The facts are more complicated (Jomo *et al.* 1997 and Jomo 2001b). There certainly was some deregulation during this period, but there also was some new private-sector-oriented regulation, more appropriate to the new industrial policy priorities of the governments of Indonesia, Malaysia, Singapore and Thailand.

East Asian differences

While many lessons may certainly be drawn from the East Asian experiences, they are far from constituting a single model. Some of the major differences in East Asia are themselves very instructive. In the case of the role of FDI, one finds tremendous contrasts, especially between Southeast Asia and the rest of East Asia. In the case of Singapore, FDI has constituted about a quarter of gross domestic capital formation. In the case of Malaysia, the proportion has been about 15 per cent. At the other end of the spectrum, in the case of Japan and the Republic of Korea, the percentage has long been below 2 per cent. Some of the other countries fall between these two extremes, with very few near the mean for developing countries of around 5 per cent. Those most successful in developing industrial capacities and capabilities in East Asia – namely Japan, the Republic of Korea and Taiwan Province of China – have hardly depended on FDI, which has only played a relatively small role.

The far greater importance of FDI in Southeast Asia has been due to a variety of reasons, which have not been entirely economic. One of the reasons for the major role of FDI in Singapore and Malaysia is political. After Singapore seceded from Malaysia in 1965, the Lee Kuan Yew government decided that to ensure its own survival, it would be best to attract foreign investment in massive quantities to Singapore, so that the major foreign powers would quickly develop a stake in the survival of the Singapore regime. Of course, this preference was subsequently justified in terms of improving access to the technology frontier. In other words, political considerations have been a very important reason for attracting, even privileging, foreign investment in Singapore. In the case of Malaysia, the country has long had ethnic rivalries and an ethnic affirmative action policy. This encouraged some policy-makers to try to limit ethnic Chinese control over the economy by encouraging FDI so as to reduce such control. Again, one finds a political motivation for the important role of FDI in Malaysia. Singapore and Malaysia are exceptions, which need to be explained politically, rather than simply by economic considerations.

Despite the much greater resource wealth of Southeast Asia, one finds that growth performance has been superior in Northeast Asia over the long term. Over the period studied by the Bank – i.e. from the 1960s until the early 1990s – the average growth rate in the former was in the region of about 8 per cent, compared to about 6 per cent for the latter. A 2 per cent difference, compounded over a period of a quarter century or more, adds up to a lot. Very importantly also, population growth, except in Hong Kong (China) owing to immigration from China and perhaps Singapore, has been much lower in the former compared to the latter. The immigration into Hong Kong (China) and Singapore involves a very high proportion of people in the labour force, thus raising the average labour utilisation rate. Political factors have also ensured far more equitable distribution of economic welfare than would otherwise have been the case in the first-tier NIEs, whereas such considerations have been less influential in the second-tier Southeast Asian NICs, except perhaps for Malaysia due to its ethnic 'social contract'.

Hence the improvements in per capita income and economic welfare have been much more significant in Northeast Asia, compared to Southeast Asia (with the exception of Singapore), despite the relative resource wealth of the latter. In other words, what Southeast Asia has achieved has been less impressive in some critical ways. Drawing from this contrast, one could argue that resource wealth is not a blessing, but a curse, insofar as it postpones the imperative to industrialise. Northeast Asia has generally had a much more sophisticated and effective industrial policy compared to Southeast Asia. This accounts, in no small way, for the very important differences in industrial and technological capabilities between Northeast and Southeast Asia. Also, industrialisation in the latter is still primarily driven by FDI, whereas industrialisation in the former is primarily an indigenous phenomenon.

It is now generally recognised that Japan and the first-generation NIEs began to industrialise in the very specific economic and political conditions of a particular Cold War historical conjuncture. Northeast Asia grew rapidly in the immediate post-war period under a 'security umbrella' provided by the Americans, especially after the Cold War began. Besides subsidising military expenditure and providing generous aid, the Americans were anxious for them to 'succeed' economically in order to be showcased as attractive alternatives to those under Communist rule or influence. Hence the Americans were quite happy to tolerate trade, finance, investment, intellectual property and other policies violating laissez-faire market or neo-liberal economic norms that they are now strongly opposed to, especially following the end of the Cold War. These favourable conditions are simply not available to others, and hence their experiences are said to be almost impossible to emulate.

There is also the claim that East Asia cannot be emulated owing to its very different initial conditions. Such differences are real, but often exaggerated. There is no doubt that Japan and the first-tier East Asian NIEs are now distinguished by high levels of education. However, the level of literacy in South Korea in 1950 was lower than the literacy rate in contemporary Ethiopia (which has one of the lowest rates in Africa today); thus the level of education achieved by contemporary Koreans reflects the tremendous investments devoted to developing human resources in East Asia in the post-war period, as the region then was generally not very advanced despite, or perhaps even because of, its (elitist) Confucian legacy. But by the end of the 1960s, literacy rates had gone up greatly for the first-generation East Asian NIEs after enormous resources had been poured into education in the preceding two decades.

In discussing initial conditions, some fortuitous circumstances must also be considered. Japan, South Korea and Taiwan Province of China all had relatively virtuous American-sponsored land reforms shortly after the end of the war (Hsiao 1996). In Japan, there also was significant redistribution of other non-land assets, most notably of the pre-war and wartime *zaibatsu* industrial conglomerates. Much of the motivation for such redistributive reforms was, of course, anti-Communist, i.e. to undermine and minimise support for the Communists by pre-emptively implementing asset redistribution.

There are important lessons to be drawn from East Asia, but clearly there is no single East Asian model as such, and most certainly, not one that can accommodate all the different experiences of Southeast Asia. Considering the historicity of the development experiences, it does not make much sense for any other country to think in terms of trying to emulate any particular economy in the Southeast region or, for that matter, East Asia more generally. There are many reasons why most will find it impossible to imitate any other country even if they wanted to. But even in drawing lessons, it will be important to recognise the distinctive nature of the Southeast Asian experiences.

Southeast Asia's ersatzness

There is considerable evidence that the three Southeast Asian economies of Indonesia, Malaysia and Thailand have some common characteristics and policies that distinguish them from the other high-growth economies of East Asia (Jomo *et al.* 1997). Most importantly, the region's high-growth economies have relied heavily on FDI to develop most of their internationally competitive industrial capabilities; government interventions have also been more compromised by considerations besides economic growth and late industrialisation, especially redistribution and rent capture. Consequently, industrial policy has also varied in nature, quality and effectiveness. Yet, it will be shown that the Southeast Asian economies would not have achieved so much without selective government interventions, including industrial policy.

Southeast Asian industrialisation has been far more dominated by foreign capital (Jomo *et al.* 1997 and Jomo 2001b), and has, as a consequence, fewer industrial and technological capabilities that may be considered indigenous or under national control. The efficacy of industrial policy has thus emerged as the primary determinant of the ability of different national economies to take advantage of transnational capital's relocation of productive capacities in the region. The distinct nature of the Southeast Asian economies and experiences (Jomo *et al.* 1997 and Jomo 2001b) offers valuable insights into various industrial policy instruments, the circumstances in which these may work, as well as the importance of relatively uncompromised, competent and effective state capacities in ensuring desirable industrial policy outcomes. Industrial policy has been less elaborate, efficient and effective in the three Southeast Asian second-tier NICs – Indonesia, Malaysia and Thailand – as compared to Japan and the first-tier East Asian NIEs, except for Hong Kong (China), but including Singapore. This is partly because state intervention in Southeast Asia has been far more abused and, hence, often seriously compromised, by politically influential business interests. Yet, it would be a mistake to 'throw the baby out with the bath water' by condemning all industrial policy in the region. Despite various abuses and other weaknesses in implementation, some industrial policy has been crucial to Southeast Asia's rapid economic growth, structural change and late industrialisation (Jomo *et al.* 1997).

Closer examination suggests that the experiences of Indonesia, Malaysia and Thailand more closely approximated the 'export-led' – but not 'open economy' (of Hong Kong (China) and Singapore) – growth model than those of Japan, the Republic of Korea and Taiwan Province of China. The latter appears to have promoted exports very actively, while also protecting domestic markets, at least temporarily, to develop domestic industrial and technological capabilities in order to compete internationally. Their strategy of temporary effective protection conditional upon export promotion (EPconEP) can hardly be equated with trade liberalisation. Recent criticisms (Baer *et al.* 1999) of attempts by an earlier generation (for example, Ian Little, Jagdish Bhagwati, Anne Krueger) to accommodate the Northeast Asian EPconEP experience within their fundamentalist free-trade-advocacy paradigm, have exposed the intellectual sophistry of neo-classical trade economists in trying to explain away the Northeast Asian success in requiring export promotion as a condition for temporary (national) market protection.

The much greater Southeast Asian dependence on FDI raises disturbing questions about the actual nature of industrial and technological capacities and capabilities in these economies, especially in their most dynamic and export-oriented sectors. This, in turn, raises concerns about the sustainability of their growth and industrialisation processes, especially if they are later deemed less attractive as sites for further FDI; for example, as more attractive alternative locations become available.

Southeast Asian weaknesses

In recent years, there has been growing recognition of major structural and systemic differences among the eight HPAEs studied by the World Bank (1993). Of these, Indonesia, Malaysia and Thailand have been increasingly grouped as second-tier or second-generation Southeast Asian NICs, with characteristics quite different from the others and, of course, even among themselves. It has been argued that industrial policy or selective state intervention has, for various reasons, been of much poorer quality and less effective in these economies. Instead, there have been other state interventions motivated by less developmental considerations, especially in Indonesia and Malaysia (Jomo *et al.* 1997). It appears that such interventions bear some of the responsibility for the vulnerability of the second-tier Southeast Asian NICs to the factors that precipitated the mid-1997 financial crisis in the region.

A longer-term view of the crisis would, of course, have to recognise the vulnerability of existing financial systems to such 'exogenous' shocks. The central banks in the region clearly fell short of the new challenges faced (Hamilton-Hart and Jomo 2001). National-level central banking faced a new situation with the new international monetary system that emerged after abandonment by the United States of the Bretton Woods framework in 1971. Further international financial liberalisation, from the 1980s on, added to the new problems for the national monetary authorities, precisely when the role of government in economic affairs was coming under greater pressures for economic liberalisation. The failure of institutional and regulatory reform to rise to new challenges posed by the changing international as well as domestic situations has to be acknowledged.

It would be erroneous to view the crises as due to 'crony capitalism' or to some similar failure of the policy and institutional framework supporting the accelerated development of industrial capacities and capabilities in the region. Yet, it would be equally fallacious to regard the concerned economies as innocent bystanders bearing no responsibility whatsoever for what was happening. Instead, the region's vulnerability to crisis was due to inappropriate and even irresponsible earlier policies, with important adverse macroeconomic implications.

While official efforts to accelerate industrial technological progress in Indonesia, Malaysia and Thailand have increased, at least since the late 1980s, the Southeast Asian trio remained well behind the Republic of Korea, Taiwan Province of China and Singapore. Domestic political priorities have often neglected technology policies, while policy initiatives have also been constrained by the weak commitments of the governments concerned. The dominant position of foreign firms in the most dynamic manufacturing sectors has also served as a major deterrent to more pro-active technology development efforts. All too often, technology policies have not been sensitive enough to sector- or industry-specific conditions. More worryingly, the scope for discretionary policies has become more constrained as global regulatory frameworks are increasingly defined by international organisations with enforcement capacities, as well as effectively co-ordinated and articulated investor demands. Nonetheless, there still is much scope and potential for informed technology policies in the region.

With accelerated globalisation and economic integration in the past decade, the international investment environment, especially in the East Asian region, has changed considerably. Taking into consideration the fresh constraints imposed by new international regulations and commitments, as well as the more sophisticated industries in some of these economies, investment policy reform was already occurring before the 1997–8 crises. However, the crises and their aftermath, including the conditionalities imposed by the IMF on Indonesia and Thailand for emergency credit facilities, have also introduced new constraints. Attracting new 'green-field' investments to restore and sustain growth as well as structural change is all the more urgent, as so much recent FDI in the region has involved mergers and acquisitions.

Most accounts of the East Asian miracle have emphasised the key contributions of educational efforts in raising the quality of human resources throughout the region. However, once again, the actual Southeast Asian record in this regard has fallen well short of the other HPAEs. With the exception of Singapore, educational achievements in Southeast Asia, including in the Southeast Asian trio, have been grossly inferior to those in the other HPAEs. While the region's earlier achievements in extending primary and lower secondary schooling have probably contributed to its rapid growth and labour-intensive industrialisation, these limited educational gains may well serve as fetters to further progress. (Ironically, the country with the highest share of tertiary education in the region – the Philippines – has not had a particularly impressive economic growth record for a complex variety of reasons.)

There is now considerable cause for concern that rapid structural change, industrialisation and productivity gains may not be achievable in the future owing to the region's poor educational efforts. Such findings and comparisons compel a reconsideration of the facile World Bank policy recommendation that governments should concentrate on enhancing human resources, but only subsidise primary schooling.

Comparing the Southeast Asian trio with the Republic of Korea and Taiwan Province of China, it is now quite clear not only that the latter two economies achieved far more in terms of growth, industrialisation and structural change, but also that income inequality in them has been significantly lower as well (Jomo 1999). While their better economic performance was probably due to more effective government interventions, especially selective industrial policy, lower inequality was probably due to significant asset (especially land) redistribution before the high-growth period, i.e. more equitable 'initial conditions'. However, there is also troubling evidence that economic liberalisation in recent years may well have exacerbated inequalities in both East Asian groups.

The East Asian debacle

Although there has been considerable work critical of the East Asian record and potential, none actually anticipated the East Asian debacle of 1997–8 (Krugman 1994). Although some of the weaknesses identified in the literature did make the region economically vulnerable, none of the critical writing seriously addressed one crucial implication of the greater role of foreign capital in Southeast Asia, in particular with regard to international financial liberalisation, which became more pronounced in the 1990s. As previously noted (Jomo 1998), the dominance of manufacturing activities – especially the most technologically sophisticated and dynamic ones – by foreign transnationals subordinated domestic industrial capital in the region, allowing finance capital, both domestic and foreign, to become more influential.

Contrary to the impression conveyed mainly by the business media as well as by the IMF, there is still no consensus on how to understand and characterise the crisis. One manifestation of this has been the debates between the IMF and its various critics over the appropriateness of its negotiated programmes in Indonesia, the Republic of Korea, and Thailand. While policy debates have understandably captured the most attention, especially with the public at large, the East Asian crises have also challenged previously accepted international economic theories. However, contrary to the popular impression – promoted by the Western-dominated financial media – of 'crony capitalism' as the main culprit, most serious analysts now agree that the crisis began essentially as a currency crisis of a new type, different from those previously identified with either fiscal profligacy or macroeconomic indiscipline. A growing number also seem to agree that the crisis started off as a currency crisis and quickly became a more generalised financial crisis, before impacting on the real economy because of reduced liquidity in the financial system and the consequences of inappropriate official policy and ill-informed herd-like market responses.

From miracle to debacle

Rapid economic growth and structural change, mainly associated with export-led industrialisation in the region, can generally be traced back to the mid-1980s. Then, devaluation of the currencies of all three Southeast HPAEs, as well as selective deregulation of onerous rules, helped to create attractive conditions for the relocation of production facilities in these countries and elsewhere in Southeast Asia and China. This was especially attractive for Japan and the first-tier or first-generation NIEs – Hong Kong (China), the Republic of Korea, Singapore and Taiwan Province of China – most of which experienced currency appreciations, tight labour markets and higher production costs. This sustained export-oriented industrialisation well into the 1990s, and was accompanied by the growth of other manufacturing, services and construction activities.

Financial liberalisation from the 1980s had major ramifications in the region, as foreign savings supplemented the already high domestic savings rates in the region to further accelerate the rate of capital accumulation, albeit in increasingly unproductive activities, owing to the foreign domination of most internationally competitive industries in the region. Consequently, several related macroeconomic concerns had emerged by the mid-1990s from the rapid growth of the previous decade. First, the savings–investment gap had historically been financed by heavy reliance on FDI as well as public sector foreign borrowings, with the latter declining rapidly from the mid-1980s. Both FDI and foreign debt, in turn, caused investment-income outflows abroad.[4] In the 1990s, the current account deficit was increasingly financed by short-term capital inflows, as in 1993 and 1995–6, with disastrous consequences later, with the subsequent reversal of such flows.[5] Many recent confidence restoration measures seek to induce such short-term inflows once again, but they cannot be relied upon to address the underlying problem in the medium to long term. Although always in the minority, foreign portfolio investments increasingly influenced the stock markets in the region in the 1990s. With incomplete information exacerbated by limited transparency, their regional presence, the biased nature of fund managers' incentives and remuneration, and the short-termism of their investment horizons, foreign financial institutions were much more prone to herd behaviour, and thus contributed most decisively to regional contagion. Second, there was an explosion of private sector debt in the 1990s, especially from abroad, not least because of the efforts of 'debt-pushers' keen to secure higher returns from the fast-growing region.[6] Commercial banks' foreign liabilities also increased quickly as the ratio of loans to GNP rose rapidly during the period.

Over-investment of investible funds, especially from abroad, in non-tradables only made things worse, especially on the current account. Only a small proportion of the lending from commercial banks and other lending agencies went to manufacturing and other productive activities. This share is likely to have been even smaller with foreign borrowings, most of which were collateralised with assets such as real property and stock. Thus, much of the inflow of foreign savings actually contributed to asset-price inflation, mainly involving real estate and share prices. Insofar as such investments did not increase the production of tradables, they actually exacerbated the current account deficit, rather than alleviated it – as they were thought to be doing. This, in turn, worsened the problem of 'currency mismatch', with borrowings in US dollars invested in activities not generating foreign exchange. As a high proportion of these foreign borrowings were short-term in nature and deployed to finance medium- to long-term projects, a 'term mismatch' problem also arose. According to the Bank for International Settlements (BIS) (*Asian Wall Street Journal*, 6 January 1998), well over half of the foreign borrowings by commercial banks were short term in nature: in Malaysia 56 per cent, in Thailand 66 per cent, in Indonesia 59 per cent, and in the Republic of Korea 68 per cent.

More generally, the foreign exchange risks of investments greatly increased, raising the vulnerability of these economies to the maintenance of currency pegs to the US dollar.[7] The pegs encouraged a great deal of un-hedged borrowing by an influential constituency with a strong stake in defending the pegs regardless of their adverse consequences for the economy. Owing to foreign domination of export-oriented industries in Southeast Asia, unlike in Northeast Asia, there was no strong domestic export-oriented industrial community to lobby for floating or depreciation of the Southeast Asian currencies despite the obvious adverse consequences of the pegs for international cost competitiveness. Instead, after pegging their currencies to the US dollar, from the early 1990s and especially from the mid-1990s, most Southeast Asian central banks resisted downward adjustments to their exchange rates, which would have reduced, if not averted some of the more disruptive consequences of the 1997–8 currency collapses.[8] Yet, it is also now generally agreed that the 1997–8 East Asian crises saw tremendous 'overshooting' in exchange rate adjustments well in excess of expected 'corrections'.

In the early and mid-1990s, some Southeast Asian economies had become excessively reliant on such short-term capital inflows to finance their current account deficits. This problem was exacerbated by excessive imports to manufacture more non-exportables, such as buildings, infrastructure and heavily protected import-substitutes. Ostensibly prudent financial institutions often preferred to lend for real property and stock purchases, and thus secure assets with rising values as collateral, rather than to provide credit for more productive ends. While foreign banks were more than happy to lend US dollars at interest rates higher than those available in their home economies, East Asian businesses were keen to borrow at lower interest rates than were available domestically. The sustained dollar pegs of the Southeast Asian currencies may have induced some moral hazard by discouraging borrowers from hedging their loans, but there is little systematic evidence of the extent of this problem. In any case, the existence of well-developed swap markets allowed Southeast Asian companies to tap into foreign capital markets, at low cost, by swapping away the currency risk. Hence, many such loans remained un-hedged as Southeast Asian currencies had been pegged to the US dollar since the 1970s, despite the official fictions of exchange rates moving with the baskets of the currencies of their major foreign trading partners. The growth in foreign banking in the region in the 1990s led to lending competition reminiscent of the loans to Third World governments in the late 1970s (which led to the debt crisis of the 1980s). However, the new belief in international policy-making circles before the crisis was that such accumulation of private sector debt did not matter as long as public sector debt was reined in. Meanwhile, portfolio investors moved into newly emerging stock markets in East Asia, with encouragement from the International Finance Corporation (IFC), an arm of the World Bank. In Malaysia, for example, they came in a big way in 1993, only to withdraw even more suddenly in early 1994, leaving most retail stockholders in the lurch. The government introduced some capital control measures, only to withdraw them later in 1994. Unfortunately, policy-makers did not learn the lessons from that experience as the new unsustainable stock market build-up from 1995 sent stock prices soaring once again, despite declining price–earnings ratios.

Perceiving the East Asian region as much more integrated than it actually is, the panicky investment decisions of fund managers were typically 'herd-like',[9] causing 'contagion' throughout the region. The very nature and magnitude of hedge fund operations tended to exacerbate these phenomena, with disastrous snowballing consequences for the region.[10] Other international, regional and, increasingly, local currency speculators and hedgers also contributed by reacting in their own perceived self-interest to supposed market trends, rather than as part of some grand conspiracy. With the currency collapses, the assets acquired by portfolio and other investors in the region depreciated correspondingly in value, precipitating an even greater sell-out and panic, causing herd behaviour and contagion to spread across national borders to the rest of the region. Meanwhile, liberalising the capital account essentially guaranteed residents and non-residents ease of exit, as well as fewer limitations on nationals holding foreign assets, thus inadvertently facilitating capital flight. Thus, financial liberalisation allowed lucrative opportunities for taking advantage of falling currencies, accelerating and exacerbating the volatility of regional currency and share markets. All this, together with injudicious official responses, transformed the inevitable 'correction' of over-valued currencies in the region into collapses of the currencies and the stock markets of the region as panic set in, aggravated by 'herd' behaviour and 'contagion'.

Some roots of the crisis

If falling exchange rates assisted export-competitiveness between 1986 and the early 1990s, the reversal from the mid-1990s had the opposite effect. The appreciation of the Southeast Asian currencies, with the decline of the yen from mid-1995, was substantial. With the renminbi devaluations of 1990 and 1994, their appreciation had especially negative impacts on exports, the balance-of-payments current account and FDI inflows. The rising currencies as well as declining tariffs and other trade controls due to trade liberalisation pushed up imports. There were no efforts to adjust exchange rates to neutralise the impact of import-liberalisation. Also, their manufacturing export structures had become somewhat rigid and were not sufficiently exchange-rate elastic. Unlike agricultural and final goods, which have competitors and substitutes, intra-firm trade (especially transnationals directly exporting assembled and processed items abroad) has accounted for much of their exported manufactures. This largely transnational-dominated trade – where demand is primarily determined in major markets abroad – meant that import demand continued to be strong.

If we consider this in conjunction with the increasing dependence on, and concurrent slowdown in, FDI, the roots of the crisis will become clearer. FDI as a proportion of gross fixed capital formation (GFCF) averaged about 15 per cent for Malaysia in the mid-1990s, with lower shares for Indonesia and Thailand, but still above the developing country average of around 5 per cent (UNCTAD 1997: figure II.19). FDI can complement limited domestic capital resources to enhance growth, although FDI's share of GFCF fell in 1996. However, the Southeast Asian share of total FDI going to South, East and Southeast Asia fell from 61 per cent in 1990–1 to only 30 per cent in 1994–6. China and India had become major rivals, especially for labour-intensive FDI. And unlike recovery after the recession of the mid-1980s, largely due to the massive relocation of East Asian investments, FDI inflows to Southeast Asia on a comparable scale seem most unlikely in the foreseeable future.

The fall in FDI to Southeast Asia from late 1996 was a consequence of a number of factors. First, the mid-1990s did not see a further massive exodus of Northeast Asian capital seeking new investment sites in the region, as had happened in the late 1980s and early 1990s. The early massive investments were neither sustained nor replaced by other sources. The falling yen from the mid-1990s also reduced the significance of the already declining Japanese FDI inflows. Second, the exhaustion of labour reserves in Malaysia and Thailand – the more attractive of the second-tier Southeast Asian NIEs for FDI – had already started to discourage prospective labour-intensive investments. Malaysia had a foreign labour force exceeding two million in 1996, which accounted for 20 to 30 per cent of the country's labour force, while Thailand probably had a similar number. The incentives had also changed in the early 1990s, so that labour-intensive firms faced pressure to relocate in less developed locations within the country, or even abroad. The crisis is likely to discourage FDI flows for years. FDI interest in the region has declined since 1996, with an increasing proportion consisting of acquisitions to take advantage of the regional 'fire sales', rather than adding new production capacity through green-field investments. The early and mid-1990s were also characterised by increased privatisation. Powerful interests captured much of the rents associated with privatisation although, initially, these abuses did not seem overly debilitating due to rapid growth. Private interests, working hand in hand with the politically powerful, began dominating financially profitable *rentier* activities. Privatisation basically involved the transfer of existing assets from public to private hands, with no necessary addition of capacity, and therefore absorbed scarce private sector financial resources without enhancing economic capacity. With 'know-who' becoming more important than 'know-how', 'cronyism' undermined the development of entrepreneurship and other capabilities.

Financial liberalisation reduced the monitoring and supervision of banking operations and transactions, including those of a prudential nature. There was also a significant increase in 'private banking' as well as increased banking transactions across borders with the proliferation of 'international off-shore financial centres' and other international banking facilities competing for business. The growing dollarisation of the world economy, including international finance, has also skewed the nature of these developments in important ways. The liberalisation of financial services as well as of investment regulations, including liberalisation of the capital account, reduced national oversight and management of financial flows, which created conditions conducive to the East Asian crises that followed. Various aspects of financial liberalisation have considerably reduced the scope for national macroeconomic, including monetary, management. Options for *rentier* as well as developmental initiatives have also been significantly reduced as a consequence.

The variety of financial regimes in East Asia does not allow for easy general-isations for the entire region. Many observers have compared the economies and regimes which have experienced major economic crises since the second half of 1997 (i.e. Indonesia, Malaysia, the Republic of Korea and Thailand) with the other HPAE economies which have not been so badly affected – namely Hong Kong (China), Japan, Singapore and Taiwan Province of China, as well as China. There is no systematic evidence that the difference lies primarily in the extent of corruption, rent-seeking, government intervention, industrial policy, export-orientation, productivity growth, FDI, or democracy. Although all the economies affected have liberalised their capital accounts, restrictions remain important, especially in China and Taiwan Province of China. In any case, capital account liberalisation may only be a necessary, but not sufficient, condition for the new type of crisis experienced. The big difference seems to have been that the East Asian four have had low foreign exchange reserves, unlike the second group of East Asian economies, which have the highest reserves in the world, and hence have been far less vulnerable to currency attack. Unlike Malaysia, the external liabilities of the three most affected economies were well in excess of their foreign exchange reserves.

Southeast Asian development after the crisis

The currency and financial crises in Southeast Asia suggest that the region's economic miracle was built on some shaky and unsustainable foundations. Growth before the crises in Malaysia and Thailand was increasingly heavily reliant on foreign resources, both capital and labour. Limited investments and inappropriate biases in human resource development held back the development of greater industrial and technological capabilities throughout the region. Southeast Asia's resource wealth and relatively cheap labour sustained production enclaves for the export of agricultural, forest, mineral and, more recently, manufactured products. However, restricted groups linked to those with political power captured much of the wealth generated. They nevertheless contributed to growth by reinvesting – albeit mainly in the 'protected' national economy – in import-substituting industries, commerce, services, and privatised utilities and infrastructure.

Most of East Asia's macroeconomic fundamentals were generally sound at the time of the crash. Low inflation and falling unemployment had characterised the economy over the preceding decade. Savings rates continued to rise despite already being among the highest in the world. However, fundamental weaknesses in the real economy more generally slowed down growth in the mid-1990s. The growing shift to knowledge- and skill-intensive production and the emergence of China and India as major low-wage production sites also threatened export-oriented manufacturing in the country. Unlike the Northeast Asian economies, the Southeast Asian three have not sufficiently developed the institutions needed to generate rapid technical change and firm progress towards the technology frontiers.

Exchange rate depreciation without increased exports

The cheaper currencies after the crisis brought little improvement in FDI trends from the mid-1990s, and especially from 1997. Unlike gradual currency depreciations, which can attract investment from abroad, especially when accompanied by strong macroeconomic fundamentals, volatile currency movements tend to discourage such inflows. The otherwise strong macroeconomic fundamentals tended to strengthen Southeast Asian currency values in the absence of earlier government devaluation efforts. The 1997–8 currency devaluations lowered domestic production costs in Southeast Asia vis-à-vis North America and Europe. However, the regional nature of the crises and the preceding Japanese economic stagnation reduced regional demand for exports, which have become increasingly important with growing regional economic integration in recent decades. Besides, because many foreign subsidiaries in Southeast Asia have low value-added production processes, with strong vertical linkages to the rest of the firm or industrial group, the devaluations neither lowered demand for imports nor increased export demand as much as might be expected from the changes in relative prices. However, the recovery in world demand for electronics since late 1998 contributed a great deal to economic recovery in the region, especially in Malaysia and the Republic of Korea. Sticky wage rates are likely to reduce the additional foreign exchange earnings to be gained with devalued currencies.

Over-expansion in construction and lending for non-productive purposes also limited Southeast Asian financing of manufacturing growth, even before the crisis. To make matters worse, the limited Southeast Asian capacities to export services and construction materials aggravated trade imbalances. Instead, construction and services were responsible for massive increases in import bills in the early and mid-1990s. Unproductive investment ventures, including property and share purchases, attracted financing from banks and other financial institutions. The decline in FDI and export growth since the crises has further reduced domestic demand for services and construction. To boost their asset markets and reflate their economies, some governments (especially Malaysia) have continued to encourage lending for asset purchases, both in the stock and property markets.

The need for technological upgrading for sustainable development

While industrial policy in the Republic of Korea and elsewhere in Northeast Asia ensured strong institutional support driving technical change, this has generally failed to materialise in most of Southeast Asia. Singapore has successfully developed and maintained the institutions necessary to sustain its leading role as the Southeast Asian regional hub for medium- to high-technology-intensive production and services. The Republic of Korea, as well as Japan and Taiwan Province of China, have successfully developed the necessary institutions, not only to speed up the absorption and development of technologies, but also to strengthen their technological capacities and capabilities more generally. Such slow technological deepening in the real sector must have limited the Southeast Asian region's growth potential. Institutional deficiencies in Southeast Asia can be seen in the institutions supporting technological deepening, human resource development, technology diffusion, as well as disciplinary mechanisms (Rasiah 2001, Jomo and Felker 1999).

Ambitious and expensive technological-deepening institutions and mechanisms were introduced in both Malaysia and Indonesia, especially in the 1990s, without much concern for ensuring international competitiveness in the medium term. While such initiatives had important technological-deepening objectives, serious failures have restricted their impact. Rising production costs and tough external competition forced Malaysia to review its export strategies and domestic capabilities. Growth in foreign-dominated export-processing activities has largely involved the expansion of relatively low value-added production. With labour reserves exhausted, the premium for skilled workers has gone up in Malaysia and Thailand. Cheap labour imports from neighbouring countries have held down unskilled workers' wages and slowed down labour-intensive firm initiatives to upgrade their process technologies (Edwards in Jomo and Felker 1999).

Achieving higher productivity inevitably requires complementary developments in human resource capabilities. Given the problems of getting firms to invest in training workers, there is a strong need to stimulate state–business collaboration in creating and co-ordinating institutions to enhance human resources for techno-logical upgrading. In Northeast Asia, the share of engineers and R & D scientists and technicians rose quickly with the strong incentives offered for increasing their number. Southeast Asia, outside of Singapore, has lacked comparable human resource support to facilitate a rapid transition to higher-technology activities. Official measures of technology transfers have undoubtedly increased in Southeast Asia. Institution-building to facilitate local technology absorption and development has, however, been weak (Jomo and Felker 1999). The region does not have enough effective mechanisms to govern and promote effective technology transfer. In Northeast Asia, governments established institutions to assist local licensees to get more favourable bargains from foreign licensers and to speed up the absorption and development of desired technological capabilities (Johnson 1982, Amsden 1989, Wade 1990). Strict conditions imposed by governments using performance standards ensured minimal waste of resources. The HPAEs in Northeast Asia have drawn heavily on foreign technology while limiting foreign ownership of industry to promote domestic industrial capital. Both the Republic of Korea and Taiwan Province of China initially invited foreign investment in order to establish new export-oriented industries such as electronics, but they restricted FDI over time while accessing foreign technology through licensing. But Southeast Asia's export-led growth boom before the crisis was driven mainly by massive foreign investments. However, passive reliance on foreign capital and technology inflows will generate little more than direct employment. Furthermore, limited domestic capabilities have meant that payments for imports and profit repatriation have reduced the potential benefits of industrialisation to the region. While transnationals have been reluctant to source more inputs locally, local firms have also not adequately developed productive capabilities to increase their participation in foreign firms' value-added chains. Industrial policies have not done much to cultivate and strengthen the capacity of local firms to take greater advantage of domestic content stipulations.

To varying degrees, the other Southeast Asian HPAEs have sought to emulate their regional neighbour, Singapore, which initiated its 'second industrial revolution' after achieving full employment in the late 1970s and, beginning in 1986, sought to establish itself as the best location for the regional headquarters of transnational corporations. Unlike the Republic of Korea and Taiwan Province of China, Singapore adopted an FDI-led path to export-oriented industrialisation in the late 1960s, partly for political reasons (Rodan 1989). Yet, despite its desire for foreign investment, Singapore is not opposed to government intervention. The Singaporean state has shaped the investment environment by providing a range of facilities, infrastructure, subsidies and complementary public investments (Low 2001, Wong 2001). Although its circumstances are very different from those of its neighbours, Singapore's experience clearly demonstrates that the scope for proactive investment policy under a liberal ownership regime is much greater than commonly presumed.

Consequently, greater attention has been given to the dynamic effects of new investment projects, even extending to matters such as market access, technology transfer and human resource development. Such considerations for evaluating investment performance became far more important during the decade-long boom prior to the 1997–8 crises. While capital-formation, employment-generation and foreign exchange earnings were not irrelevant, governments did become more selective in their investment-promotion efforts, largely with a view to maximising value added and positive externalities over time. The new emphasis on investment externalities has, in some countries, shifted the objective of investment-promotion policies from particular industries to industrial clusters of complementary assembly, component production, and producer-service activities. Emphasis has shifted from maximising new green-field FDI in export-oriented industries to encouraging reinvestment by established producers in deepening their local operations, upgrading skills, forming domestic economy linkages, and gaining a larger share of their parent companies' global operations.

Investment regime in an integrated global economy

Investment-policy regimes are usually seen as lying somewhere along a continuum from the restrictive to the more liberal and incentive-neutral, with the analytical focus on regulations that shape entry barriers. From this perspective, the main trend since the mid-1980s has been the relaxation of restrictive regulations on foreign ownership. So-called trade-related investment measures – such as local content, foreign exchange balancing and technology transfer requirements – have also been relaxed. However, three issues have compromised this regional trend towards open investment regimes. First, liberalisation has occurred unevenly across sectors and countries. Although general investment barriers have been relaxed, the remaining restrictions have become more significant, sending clearer signals about policy priorities and concerns. After Singapore, Malaysia has the most open investment regime, allowing wholly foreign-owned firms to operate in the export-oriented manufacturing sector with minimal restrictions. However, following the crises, Thailand and Indonesia have opened their financial and other services to foreign mergers and acquisitions, while Malaysia has liberalised more cautiously in this regard. Second, exemptions from (national) equity ownership requirements in the Southeast Asian HPAEs have usually been tied to exports and, sometimes, other more specific policy goals. For example, unlimited foreign ownership was allowed in export-oriented industries, but not for import-substituting production. Integration into the global economy in the 1980s and 1990s did not involve incentive-neutrality and market-determined specialisation. Instead, government initiatives responded to fresh opportunities offered by firms' new strategies vis-à-vis the globalisation of industrial production. Third, Southeast Asian HPAEs have been using investment *subsidies* such as tax holidays, exemptions and deductions, rather than entry restrictions (Felker and Jomo 1999). Incentives have been used to promote particular industries or to impose specific performance requirements. Such subsidies have been conventionally viewed as due to (socially inefficient) competition among prospective host governments. Nevertheless, they have enabled host economies to promote certain industries to some advantage when investment externalities exceed subsidy costs, owing, for example, to scale or agglomeration economies. It has also been argued that investment incentives compensate transnational corporations for their search costs and extra risks involved in transferring advanced production activities to new locations (UNCTAD 1998: 97–106). Generally, governments in the region have used investment incentives to signal their commitment to attracting and retaining investors. Unlike investment restrictions and direct export subsidies, many investment subsidies are not proscribed by existing WTO provisions.

Current reform programmes, as prescribed by the IMF, exclude a priori the possibility that government investment policies can encourage technology transfer, linkage formation, skill development and other externalities. An important requirement for sustainable recovery is stronger expertise and more flexibility in public agencies overseeing industrial development. In the wake of the East Asian crisis, the IMF has urged or even required countries to dismantle or reduce such subsidies. However, as they lose some policy instruments for promoting and shaping industrialisation, Southeast Asian countries will need to retain and hone the remaining instruments in order to cope with new challenges.

As investment policy goals have shifted, policy instruments have changed accordingly. Negative restrictions, such as foreign ownership limits and local content requirements, have been or are currently being phased out in most sectors, although significant exceptions remain. Tax holidays have also become less important insofar as most governments offer them to varying degrees. Instead, some governments have begun providing infrastructure and services designed to enhance their investment environments, attract desired investments, and induce positive externalities such as:

1   One-stop facilitation of administrative approvals;
2   Provision of specialised physical, customs-related, and technical infrastructure;
3   Support for labour procurement and skills development;
4   Matching of investors with local suppliers;
5   Other services relating to investors' routine operations, such as immigration, customs and other tax services, as well as trouble-shooting administrative problems with other government bureaucracies.

Implementation of these new investment policies has involved daunting political and administrative challenges, requiring government investment agencies to develop greater expertise and flexibility, rather than a sector-neutral and passive policy stance. Reshaping national investment environments in line with new investor demands requires understanding the great variation within particular industries, the logistical needs and strategic concerns of transnational businesses, and the rapidly changing international investment environment. Changing the main task of investment policy from *regulation* to *promotion,* and now *services,* requires changing often deeply entrenched institutions and organisational cultures within the relevant bureaucracies. Hence, new investment policies have often involved creating new specialised agencies, authorities and administrative zones.

This situation poses difficult challenges for countries with weak skill endowments, particularly related to engineering. For them, foreign investment is expected to catalyse industrial development, but these countries have limited complementary capabilities to offer. They have few technologically-advanced producers able to integrate easily into the international supply chains of transnational corporations. Similarly, the efforts of transnational corporations to develop internationally-integrated production specialisations may constrain host-country efforts to promote domestic linkages and spillovers. Although some transnational corporations have begun to devolve functions like procurement, marketing, design, and even R & D to their Southeast Asian operations, certain functions remain centralised in regional headquarters in Singapore or Hong Kong (China). Most subsidiaries in other Southeast Asian countries lack the authority to make important decisions in close proximity to a regional headquarters. As a consequence, they may not even have the independence to develop new supply sources for anything other than the simplest components. These challenges point to the potential scope for policy initiative by governments and private entrepreneurs in enhancing the gains from FDI under a liberal investment regime. However, government efforts to foster linkages, skill formation, and technology spillovers have so far met with considerable difficulties. Clearly, FDI alone cannot ensure the development of capabilities, as is often presumed. Instead, dynamic externalities from foreign investment are more likely in host environments with appropriate skills, infrastructure, and supplier and technical capacities. In less conducive investment environments, export-manufacturing FDI may not generate the desired consequences, remaining primarily low-skill, import-dependent enclaves, as in Mexico.

A country's comparative advantage as a location for production linked to transnational corporations increasingly depends on factors that affect those corporations' costs and competitive advantages. Besides political stability and investment security, transnational corporations are increasingly concerned about the quality of physical infrastructure and administrative systems, skill endowments, and proximity to quality suppliers. Host governments require considerable public expertise, institutional flexibility, and judicious investments in skill and technical capacities to ensure a mutually advantageous investment environment. Authorities will undoubtedly continue to seek new ways of encouraging industrial and techno-logical progress. Over-capacity in several manufacturing sectors and slow recovery in Japan probably mean that the new manufacturing FDI will not quickly resume the dizzy growth rates of the decade preceding the crisis. More worrying is the shift in FDI flows towards mergers and acquisitions, and away from new green-field investments or even the reinvestment of profits. Such trends have important implications for the development of industrial and technological capabilities. While facilitating investments has become central to recovery throughout the region, the new situation also poses significant downside risks. For example, opportunities for more value-added activities, such as design and R & D, may be constrained by the new strategies and internal organisation of transnational corporations.

For other reasons too, it is unlikely that nuanced proactive investment policies will continue to shape new investment trends. The region's opening to export-oriented FDI in the past did not result in the same sort of industrial linkages and technology development found in the Republic of Korea and Taiwan Province of China, because of poorer policy, weaker institutional support and fewer capabilities. Whatever the potential advantages of mergers and acquisitions, it is unlikely that these will be fully realised without appropriate institutional support, skills, policy incentives, and the ability to extract and capture rents. Building new investment-management capabilities continues to face formidable difficulties. Assisting governments to regulate foreign investment is low on the agenda of the powerful international financial institutions, as well as that of most domestic reformers. In Indonesia, the desire to restore investor confidence is likely to constrain government policy activism for some time. Although there are some signs of emerging public–private co-ordination in fostering the development of skills and technology in Thailand, some of the indigenous industrial capacities built up in recent years have been lost with the financial liquidation of many manufacturers. Malaysian Prime Minister Mahathir's rejection of orthodox prescriptions for economic restructuring in Malaysia has mainly protected financial and other non-manufacturing interests. Although the government retains important policy instruments, efforts to revive growth in the short term have forced Malaysia to liberalise its de facto investment-policy regime. Prospects for rebuilding investment-management capacities have also been clouded by current multilateral efforts to proscribe discretionary government interventions and regulations affecting investment flows. Establishing a multilateral investment regime even more restrictive of national government initiative may reduce the potential for abuses of investment policy. The main effect will be the loss of an important tool for fostering long-term industrial development.

Concluding remarks

Some popular accounts of the East Asian miracle economies portrayed them as geese flying in the slipstream of the lead goose, Japan. Many went further to imply that they were Japanese clones or at least 'wannabes'. Even serious scholars of the region have written of a yen bloc, for instance, despite the fact that most Japanese corporations used the US dollar to denominate their internal transactions, and most monetary authorities in the region, including Japan, never sought the internationalisation of their currencies. In short, the picture of East Asian homogeneity has long been grossly exaggerated.

Although there was no one development model for the eight HPAEs, all experienced rapid growth due to high savings and investment rates as well as labour utilisation and human resource development. Exports were also important in all these economies, although most were far from being open economies. It is now generally agreed that international financial liberalisation was the principal cause of the crisis, though those in favour of such liberalisation would argue that the problems involved improper sequencing and/or inadequate prudential supervision, rather than liberalisation per se. Such international financial liberalisation generally began in the region from around the mid-1980s, and certainly cannot be considered part and parcel of the development strategies responsible for the rapid growth, industrialisation and structural changes before that.

Returning to the various institutional features that made possible the East Asian miracle in the past is, for several reasons, no longer an option. The international economic environment has changed quite radically in the past fifteen years. International economic governance profoundly altered with the IMF's stabilisation programmes and the World Bank's structural adjustment packages in the wake of the debt crises of the 1980s. New conditionalities have been imposed in the region by the Bretton Woods institutions, together with the emergency credit facilities provided to Indonesia, the Republic of Korea and Thailand during the 1997–8 crises. It is increasingly recognised that economic liberalisation and such conditionalities have had adverse consequences for growth, as well as for distribution. International economic liberalisation has been further advanced by other institutions and processes, most notably the conclusion of the Uruguay Round of international trade negotiations with the advent of the WTO in the mid-1990s.

Furthermore, the needs and requirements of the HPAEs have changed over time; given their variety, there is no single universal set of institutional reforms for all these economies. However, bank-based financial systems are still more likely to serve the developmental finance requirements of these economies. But the scope for directed credit (praised in World Bank 1993) and financial restraint has been considerably reduced by internal as well as international financial liberalisation. Instead, with the Financial Services Agreement under the General Agreement on Trade in Services (GATS) and the imminent broadening of the IMF's mandate to cover the capital account as well, there is likely to be greater pressure to promote and open up capital markets in the region.

As with finance, there is also little conclusive evidence of the superiority of Anglo-American corporate governance. Nevertheless, the Fund and the World Bank continue to press for corporate governance reforms and corresponding conditionalities imposed during the East Asian crises, insisting that such changes are necessary for economic recovery. However, the relatively stronger economic recoveries in Malaysia and the Republic of Korea have had little to do with such reforms and were primarily due to successful, Keynesian-style, counter-cyclical reflationary policies. East Asian business relations – once celebrated as synergistic social capital – have since come to be denounced as 'crony capitalism' ostensibly responsible for the crisis. The family firm, a feature of early capitalist development in much of the world, has also been targeted for reform as if it were responsible for the abuses associated with parasitic 'cronyism'.

Economic liberalisation more generally has greatly reduced the scope for industrial policy or selective government interventions. Yet, the World Bank's advocacy of targeting poverty – for example, in connection with its social safety net programmes – has underscored the legitimacy of such selectivity, while implicitly acknowledging government capacity to do so reasonably well. Despite the recent push for trade liberalisation as well as the abandonment of several GATT arrangements that acknowledged and sought to compensate for different national economic capabilities, UNCTAD's annual *Trade and Development Report* has continued to affirm the remaining scope for trade-related industrial policy. Similarly, the works of Stiglitz and others have reiterated not only the need for but also the potential for finance-related industrial policy.

This chapter has considered some recent developments in Southeast Asian investment regimes in line with industrial policy against the advice of the international organisations. The scope for corresponding technology policy has also been identified despite the strengthening of corporate intellectual property rights. Human resource development is probably the area for industrial policy initiatives least fettered by recent liberalisation trends, despite the World Bank's advocacy of non-subsidisation of post-primary education and recent trends in education and health-care privatisation. Ensuring a return to the high productive investment rates of the past is helped by the continued high domestic savings rates in the region, in spite of the devastating social impacts of the 1997–8 crises in the East Asian region. It is now generally acknowledged that much of the additional funding made available by foreign bank borrowings, as well as portfolio investment inflows into the region, helped fuel asset-price bubbles, which later burst with such catastrophic consequences. Yet, financial liberalisation in the region has been furthered – rather than checked – in the aftermath of the crises, mainly due to the conditionalities imposed by the Fund as well as the urgent need for foreign funds to help economic recovery.

In the unlikely event that the Europeans and the Japanese do not resist the continued promotion of the Anglo-American capitalist norm for the rest of the world, it is quite likely that we will witness a greater degree of conformity and uniformity in the formal rules and institutions of the economy. But such conformity may remain superficial, rather than become substantial or, as is perhaps more likely, the Anglo-American forms may take root unevenly in different situations, depending on changing historical, economic, political, cultural, social and other environmental factors. In the same way that Islam once spread rapidly across North Africa, providing a common legal and cultural basis for long-distance trade, the English language and Anglo-American norms may well become universal in the forthcoming era. But just as the acceptance of Islam has resulted in a great variety of Muslim cultural expression and behavioural norms, a twenty-first century Anglo-American global capitalism may still be quite diverse. Neo-liberal globalisation of Anglo-American capitalism seems likely to continue in the near future. These trends will probably be led by the two Bretton Woods institutions as well as the WTO. Nevertheless, there continues to be some diversity of opinion within as well as among these institutions, which is likely to be reflected in policy prescriptions. The WTO's formal democracy provides some basis for reformist initiatives, while the Fund and the World Bank will continue to be under pressure to become more accountable, if not democratic.

As noted earlier, the aftermath of the debt crises of the early and mid-1980s saw stabilisation programmes and structural adjustment packages begin this process, especially in the most heavily indebted economies which had to approach the Bretton Woods institutions for emergency credit facilities, and were therefore obliged to accept the accompanying conditionalities. The currency and financial crises of the 1990s have seen similar outcomes, with East Asian governments obliged to accept, implement and enforce conditionalities imposed by the Fund, the United States Treasury, and other foreign government agencies. But such circumstances for the extension of the neo-liberal globalisation agenda underscore the constraints it is subject to. Not only is there growing resentment over such impositions within the countries concerned, but there is also growing international understanding and wariness of the underlying interests and agendas involved. In other words, every success also hardens resistance. This alone will ensure that the future of liberalisation is far from assured and unlikely to be either smooth or even. Even in the improbable scenario that all developing countries are compelled to subject themselves to such conditionalities, the outcomes are unlikely to be the same. Initial conditions can account for many variations, as we have seen from our very limited sample of four East Asian economies. Different economies have developed different capacities and capabilities, and may therefore be affected rather differently by liberalisation and globalisation. Sequencing will also give rise to differences. There are several different sequencing issues, of which one alone, the different aspects of domestic and external liberalisation, may involve many different permutations. Policy-makers for those economies that liberalise later are also in a position to learn from the experiences of those before them, and thus to anticipate and prepare themselves better.

The mixed consequences and experiences of liberalisation and globalisation thus far have also greatly undermined the previously smug self-confidence of what has been termed the Washington Consensus. With the benefit of hindsight, Stiglitz's (1998) predictions of a post-Washington Consensus may well have been premature. The circumstances of his departure from the World Bank and the more recent controversy over the contents of the *World Development Report* for the year 2000 on poverty are important reminders of the continued hegemony of the Washington Consensus, albeit slightly chastened. Hence, it is not a self-confident, unchallenged and unproblematic consensus, but rather one that is increasingly vulnerable, not least because of developments in East Asia. The earlier appreciation of the East Asian miracle posed an important challenge to the economic neo-liberalism under-lying the stabilisation programmes and structural adjustment packages of the 1980s and 1990s. While the East Asian debacle of 1997–8 has been invoked to negate much of that earlier analytical challenge, it has also raised troubling questions about financial liberalisation. While much of the earlier criticisms of liberalisation and economic globalisation came from outside the mainstream of contemporary economic thinking, much of the recent debate and dissent over financial and capital account liberalisation, as well as the role of the Bretton Woods institutions, has involved orthodox economists, including many who have been strong advocates of liberalisation with regard to international trade, investment and other economic areas.

And while there is unlikely to be any imminent radical change in the international financial architecture, as the threat posed by and the memory of the East Asian financial crises recede, it is unlikely that there will be a simple return to the smug and simple-minded advocacy of economic liberalisation on all fronts, as in the recent past. Much more nuanced and sophisticated understandings of economic liberalisation and its consequences may therefore have a greater intellectual and policy-making impact. However, while the economic convergence promised by neo-liberal economic globalisation is unlikely – not only because it is mythical, but also because there can never be the truly level playing field promised by liberalisation – one cannot deny that even partial liberalisation has limited the range of options as well as the variety of possible economic arrangements. The changed institutional or systemic ecology permits fewer species to survive. But variety, albeit increasingly limited, there can and will be. In these circumstances, it is increasingly probable that systemic differences will be less stark and obvious. But this will perhaps compel closer attention to the remaining variety as well as the remaining scope for diversity, which should in turn lead to more careful attention to detail and to greater appre-ciation of the sources of efficacy of policy instruments, for example. Hence, it seems likely that there will be less interest in alternative economic models or systems, but more consideration of the microeconomic bases for the viability of particular policies and institutions. This could, in turn, lead to a much more eclectic mixture of policies and institutions and, hence, to a greater variety of systems or models.

Notes

1   This chapter draws heavily from previously published work (e.g. Jomo 2001a, 2001b, 2002).
2   Namely Hong Kong (China), Indonesia, Japan, Malaysia, the Republic of Korea, Singapore, Taiwan Province of China and Thailand.
3   This section and the next draw from the introductions to Jomo (2001a) and Jomo (2001b).
4   Of course, the availability of cheap foreign funds – for example, owing to a low real interest rate – can help to temporarily close both domestic savings–investments as well as foreign exchange gaps, especially if well invested or deployed.
5   Financial analysts had become fixated with the current account deficit. This indicator, almost alone, had become the fetish of financial analysts, especially since the Mexican meltdown of early 1995. In earlier, different times, some economies sustained similar deficits for much longer, without comparable consequences. As noted in the immediate aftermath of the Mexican crisis of 1995, several Southeast Asian economies already had comparable current account deficits then, despite, or rather because of, rapid economic growth.
6   In some countries, government-owned non-financial public enterprises (NFPEs) have been very much part of this supposedly private sector debt-growth phenomenon.
7   While the United States economy was strengthening, the Southeast Asian economies were growing even faster.
8   In the mid-1990s, as the US dollar strengthened along with the United States economy, both the Japanese and the Germans allowed their currencies to depreciate against the US dollar, with relatively little disruption, in an effort to regain international competitiveness.
9   In the face of limited information and a rapidly changing situation, such behaviour is often considered rational by market players, even if unfortunate.
10   Hedge funds may, however, go in different directions, such as when the currency sell-off of one fund provokes another fund to snap up bargain equities – for instance, foreigners were often persistent net buyers of Japanese stocks throughout the bursting of the bubble in Japan in the 1990s.

Bibliography

ADB (1997) *Emerging Asia*, Manila: Asian Development Bank.
Amsden, A. (1989) *Asia's Next Giant: South Korea and Late Industrialisation*, New York: Oxford University Press.
Backman, M. (1999) *Asian Eclipse: Exposing the Dark Side of Business in Asia*, Singapore: Wiley.
Baer, W., Miles, W.R. and Moran, A.B. (1999) 'The end of the Asian myth: Why were the experts fooled?', *World Development* 27,10: 1,735–47.
Bhagwati, J. (1998) 'The capital myth', *Foreign Affairs* 77, 3 (May/June): 7–12.
BIS (1998) *Report on the Maturity and Nationality of International Bank Lending*, Basel: Bank for International Settlements, January.
Booth, A. (1999) 'Education in Southeast Asia,' paper presented at the Second Malaysian Studies Conference, Malaysian Social Science Association, Kuala Lumpur, in Jomo K.S. (ed.) (2002), *Southeast Asian Paper Tigers? Behind Miracle and Debacle*, London: Routledge.
Clifford, M.L. and Engardio, P. (2000) *Meltdown: Asia's Boom, Bust and Beyond*, Paramus, NJ: Prentice Hall.
Felker, G. and Jomo K.S. (1999) 'New approaches to investment policy in the ASEAN 4', paper presented at the Asian Development Bank Institute Second Anniversary Workshop on Development Paradigms, Tokyo, 10 December.

Furman, J. and Stiglitz, J.E. (1998) 'Economic crises: Evidence and insights from East Asia', *Brookings Papers on Economic Activity* 2: 1–135, Washington, DC: Brookings Institutions.

Hamilton-Hart, N. and Jomo K.S. (2001) 'Financial regulation, crisis and policy response', in Jomo K.S. (ed.) *Malaysian Eclipse: Economic Crisis and Recovery*, London: Zed Books.

Hsiao, M.H.H. (1996) 'Agricultural reforms in Taiwan and South Korea', in J. Borrego, A. Bejar and Jomo K.S. (eds) *Capital, the State and Late Industrialisation*, Boulder, CO: Westview.

Johnson, C. (1982) *MITI and the Japanese Miracle*, Stanford: Stanford University Press.

Jomo K.S. (ed.) (1998) *Tigers in Trouble: Financial Governance, Liberalisation and Crises in East Asia*, London: Zed Books.

—— (1999) 'Globalisation and human development in East Asia', in *Globalisation with a Human Face: Human Development Report 1999. Background Papers*, 2, New York: Human Development Report Office, United Nations Development Programme.

—— (ed.) (2001a) *Malaysian Eclipse: Economic Crisis and Recovery*, London: Zed Books.

—— (ed.) (2001b) *Southeast Asia's Industrialisation*, Basingstoke: Palgrave.

—— (ed.) (2002) *Southeast Asian Paper Tigers? Behind Miracle And Debacle*, London: Routledge.

Jomo K.S. *et al.* (1997) *Southeast Asia's Misunderstood Miracle: Industrial Policy and Economic Development in Thailand, Malaysia and Indonesia*, Boulder, CO: Westview.

Jomo K.S. and Felker, G. (eds) (1999) *Technology, Competitiveness and the State: Malaysia's Industrial Technology Policies*, London: Routledge.

Krugman, P. (1994) 'The myth of the Asian miracle', *Foreign Affairs* (November–December): 62–78.

—— (1999) *The Return of Depression Economics*, London: Allen Lane.

Low, L. (2001) 'The role of the government in Singapore's industrialisation', in Jomo K.S. (ed.) *Southeast Asia's Industrialisation*, London: Palgrave.

Perkins, D. (1994) 'There are at least three models of East Asian development', *World Development* 2, 4: 655–61.

Radelet, S. and Sachs, J. (1998) 'The East Asian financial crisis: Diagnosis, remedies, prospects', *Brookings Papers on Economic Activity* 1: 1–90.

Rasiah, R. (2001) 'Pre-crisis economic weaknesses and vulnerabilities', in Jomo K.S. (ed.) *Malaysian Eclipse: Economic Crisis and Recovery*, London: Zed Books.

Rodan, G. (1989) *The Political Economy of Singapore's Industrialisation*, Kuala Lumpur: Forum.

Stiglitz, J.E. (1998) 'The role of international financial institutions in the current global economy', address to the Chicago Council on Foreign Relations, Chicago, 27 February (www.worldbank.org/html.extme/jssp022798.htm).

UNCTAD (various years) *Trade and Development Report*, United Nations sales publication, New York and Geneva: United Nations Conference on Trade and Development.

Wade, R. (1990) *Governing the Market: Economic Theory and the Role of Government in East Asian Industrialisation*, Princeton, NJ: Princeton University Press.

Wong, P.K. (2001) 'The role of the state in Singapore's economic development', in P.K. Wong and C.Y. Mg (eds) *Industry Policy, Innovation and Economic Growth: The Experience and the Asian NIEs*, Singapore: Singapore University Press.

World Bank (various issues) *World Development Report*, New York: Oxford University Press.

—— (1993) *The East Asian Miracle: Economic Growth and Public Policy*, New York: Oxford University Press.

Yoshihara, K. (1988) *The Rise of Ersatz Capitalism in Southeast Asia*, Singapore: Oxford University Press.

10 Epilogue: rest in peace or a relevant piece for the rest?

Industrialisation models and the new regional division of labour in Asia-Pacific

Martin Andersson and Christer Gunnarsson

Introduction

Standard interpretations of the Asian financial crisis tend to be focused on the role of government policies and 'quality' of institutions. The crisis is taken to be an effect of either too much government regulation and lack of transparency within the realm of an Asia-Pacific developmental state, or weakened national institutions under increasing financial globalisation. So the issue is either that the state has been too encompassing and unrestricted by legal institutions (rule of law), or that a gravely weakened state has been unable to set up a functioning regulatory framework for financial markets. Regardless of the potential merits of such interpretations, the fact is they have contributed to shifting the analysis away from the dynamics of economic development proper towards a search for the 'right' set of institutions. A consequence of this analytical shift is that the historical significance of the Asia-Pacific development experience is toned down in the search for a universal model of the market economy. Thus, we are no longer encouraged to generalise the Asia-Pacific economic miracle into a development model, but rather instructed to search for ways in which the institutional underpinnings of the Asian economies can replicate an alleged Western type of market institutions.[1]

It is also clear that not only speculators and market analysts, but also scholars, regardless of whether they belonged to the market-friendly (MF) or the state-led (SL) camp, ran into problems when the financial crisis blew open. The MF approach had a problem in explaining how the crisis could have been caused by harmful policies and poor institutions when, not long ago, the region had been held up as an example to the world demonstrating the virtues of free trade, low taxes and modest government spending (see Baer *et al.* 1999). The problem for the SL approach, on the other hand, was to explain how economies that had industrialised through strong and effective state intervention suddenly proved to be extremely vulnerable to market forces.

In this chapter we shall try to reverse the perspective and relate the financial crisis to the actual development pattern in the region during the last four to five decades. The intention is not to resuscitate the notion of an Asian model, which

· has been 'officially' declared dead.[2] A uniform Asia-Pacific development model has never existed and, therefore, the crisis did not reveal weaknesses in a homogeneous and invariable development model. The economies in the region have certainly not followed identical development patterns, let alone identical policies, and substitution and variation rather than imitation characterised the diffusion of industrialisation from pioneers in the 1950s and 1960s to latecomers in the 1970s and throughout the 1990s. Thus our purpose is to place the current discourse on institutions and policy in a structural and historical perspective. Two propositions are made. First, the development experience in the region can be historically divided into two distinctly separate periods, one before the mid-1980s and one after. Second, within both periods the development patterns that have evolved vary a lot between Northeast Asia and Southeast Asia depending on the forms of substitution undertaken in the process of industrialisation.

Periodising the development process

With respect to periodisation, the first development phase that lasted some thirty years, from the 1950s to the early 1980s, was characterised by economic nation-building programmes formulated and carried out within national borders and with national governments – developmental states – as leading policy actors. Government control over national financial systems and a relative immobility of industrial and financial capital were major characteristics of this period. During the phase that began surfacing in the 1980s and came into bud in the 1990s, the role of national governments changed dramatically as private international financial markets developed and manufacturing capital turned global.

The evident and distinctive structural differences between Northeast and Southeast Asia had already developed during this first phase. Although mercantilist in their policy outlook, Taiwan and South Korea built their early industrial economies on a strong and growing home market that was initially nurtured by productivity improvements in the agricultural sector, and it was only after this first industrial phase that they became decidedly export-oriented. Most of the efforts of the Northeast Asian developmental states focused on technological and organisational improvements in agriculture and on investments in infrastructure and human capital. The ASEAN experience of early industrialisation in the 1960s was more a typical case of import-substitution industrialisation (ISI).[3] Manufactured exports were negligible – except for processed raw materials – and the rise in domestic demand was fairly slow, indicating a weak transformation pressure in the agrarian economy. Foreign direct investments (FDI) in manufacturing usually catered for the local protected markets.

In the 1970s, efforts were intensified to build strong export economies all over the Asia-Pacific region. A mercantilist trade orientation became a typical trait of the Asia-Pacific developmental states. Mercantilist tendencies were intensified in Taiwan in the country's second phase of industrialisation, during the move to more sophisticated production technologies and the drive to spur export industries. This tendency was even more pronounced in Korea under the heavy-industry programme of the early 1970s. The ASEAN economies, too, gradually embarked on the road to a more outward-oriented type of industrialisation, and various types of export-promotion schemes were set up all over the region in attempts to build industrial capabilities. During this period, however, agricultural modernisation had also gained momentum in Southeast Asia. Land and labour productivity was rising from the mid-1960s, particularly in Malaysia and Thailand, although it sometimes did so from very low initial levels.[4] This indicates that it may not only have been the increasing export orientation as such, but perhaps also the modernisation of agriculture that contributed to the industrial take-off among the ASEAN countries in the 1970s (see Figure 10.1).[5]

In the 1980s, things changed dramatically in two ways that were to have far-reaching consequences for the structure of the Asia-Pacific economy. This was the beginning of a new period with distinctively different structural characteristics. First, the world financial system underwent revolutionary changes as national systems were being gradually deregulated and partly privatised, and restrictions on cross-border capital movements were being eased. The effects on the structure of and preconditions for national economic organisation were no less dramatic. Formerly, a fundamental task of the state had been to control the process of capital accumulation and investment allocation through its command over the financial system. From the mid-1980s, the national financial systems were gradually opened to international capital flows and an enormous amount of capital began circulating on private markets seeking profitable investment opportunities. After having been restrained by a capital-rationing system monitored by the national governments, investors now had access to an abundant supply of capital in international capital markets. This marked, in effect, the beginning of the end for the Asia-Pacific developmental state.

Second, the Plaza Accord of 1985, which forced Japan, Korea and Taiwan to appreciate their currencies and to accept voluntary export restraints (VERs), was to have a dramatic effect on the division of labour within the Asia-Pacific region. Japanese, Korean and Taiwanese export firms, which had already begun to experience lower returns and weakened comparative advantages due to rising domestic production costs, were now given good reasons to seek production locations elsewhere. To move production to the ASEAN region was, from this perspective, a reasonable alternative. Product life cycles could be prolonged, at the same time that exporting from the ASEAN area opened up new market opportunities, especially in Europe. In the second half of the 1980s, the large influx of FDI from Northeast Asia made possible a dramatic expansion in manufacturing production and exports, especially in Malaysia and Thailand. In the latter half of the 1980s Malaysia and Thailand entered the second phase of industrialisation and in the 1990s they were joined by Indonesia, the Philippines (see Figure 10.2) and China. Again, this had an enormous impact on the economic organisation of the Asia-Pacific region and the scope for national economic policy-making. If the governments have continued to play a leading role, it is decidedly neither by control over the financial system, nor by regulation of FDI. However, although the developmental state may be in demise under the new phase of globalisation, clearly the huge influx of private capital in many forms has opened up new opportunities for government participation in the economic sphere. In fact, governments may have taken on the role of *'rentiers'* in the new division of labour (see Figure 10.3).

Thus we interpret the financial crisis as part and parcel of a long-term development process and as a consequence of events that occurred ten to fifteen years prior to its eruption. The crisis is historically then determined in reference to the structural change affecting the region and its economies during the 1980s, a change symbolised by the new division of labour between the first-tier industrialisers (Taiwan and South Korea plus Japan) and the second-tier (ASEAN and later China). This change involved an intensified integration of the economies in the region and was a consequence of a combination of factors such as: the external pressure for liberalisation; the need for Korea and Taiwan to take further steps up the value-added ladder; and the simultaneous chance it gave to the ASEAN countries to acquire capital for the expansion of their manufacturing industries.[6] This integration, regardless of what sequence of industrialisation the economies were involved in, was perhaps not a major cause behind the crisis as such,[7] but it is surely a chief explanation for the multiplying of the Thai baht crisis throughout the region. It is also the main explanation for the demise of the developmental state. This means that, in effect, this structural transformation is a more important factor behind the development of the region than the crisis per se, the causes and effects of this transformation therefore being the principal issues we are concerned with here.

As history proceeds, new circumstances evolve that are quite ruthless to any claims locked into ideological paradigms or dogmatic theoretical schemes. We therefore propose a historical approach, which focuses on causality and processes in the real economy rather than on universal laws or historical 'necessities'. As an analytical point of departure we consult Gerschenkron's framework for the study of industrialisation in 'backward' economies. This framework is particularly relevant in the context of industrial development in the Asia-Pacific region since Gerschenkron is sometimes said to have proposed that state leadership is a necessity in the catching-up process.

A Gerschenkronian analysis of substitution and mercantilism

When we search for the inner logic or dynamism of an all-encompassing Asia-Pacific development model, it is useful to start off with the reminder that there is no reason to believe that the Asian experience of industrialisation has been any more homogeneous or model-conformist than the European nineteenth-century experience. If 'prerequisites' for industrialisation, e.g. markets or capital, are missing, alternatives may be substituted for them. Backwardness could thus be mitigated by, for instance, state intervention, or by an influx of foreign investments. Industrialisation is a historical process where necessary prerequisites are impossible to define a priori. It is, therefore, an inadequate simplification to sum up Gerschenkron's approach as 'the *later* a country industrializes in chronological history, the greater the economic interventions of its government' (Amsden 2000: 284, our italics). The real lesson from Gerschenkron's methodology is that there is no singular way towards prosperity, i.e. if market dynamics are too weak to propel the industriali-sation process, there are ways by which substitutions may be made and it is the relative degree of backwardness of an economy that might indicate what forms of substitution the process is likely to contain. Gerschenkron acknowledges that 'special institutional factors designed to increase the supply of capital' are likely to play an important role in a vastly backward country (Gerschenkron 1962: 354). State intervention to raise the capital needed for industrial investments *might* therefore be a key factor, but its importance will depend on the relative degree of backward-ness of the economy and on the availability of other forms of substitution. 'Lateness' has nothing to do with substitution. In fact, it may lead our thoughts in the wrong direction in indicating that latecomers can and will imitate forerunners. In fact, substitution is the reverse of imitation; it is what gives rise to variety rather than uniformity in development.

Throughout history, the state has to varying degrees played an active role in institutional change (e.g. emancipation of the peasantry and establishment of banking systems), in market integration (e.g. infrastructure investments) and also in capital accumulation when the degree of backwardness is high. But regardless of the initial degree of backwardness, in the longer run the role of the state as the vehicle of growth – the developmental state – has to be transitory. If, in the longer run, a capitalist market economy is to emerge, state interventions should contribute to creating market dynamics (including institutions, entrepreneurship and skills) so that the economy can function without state leadership. Unless that is done, substitution will be permanent and the economy has to be run by command. As we have argued in Chapter five, the presence of a developmental state is no guarantee for success. The long-term effects of its actions will depend not only, and not even primarily, on its ability to accumulate and relocate capital in the shorter run, but in the longer run, and more importantly, on the measures taken to integrate internal markets, i.e. on the extent to which the traits of backwardness are eradicated. In the real world states might indeed fail to make substitutions for such defectiveness, or over-do the substitution so that market forces suffocate.

Gerschenkron argued that in relatively backward economies there would, *for political reasons*, be an urge to speed up development and to catch up with neighbours and enemies. Thus when the state steps in, it does so for the purpose of economic nation-building. During the Cold War era, development, meaning industrialisation, became a necessary means for survival for most political regimes in the Asia-Pacific region. In the 1950s developmental states emerged throughout the region, i.e. regimes that used their command over the financial system to direct national savings into productive investments. Initially, they all made substitutions for missing market institutions, but their development paths took different directions. In Southeast Asia, the first attempts towards industrialisation were taken within the realm of ISI regimes. During the 1960s, industrialisation proceeded slowly and the domestic market remained limited. Government substitutions did not contribute to eradicating backwardness or to fostering domestic markets, basically due to the fact that the agricultural sector remained relatively backward. In Taiwan and South Korea, substitutive measures were taken as well, but more important were the investments made to remove backwardness in the rural economy, measures which spurred the rise of the internal market economy. These two countries went though the industrial 'great spurt' during this period. Thus modernisation of agriculture was not a 'necessary background' to industrialisation, but actually its very starting point. The major effect of state intervention during this period was to make the process of industrialisation less substitutive by lowering the degree of backwardness.

In the 1960s, Taiwan and South Korea gradually became more export-oriented. Mercantilist trade strategies dominated in the drive towards upgrading industry in the second phase of industrialisation. Similar strategies were also adopted in Southeast Asia and contributed to the industrial take-off in the 1970s. The paradox is that in this period the interventions of the state sometimes became more sub-stitutive, in spite of the change in strategy from import-substitution to export-orientation. The Asia-Pacific developmental states turned increasingly mercantilist. In political economy mercantilism stands for protectionism, state control, privilege economy and rent-seeking activities. The concept is often used to describe conditions of economic stagnation in Latin America and Africa, which are contrasted with the free trade that is thought to have created flexibility, dynamism and growth in Pacific Asia (see De Soto 1989 and 2000). But, as discussed in Chapter seven, mercantilism also denotes trade-orientation deliberately biased towards enjoying a surplus for nationalistic reasons. Thus, if mercantilism is analysed in terms of *economic nationalism, national integration* and *economic nation-building*, concepts deeply rooted in the economic thinking in Japan, Taiwan, South Korea, Malaysia and (perhaps) Indonesia, it is easier to understand why the state intervened to promote the development of the national economy under phases of increasing export-orientation as well. These are also some of the major lessons delivered by Adelman in her chapter. One should bear in mind, however, that in this process there is always tension between tendencies to overdo the substitution, e.g. an excessive transfer of resources to heavy industry as in Korea and Malaysia, and the call for reforms to reduce backwardness, especially in rural areas. This is also one important lesson from Ishak's contribution to the present volume. So the effects of the mercantilist strategy may not necessarily have been to widen the gap between an advanced export economy and a backward rural society, although this was decidedly much more the case in Southeast Asia than it had been in Northeast Asia.

As for the causes and effects of the structural change, all countries in the region – Taiwan, followed in order of relative backwardness by Korea, Malaysia, Thailand the Philippines and Indonesia – joined the development process, although in different phases, as they entered a common orbit of regional economic integration. Most important, however, is the fact that Taiwan and Korea constitute a separate type of development distinctly different from most other cases in the region, as Booth and Jomo convincingly point out (see also Booth 1999). The economic intertwining in the 1980s and 1990s was not only a logical consequence of the emerging industrialisation processes within the region. It also represented a change in the conditions for further industrialisation, in particular in terms of access to capital. Hence the possibilities for Gerschenkronian substitution effects were altered. From the late 1980s access to foreign capital removed one of the restrictions (capital shortage) and opened up for a new form of substitution by which export markets replace home market demand as the driving force in the industrialisation process.

We date this stage of increasing integration to the years around 1985. The Plaza Accord of 1985 resulted in the appreciation of the yen vis-à-vis the US dollar. The values of the Taiwanese and Korean currencies were also raised vis-à-vis the US dollar after 1985, while the opposite occurred in the rest of the region. At the same time, the costs of production were on the rise in Japan, and Japanese investors became increasingly attracted to the ASEAN economies. Japanese FDI to Malaysia, Indonesia, Thailand and the Philippines had increased markedly by the late 1980s, especially in labour-intensive production in the electronics and automotive industries. In the early 1990s, China also became an increasingly important destination for Japanese investments. The mid-1980s was also a period when the financial systems in Japan, Taiwan and South Korea were deregulated.

The wave of deregulation and liberalisation sweeping across East Asia in the early 1980s and the change of the terms of trade following the Plaza Accord, therefore, justify the years around 1985 as being seen as a major break with national development and the commencement of more integrated regional development. These policy changes are, however, not necessarily the causes behind the change but rather the expression of speeding up the structural change that was waiting in the wings. Therefore, let us take a look at how the different economies arrived at this point under different preconditions and processes.

The first-tier type: industrialisation through the domestic market

When Taiwan and South Korea gained their independence and started to industrialise in the late 1950s to early 1960s, they had, compared to many other newly independent nations in the Third World, a clear advantage that made the need for substitution less urgent: the agricultural sector had already been institutionally transformed and the domestic market was on the rise. In the following, the Taiwanese case will be used to exemplify industrialisation through the domestic market, since it illustrates this type somewhat clearer than does the case of Korea.

During Japanese colonisation, productivity in Taiwanese agriculture rose substantially, not least due to intensified land use. Moreover, institutional change involved the implementation of a nation-wide network to organise the farmers and the establishment of financial institutions. The huge profits earned did not benefit the Taiwanese directly through rising real wages, and the level of private consumption was kept low. However, the Japanese invested part of the surplus in the education and health systems and in agriculture. Although the Japanese controlled, through taxation, the profits made in the agricultural sector and in the nascent industry, ownership of small industries (such as rice mills and noodle factories) remained in the hands of the local Taiwanese. When the KMT seized power, a thorough land reform was undertaken in the early 1950s. This three-staged land reform changed the structure of ownership dramatically. However, in the light of the process that was already set in motion, the land reform could rather be seen as a late stage, not a first stage, in the agricultural transformation. It was also the centrepiece of the deepening of the market that was to set in motion the extraordinary subsequent growth record. The equalisation of land played an important role in increasing agricultural productivity further, through a new set of incentives when farmers became owners and the land rent was lowered.[8]

The modernisation of agriculture had a direct impact on the rural economy at large, not least evidenced by the mushrooming of rural small industry. Rural small industry created off-farm employment opportunities for farm households on a part-time basis. While agricultural productivity rose and the demand for labour decreased, landless agricultural labour could find work in industry, thereby avoiding being marginalised or falling into poverty. Additionally, the pressure of migration to the cities was not particularly strong. Agricultural development could also, in this way, develop at its own pace in the sense that demand for seasonal work could be met, and at the same time even compete with industry with regard to wages (at least up to the mid-1960s).[9] Total equality increased, since the income gap between the two sectors did not widen and small firms hindered a concentration of capital. The production process was labour-intensive production and produced goods with agricultural products as inputs. Thus, the *domestic market* seems to have played a crucial role in Taiwan before the shift towards export-orientation.

The first-tier type going global

In Taiwan, state ownership remained an important element in the mercantilist strategy in the 1960s (Chou 1991). Another important factor was the KMT, the ruling party, and its involvement in industry and business. Even more important was the fact that the state kept control over the banks, and most commercial banks remained under state control even during the process of liberalising interest rates, capital flows and currency trade after the mid-1980s. The Taiwanese economy nevertheless has undergone a dramatic and remarkable transformation over the last fifteen years. Industrial productivity has grown spectacularly, and knowledge- and technology-intensive industries are today totally dominating the manufacturing sector. The Taiwanese economy is greatly involved in the process of globalisation and, as such, it is certainly becoming more and more open. Taiwanese investments in ASEAN countries (especially Malaysia) were increasing in the mid to late 1980s and mainland China has received the bulk of outward investments since the early 1990s (TSDB 1997).

The increasing openness of the 1980s is indicated by the fact that the revenues from customs duties as a percentage of total tax revenues were cut in half between 1980 and 1990 (TSDB 1997). Business and income taxes instead became the principal sources of public financing. In order to secure its revenue base, the Taiwanese government supported the spearhead companies and kept control over the commercial banks, while still ignoring the traditional SME sector (the labour-intensive and semi-formal small-scale producers). This sector, once the backbone of the Taiwanese manufacturing sector, is deeply involved in the industrial development of Southeast Asia and mainland China. Its behaviour illustrates the drive towards a regional division of labour during the late 1980s. When the costs of production became too heavy at home, particularly after the Plaza Accord, they simply left for relatively less costly economies in the region. It is also important to note that this sector was never formally integrated into the Taiwanese economy in the sense that it was never supported by the KMT developmental state, with the result that the firms developed special skills with respect to tax evasion (see, for instance, Lam and Lee 1992).

Taiwan also received large and increasing amounts of investments from abroad during the latter part of the 1980s, before these came to a halt in the early 1990s only to expand again before and during the crisis (TSDB 1997 and MOEA 2002). It is also interesting to note that in 1984 almost 50 per cent of Taiwanese exports went to the US. In 1996 this fell to less than a quarter. Exports to Hong Kong developed in the opposite direction, going from 7 to 23 per cent, indicating the increasing importance of the mainland not only as a host for foreign investments but also as a market, especially for machinery and electrical equipment.[10] Three important aspects deserve special comment. First, although export shares of GDP fell in the 1990s, the Taiwanese economy maintained its trade surplus and never experienced the capital account deficits that became a typical feature of other export-dependent economies in the region during the 1990s. Second, Taiwan became a large capital exporter and, unlike other Asia-Pacific economies, it did not rely heavily on inward capital movements. Third, the state kept tight control over the financial sector throughout the period. Before the financial crisis, the Taiwanese reluctance to ease control over the banking system was referred to as a 'special case', certainly not a case worth replicating (Asian Development Bank 1995: 224). Thus, paradoxically enough, the most internationalised and advanced economy of the region remained the only case of a still reasonably functioning developmental state.[11]

If the structural change towards a more economically open region was relatively smooth in Taiwan, things were clearly different in South Korea. First of all, the Korean development has been more 'explosive', unbalanced and substitutive compared to the Taiwanese, and the state has been actively involved in the rise of large-scale capital-intensive industry (e.g. steel, machinery, chemicals and shipbuilding). In contrast to Taiwan, this sector became the most salient trait of Korea's industry. The *chaebols* were in many ways creations of the state and were kept under supervision through control of the credit-granting institutions. When the military took over the rule of Korea in 1961, one of its first major policy measures was to nationalise the banks. It was via lending through these state-owned banks that the huge conglomerates were established in a mercantilist partnership with the state. In contrast to Taiwan, the smaller firms remained subordinated to the *chaebols* and were confined to a role as subcontractors. In 1983 the banks were privatised. From then onwards Korea followed a vigorous privatisation programme and only a negligible portion of the financial sector remained in public control (Asian Development Bank 1995: 219). Instead, the large conglomerates could control the credit flows by influencing the banks and the government. Thus Korea moved towards a system where oligopolies seemed to be running the state and where cronyism prevailed. The Korean developmental state clearly vanished in the process of liberalisation, and the mercantilist nationalist vision was replaced by more narrow and private goals. As Chang notes: 'It can even be said that the demise of the industrial policy critically contributed to the crisis, by removing the restraints on duplicative investments and possibly creating more room for cronyism'. Moreover, 'if industrial policy was largely absent, it seems rather difficult to blame the Korean crisis on it' (Chang 2000: 779). Ironically, it seems that the reform programmes implemented after the crisis under IMF supremacy have to some extent helped to restore the principal /agent structure in Korea.

But, although the state–industry arrangements and certain characteristics of their industrial development constitute structural differences between Taiwan and Korea, the two economies had, prior to the liberalisation of the mid-1980s, developed by means of a thorough modernisation of the agricultural sector, in which the rural economy not only provided labour and capital, via channelling savings through the state-run banking system, for industrialisation, but also helped to develop the domestic market. Taiwan was in this regard the more successful of the two, but Korea also managed to industrialise along those lines. Hence the state in Korea and Taiwan did not make substitution for missing markets in the early phases of development due to an absence of productivity growth in agriculture. This may, however, have happened during the next sequence, when industrialisation gained momentum and industry required large amounts of capital that were not readily available from abroad. In the 1970s when industry became more oriented towards, and also more dependent on, export markets, the mercantilist strategy to control domestic capital flows and accumulate foreign currency reserves through trade surpluses became important. The mercantilist strategy served this purpose well as world demand expanded. Perhaps too well, one might argue, since it brought with it the pressure for lower tariffs, flexible exchange rates and the deregulation of domestic financial systems that speeded up the regional division of labour. Taiwanese and Korean capital had higher returns in relatively lower-cost economies and, as opportunities for overseas investment arose, the state could do little about it.

Although Taiwan and, especially, Korea were very poor countries in the 1950s, it is doubtful if we can characterise them as extremely backward in the Gerschenkronian sense, since their agricultural sectors and domestic markets were indeed progressing. It was rather the success of this early development that created the need for increasing amounts of capital. The developmental states could help to solve the problem of scarcity of capital during this phase. After the mid-1980s, however, this particular function became obsolete.

The second-tier type(s): open-market industrialisation

The golden age of the developmental state was the period of export-orientation of the 1970s and early 1980s, when export-promotion policies could be pursued by means of mercantilist strategies. The irony of the matter is that, when the economies in the region were rapidly becoming more export-dependent in the context of capital liberalisation and foreign investments from the end of the 1980s, the preconditions for the developmental state were gradually eroded. Thus one might argue that the life span of the Asia-Pacific developmental state was rather short, especially in its mercantilist form in Southeast Asia. As opposed to the pre-1985 period, private interests who have access to abundant and cheap capital in private capital markets can now take most of their investment decisions on their own. This is a fundamental institutional and organisational change. The industrialisation in the 1990s in Thailand, Indonesia, the Philippines and Malaysia, but even more in China and Vietnam, has been greatly spurred by an influx of foreign (i.e. mostly Japanese, Taiwanese, Korean and Hong Kong) capital. This is de facto a new phenomenon, which means that a comparison with the experience of the early Northeast Asian miracle countries is no longer particularly valid.

The push for industrialisation and the rise of the manufacturing sector were greatly facilitated by the availability of foreign capital in the region. Hence the need for *the state* to make substitutions for missing capital resources might not have been as urgent as it had been in Korea and Taiwan in the 1970s, but since the home market was less developed the extent of substitution ought to have been higher. But the increasing availability of international capital solved the problem and the conditions for industrialisation thus changed dramatically. In the Southeast Asian economies agriculture remains the largest sector, although to varying degrees, as far as employment is concerned. The striking difference in terms of *growth with equity* between, for instance, Taiwan and Thailand has to do with these circumstances. In Thailand, a large agricultural sector, with a potential abundance of labour, was not exposed to modernising pressure, largely because of the easy access to regional capital. At the same time, it seems that the annual growth rate of productivity per worker in Thai agriculture speeded up after 1987 (see Figure 10.2). Even if this was only a small change, it lends some support to the notion of export-led growth pushing up productivity in Thai agriculture, i.e. the reversal of the first-tier type.[12]

Malaysia, on the other hand, might be considered a case that in certain ways combines the domestic market *and* open market types of industrialisation. Although Malaysia, more than any other country, has relied on export markets and the inflow of foreign direct investment, the agricultural sector has changed dramatically since the early 1970s (as Ishak demonstrates, the state played a significant role in increasing the standard of living for the Bumiputeras, which was a central aspect of the nation-building process in Malaysia).[13] When the large plantations were reorganised and mechanised and deliberate efforts were made to increase both land and labour productivity on smallholdings, the rural industrial sector absorbed the released labour. As a result, poverty was greatly reduced. The rise of this stratum of middle-class peasants is also an important political factor. In fact, it has the real base for political power in Malaysia, where the creation of a strong peasantry is one of the goals of that particular regime. The switch from ISI towards the open market in the mid-1980s was also a shift from exports of processed raw materials to exports of manufactures. The evidence for Malaysia, regarding type of industrialisation, is therefore somewhat mixed. If any case should be characterised as an intermediate case, Malaysia is the one.

Concluding remarks

The industrialisation model attempted after the mid-1980s in Southeast Asia is clearly different from the 'original' Asia-Pacific model. Contrary to Northeast Asia, it has been built on capital imports and led by companies catering for foreign markets. Obviously, the role of the state has turned out quite differently as well. It is also possible that the switch towards export-oriented growth implied in this new model has also led to higher income inequality because of growing income differences between sectors; in particular, since agriculture has played a rather passive role in the process of industrialisation. Thus we find the new regional division of labour and concurrent dismantling of the developmental state after 1985 to be a crucial aspect of the industrialisation process in the region. Lamentably, these aspects have been largely ignored by the standard explanations of the rise of Asia-Pacific, and they seem to have been left out of most interpretations of the roots of the financial crisis.

The forces of globalisation and liberalisation affected both Northeast and Southeast Asia, but since the economies of the latter region at the time were in a fundamentally different phase in the industrialisation process, it is difficult to argue that the engines of growth have been identical in all economies in the region. The opening up of the Asia-Pacific economies increased capital exports to the region, and the large influx of FDI to Southeast Asia from Japan and the NICs facilitated the industrial boom in the ASEAN economies. Previously informal markets for credits were legalised and private savings were channelled to the new open credit market. In the transformation from the mercantilist to the open trade regime, the trade in stocks and bonds has soared and exchange rates have become more flexible. This structural change, which began to take shape around 1985, should thus be seen as a fundamental condition helping to explain the extent of the Asian crisis of 1997.

During the present period of recovery, Southeast Asia will perhaps continue to rely on FDI and on the international financial markets, but it remains to be seen if this will help to bring its large agricultural population into the process of industrialisation. It also remains to be seen how the former mercantilist states in Taiwan and South Korea will act as their economies become more open and technology-intensive. An additional big question is, of course, whether China will lean towards the Northeast Asian trajectory or the Southeast Asian one. The fact is that China so far has remained fundamentally a mercantilist trade regime, largely due to the fact that the state has retained its control over the financial system even during conditions of increasing inflows of capital. To paraphrase Gerschenkron, the answers are perhaps hidden in the understanding of the basic peculiarities of relative backwardness. These peculiarities are, according to our analysis, fundamentally conditioned by the division of labour in the regional economy, the productivity of the agricultural sector and the available means of procuring capital.

Our conclusion is, therefore, that the industrialisation types, in the light of the structural change in the region, provide relevant lessons for development, both within and beyond Asia-Pacific. It is, however, unlikely that the traditional 'miracle' explanations will be able to contribute toward this end. These explanations have shown to be too stiff to encompass and account for a number of important events, structures and processes in the real economies of the Asia-Pacific. And like all stiffs, they should rest in peace.

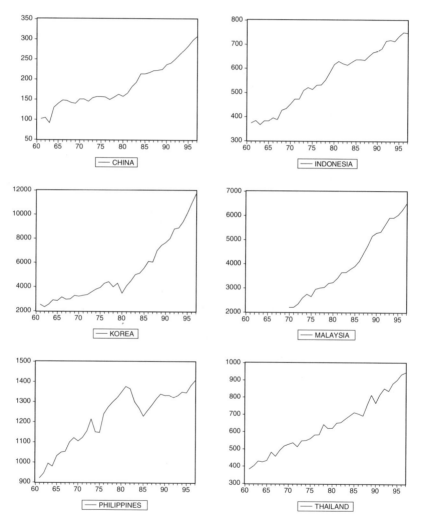

Figure 10.1 Agricultural value added per worker 1961–97 (in $US 1995)

Source: World Bank (1999).

Data for Malaysia 1961–70 n.a.

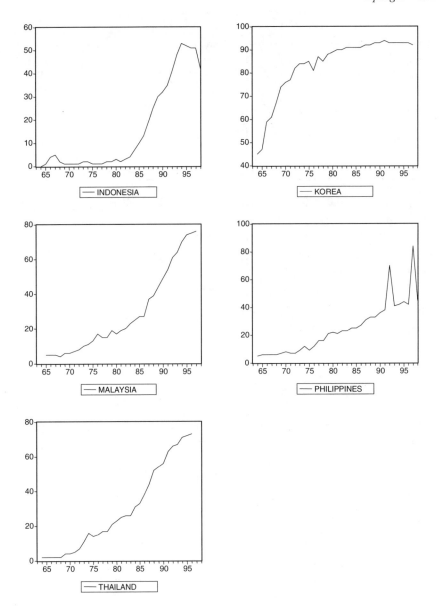

Figure 10.2 Share of manufactures in total exports 1964–96 (in percentages)

Source: World Bank (1999).

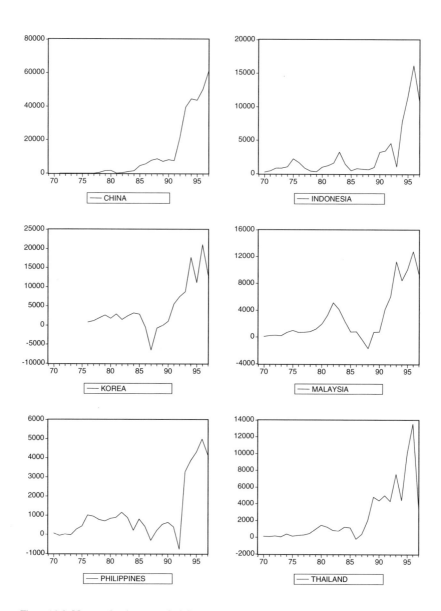

Figure 10.3 Net total private capital flows 1970–97 (current mill $US)

Source: World Bank (1999).

Data for Korea 1970–6 n.a.

Notes

1 Western institutions are often defined in terms of the Anglo-American common law tradition. For a strong critique see Woo-Cumings (2001). For a thorough critique of current crisis explanations, see Wade (2002).

2 At least this seems to be the received wisdom of the Washington Institutions and the US Federal Reserve.

3 Although the case of Malaysia indicates that growth of domestic demand played a not insignificant role for the growth of manufacturing also in the 1960s. See Hoffman and Tan (1980).

4 Agricultural productivity was already then much higher in Malaysia. Value added per worker had reached $US 2,000 in 1970, which may be compared to US$ 500 in Thailand and below $US 450 in Indonesia. However, poverty among smallholders was widespread indicating that development efforts so far had been insufficient to elevate productivity in the smallholder sector.

5 All figures appear at the end of the chapter.

6 Although Edwards and Medhi disagree on the virtues of the post-1985 liberalisation and the rise of financial capital, they both acknowledge its extreme impact.

7 We shall leave this possibility unexplored. The integration in Asia had not made the macroeconomic fundamentals unsound. On the other hand, the integration might have caused an increase in the relative importance of the actors on the financial markets, whose behaviour, as argued by Weeks, might be irrational and therefore crisis-provoking. While this is a plausible inference, we are merely interested in what made the crisis possible as distinct from what triggered it.

8 While agricultural employment increased by 12 per cent from 1952 to 1964 and man-days of labour by 17 per cent, agricultural production increased by 79 per cent (Fei *et al.* 1979).

9 Wage-employment was particularly significant for families with the smallest plots of land. During the 1957–67 period, wage-income contributed to around 45 per cent of total income (over 60 per cent if we include property income) for farmers with the smallest holdings. For farm-families with the largest plots (2–4 chia) wage-income just contributed 12–13 per cent of the total (25 per cent including property) (Fei *et al.* 1979).

10 The trade surplus became significant during the early 1980s and reached its peak in 1987, and the foreign exchange reserve was fifty times higher in 1987 than in 1979!

11 This concurs with Wade's view that the developmental state is largely intact in Taiwan as opposed to the case of Korea (Wade 2002: 5).

12 From 1961 to 1984, the annual productivity growth was 2.6 per cent. From 1987 to 1997 the annual growth rate was 3.2 per cent (World Bank 1999).

13 The annual growth rate of agricultural productivity per worker in Malaysia was roughly 4 per cent between 1970 and 1997 (World Bank 1999).

Bibliography

Amsden, A. (2000) *The Rise of 'the Rest' – Challenges to the West from Late-Industrializing Economies*, New York: Oxford University Press.

Asian Development Bank (1995) *Asian Development Outlook 1995 and 1996*, Hong Kong: Oxford University Press.

Baer, W., Miles, W. R. and Moran, A. B. (1999) 'The end of the Asian myth: Why were the experts fooled?', *World Development* 27, 10: 1,735–47.

Booth, A. (1999) 'Initial conditions and miraculous growth: why is South East Asia different from Taiwan and South Korea?', *World Development* 26, 2: 301–21.

Chang, H. (2000) 'The hazard of moral hazard: untangling the Asian crisis', *World Development* 28, 4: 775–88.

Chou, Y. (1991) 'The role of state in revising Taiwan's neo-mercantilist trade strategy', *The Chinese Journal of Public Policy Studies* 13: 31–57.

De Soto, H. (1989) *The Other Path – The Invisible Revolution in the Third World*, New York: Harper & Row Publishers Ltd.

—— (2000) *The Miracle of Capital – Why Capitalism Triumphs in the West and Fails Everywhere Else*, New York: Basic Books.

Fei, J.C.H., Ranis, G. and Kuo, S.W.Y. (1979) *Growth with Equity – The Taiwan Case*, Washington DC: Oxford University Press.

Gerschenkron, A. (1962) *Economic Backwardness in Historical Perspective*, Cambridge MA and London: The Belknap Press of Harvard University Press.

Hoffman, L. and Tan, S.E. (1980) *Industrial Growth, Employment, and Foreign Direct Investment in Peninsular Malaysia*, Kuala Lumpur: Oxford University Press.

Kuo, S.W.Y. and Liu, C.Y. (1998) 'Characteristics of the Taiwan economy in the context of the Asian financial crisis', *Industry of Free China* 88, 7 (July): 57–81.

Lam, K.D. and Lee. I. (1992) 'Guerrilla capitalism and the limits of statist theory: comparing the Chinese NICs', in C. Clark, and S. Chan (eds) *The Evolving Pacific Basin in the Global Political Economy*, Boulder and London: Lyenne Rienner Publishers.

MOEA (2002) *Ministry of Economic Affairs*, www.moea.gov.tw.

TSDB (1997) *Taiwan statistical data book*, Republic of China: Council for Economic Planning and Development.

Wade, R. (2002) 'Gestalt shift: from "miracle" to "cronyism" in the Asian crisis', *Destin Working Paper Series* No. 02-25, London School of Economics.

Woo-Cumings, M. (2001) 'Diverse paths towards "the right institutions": law, the state, and economic reform in East Asia', *ADB Institute Working Paper* 18, Asian Development Bank Institute, Tokyo.

World Bank (1999) *World Development Indicators* (CD-ROM), Washington, DC: World Bank.

Index